Help People

Overcome

the Past

Spiritualizing the World, vol 3

Help People Overcome the Past

KIM MICHAELS

Copyright © 2016 Kim Michaels. All rights reserved. No part of this book may be used, reproduced, translated, electronically stored or transmitted by any means except by written permission from the publisher. A reviewer may quote brief passages in a review.

MORE TO LIFE PUBLISHING

www.morepublish.com

For foreign and translation rights,

contact info@ morepublish.com

ISBN: 978-87-93297-35-7

The information and insights in this book should not be considered as a form of therapy, advice, direction, diagnosis, and/or treatment of any kind. This information is not a substitute for medical, psychological, or other professional advice, counseling and care. All matters pertaining to your individual health should be supervised by a physician or appropriate health-care practitioner. No guarantee is made by the author or the publisher that the practices described in this book will yield successful results for anyone at any time. They are presented for informational purposes only, as the practice and proof rests with the individual.

For more information: *www.ascendedmasterlight.com and www.transcendencetoolbox.com*

CONTENTS

Introduction 7
1 | A Higher level of Service 11
2 | Awaken People to the Reality of Free Will 27
3 | Looking at Everything from Love 59
4 | Helping People Look at Everything from Love 73
5 | Introduction to Saint Germain 111
6 | An Alchemical Shift in people's perception 117
7 | Invoking an Alchemical Shift in perception 133
8 | Invoking Forgiveness of the German People 153
9 | Freeing people from the Burden of Christianity 173
10 | Invoking the Judgment of False Christianity 197
11 | Setting People Free from False Christianity 227
12 | A Significant Clearing of the Astral Plane 257
13 | Invoking the Clearing of the Astral Plane 263
14 | The mental and identity illusions of Europe 287
15 | Clearing the Mental and Identity Realms 303
16 | How You Can be Free from Your Past 331
17 | Helping People Let Go of the Past 343
18 | A Mighty Action of soul healing 377
19 | Healing people's past traumas 397
20 | Healing people from hatred of the Mother 439
21 | A Buddhic perspective on overcoming the past 457
22 | Helping people attain non-attachment 481
23 | Helping people attain non-reactiveness 505
24 | Protection from Dark Forces 539

INTRODUCTION

This book belongs to the series *Spiritualizing the World*. The books in this series are given by the ascended masters as workbooks that provide the knowledge and practical tools we need in order to make a contribution to solving concrete world problems. This book obviously contains the knowledge and the tools we need in order to help peoples, nations or even the world let go of the past. These books do not contain foundational knowledge about ascended masters and their teachings. In order to make the most efficient use of this book, you need to have a general knowledge of the following topics:

- You need to know who the ascended masters are, how they give their teachings and how you can make the best use of them on a personal and planetary level. You can find extensive teachings on this in the books: *How You Can Help Change the World* and *The Power of Self*.

- You need to know how the earth functions as a cosmic schoolroom. You need to know your own role and the authority you have as a spiritual being in embodiment. You need to know the role of the ascended masters and how only we who are in embodiment can give them the authority to use their unlimited power to affect change on earth. You can find more on these topics in the first book in this series: *How You Can Help Change the World*.

- You need to know how to use the practical tools given by the ascended masters. You can find more on this topic in: *How You Can Help Change the World* and on the website: *www.transcendencetoolbox.com*.

- You need to know about the existence and methods of the dark forces who are ultimately responsible for creating war on earth. You can find foundational teachings on this in: *Cosmology of Evil*.

How to use this book

There is no one way of using the teachings and tools in this book. However, if you want to make a significant contribution to stopping war, it is suggested that you start by following this program:

- You read one of the chapters in the book completely in order to increase your understanding of the topic.

- You give the invocation associated with that chapter once a day for nine days while studying the same chapter again.

The reasoning behind this program is that the chapters in the book form a progression. As you give an invocation for one chapter, you are also clearing your own consciousness from certain energies and illusions. This makes it easier for you to absorb and apply the teachings from the next chapter.

You can, of course, also read the book all the way through and then select one or more invocation(s) that you give several times. It is always more powerful to give an invocation once a day for nine or 33 days.

Please note that even though the dictations in this book were given at a conference in Europe (and therefore talk about the European continent and nations), the teachings are universal, as people everywhere are burdened by the past. You can therefore use this book to help people anywhere on earth overcome their past.

The invocations have generally been made universal. In some cases, they do mention specific nations or events that took place in Europe. You should feel free to change these names to work for other parts of the world. When changing an invocation, make sure you keep the total number of verses. You can repeat the name of nations several times in order to maintain the structure of the invocation. You can also give an invocation for just one nation or one group of people.

If you feel burdened

The purpose of this book is not to merely give you intellectual knowledge. The real purpose is that you give the invocations, whereby you give the ascended masters the authority to remove the dark forces and energies that cause people to be stuck in repeating old patterns. These forces will not be happy that you contribute to the process of removing them from the earth. They may therefore seek to direct energy at you that can make you feel burdened in various ways. Their purpose is to make you stop (or prevent you from starting) your efforts.

If you feel burdened, please read the last chapter in the book and use the invocation associated with that chapter to make the calls for the protection of yourself and all people around you. As stated in that chapter, most people can quickly come to a point where they are no longer vulnerable to the attacks from dark forces.

The dark forces will always seek to inflate any condition in our personal lives that makes us vulnerable. If you have particular issues, it may be helpful to use other tools that address those issues in a more direct manner. The ascended masters have given many invocations and decrees that can help you deal with specific topics, and you can find most of them on *www.transcendencetoolbox.com*. Some tools are found in the other books by Kim Michaels, and you can see them on *www.morepublish.com*.

As stated in this book, it is important that a certain number of people give the invocations and transcend the consciousness behind war. It is highly recommended that you talk to other people about this book, including using social media. As Mother Mary states, if enough people use this book and its invocations, it will be possible for the ascended masters to remove war from earth within the foreseeable future. *Isn't that a message worth spreading?*

1 | A HIGHER LEVEL OF SERVICE

I AM the Ascended Master Archangel Michael, and I AM here. Where is here? Is there a particular location on earth that can hold me, that can limit me, that can imprison me? Nay, I am everywhere in the mind of God, and that is why I am here. That is also why you are here. You can only be "here" if you are "everywhere." Of course, when you are in a dense physical body, it is difficult to be aware that you are everywhere in the mind of God.

You have chosen to enter the body to have that particular perspective. It is not wrong. It is not sinful. Your body is not sinful. You are not a sinner because you are in the body. You are not a sinner because you have an outer self. You are still everywhere in the mind of God. The barrier that seems to exist is not created by God. It is not created by the ascended masters. It is only an illusion, a veil of energy that separates you from me. It does not separate you from me in a real sense. It only *seems* to separate you from me.

This veil of separation has two aspects, a personal and a collective. In your own mind there is a belief that causes you to see yourself as a distinct, separate being. This is partly necessary, as Mother Mary said, in order to keep you in the physical body. Again, this is not a sin, this is not evil, this is not wrong. It simply is the condition that needs to be fulfilled in order for you to take embodiment in a sphere on a planet as dense as earth. It can be no other way. Of course, what the false teachers and the fallen beings have tried to make you believe is that this is inherently sinful, that this is somehow wrong, and that you need to run away from it.

Then there is the collective aspect, which is that humankind has collectively created so much energy of a certain vibration that it literally forms a veil. You cannot, with the outer senses and the outer mind, sense that there is anything beyond the veil. You cannot see us directly with the physical senses. I am here, my beloved. I am here right now as you are hearing these words. Wherever you are when you hear a recording of this or read it in a book, I am here with you. You cannot see me physically because your eyes cannot see beyond the vibrations that make up the spectrum of light that your eyes are capable of detecting.

Why we do not see the masters

You also cannot see me because your mind holds an image of a form, and you are trying to see that form, rather than trying to see the formless being that I am. Your eyes, your physical eyes, are actually capable of seeing me, seeing the light that I am, but your mind has for so long superimposed these images on what your eyes are supposed to see. If you have a strong image of what Archangel Michael, or any ascended master, is supposed to look like, if you have imprisoned us in a form in your own mind, then you are trying to see that form. Do you see, my beloved, if we actually were to take on that form, so that you could see us as having the form you have in your mind, what would we do? Would we help your liberation from form, or would we hinder your liberation from form? We would indeed hinder your liberation by conforming to the mental image you have. For what is it that keeps you imprisoned in form? It is the mental image you have of yourself, of God, of the world. There is nothing else that keeps you imprisoned but the mental images that your mind is superimposing upon what we might call reality.

Form is not sinful

What does it mean to be a fallen being? It means to be a being that is completely identified with an image and has lost touch, lost contact, with reality. Most people on earth have been affected by this state of consciousness, and they see themselves as human, limited, sinful beings. This is truly one of the most subtle and most powerful manifestations of anti-love in Europe and elsewhere. It is the entire idea that you are trapped in the form you have right now. You see, my beloved, there is nothing sinful or wrong about form when you realize that any form is temporary, is constantly in the process of moving with the River of Life, transcending itself.

Do you understand that you have been programmed by the dualistic mind – and those who are trapped in the dualistic mind and those who seek to trap you – to believe that certain forms are evil and certain forms are good? The reality is that form is just form. No form is permanent. Every form is in the process of transcending itself. It will either be pulled up by the upward movement of the rest of the universe, the River of Life, or it will go into a self-destructive spiral, where what we have called the second law of thermodynamics will ensure that the form breaks down. Even a form that is being broken down is also transcending itself, whereby I mean that no form can be permanent.

If you understand this, then you realize that you cannot be trapped in form for an indefinite period of time and certainly not forever, as the Catholic church would have you believe that sinners will suffer in hell for eternity. Truly, a meaningless concept, for if something is eternal, where is time? You cannot really talk about an eternal time period, an eternal time span. You cannot measure eternity by time. The idea that your suffering could last for all eternity is truly meaningless when you make that switch in the mind and realize that nothing could be permanent.

You are not a permanent being either, in the sense that you are in embodiment to go through the process of transcending yourself. When you realize this and realize that no form can trap you, you can start freeing yourself, liberating your mind from the illusion created by the dualistic consciousness. The challenge of taking embodiment in an unascended sphere, especially on a very dense planet like earth, is that, when you are in the dense body and you look at some of the limitations that you face and that cause you to suffer, it is so easy to think that you do not have the power to change these conditions,. Therefore, you are trapped in them indefinitely, or at least for the rest of this lifetime.

No limitations are permanent

What the fallen beings really want you to believe is that some of the limitations you see on earth are permanent. They are either created by God or by some immovable laws of nature. You also know from science that there has been an evolutionary process, that things do not stay the same. Even in the very short time span of what you now call recorded history, you see how much change there has been. If all of these conditions can change, is it logical to believe that there are some conditions that cannot be changed?

You see the trick of the fallen beings. They are allowed to embody on a planet like earth because the original inhabitants have already gone into a certain state of blindness. Then the fallen beings embody here, or come in the other three octaves, and they start creating even more limiting conditions. Then they want you to believe that the conditions that have been co-created by the fallen beings and the inhabitants of earth are somehow permanent, that what you have co-created you cannot uncreate. They even want you to believe that either God has created these conditions or God does not have the power to change them. As one person was saying this morning, so many people look at the evil and the problems going on on this planet, they look at the suffering of innocent children, and they say: "Where is God in all of this? Why doesn't God step in and change this?"

The reason why these manifestations can occur on earth is that in the past, in the distant past, the inhabitants of the earth decided that they wanted to experience what it was like if they did not feel the Presence of God and the ascended masters with them on a daily basis. They wanted to experience what it was like to create something seemingly on their own. In reality you cannot create anything on your own because you need energy from which to create it, and this energy comes from the ascended masters.

Of course, you can lower the energy in vibration so it cannot flow up to us and be multiplied. You can take this lower energy, this fear-based energy, and you can use it to create horizontally. You can create conditions that are not what you would create from the higher light that you receive directly from us. This is what has made it possible to create all of these limitations that you face. When you create from the lower light, from the fear-based energy, there *will* be limitations. There will be built-in limitations because fear springs from duality, and duality always has two opposing polarities.

How the masters look at free will

There will always be a tension. There will always be a struggle. Where is God in all of this? Well, God respects your free will. The inhabitants of the earth have said: "We want to experience what it is like without having God or the ascended masters interfere," as they saw it, "with what we are doing. We want to be able to hide from God. We want to not have the ascended masters look over our shoulders," as they felt. It is not that we are micro-managers or that we are seeking to force you. We respect free will. We are there to guide you, to help you make better choices. We allow you to make any choice you need to make so that you can have the experience you need to have in order to grow in awareness.

We know when to step back, and we allow you to withdraw so that you can feel you have a space on your own. This is part of the path. It is part of the initiation. We are not in any way condemning anyone for making that choice. It is not evil. It is not sinful. It is just a choice that gave the inhabitants of earth a certain experience. It is not logical, and it certainly is not helping anyone, to then come out and blame God for the conditions that you have co-created by saying you did not want God to interfere. You cannot expect God to let you create any problem you want, and then when you face consequences you do *not* like, God is supposed to step in and clean up your mess. This is not logical, it is not rational. This is the lie that the fallen beings have made you believe: That God somehow is responsible for what they have misled you into creating, and that God should then step in and clean up the mess.

My beloved, you asked for space to experiment with your free will in a seemingly separate environment. You asked for this because you wanted that learning experience. How would it facilitate your learning if God or I would step in and clean up your mess because you no longer like the consequences? Of course, it would not in any way help your learning. You need to take responsibility, and when I say "you," I speak to the mass consciousness. You need to take responsibility and realize that you have co-created the current conditions.

God has allowed you to do this because of free will. Therefore, you can pray until you are blue in the face, as they say, but you will not magnetize the Blue Flame Presence of Archangel Michael. I am not here to undo your choices. You have made the choices. I respect your free will. I will not undo your choices for you, nor will I clean up the consequences that you don't like. If you don't like the consequences, undo the choices in your own mind. This is truly taking back your power to choose.

You are not a slave of your own creation

The most subtle manifestation of anti-love, the most subtle abuse of power on earth, is that the fallen ones have made you believe that you are a slave of your own co-creation, that you cannot uncreate what you have created. This is the lie, the basic lie. If you can create something, surely you can uncreate it.

There is no condition manifest on earth right now that is not in some way affected by the collective consciousness. The Elohim did not create the earth as you see it today, with all of the limitations and all of the density. It is all a manifestation of the collective consciousness. Therefore, it can be uncreated by the collective consciousness.

Surely, I realize that the relatively few people on earth who are open to ascended master teachings do not yet have the numbers where you are allowed to uncreate the conditions on earth. There needs to be a greater number of people who realize the dynamic and take responsibility. What you certainly *can* do is free your own minds from these illusions, and when you do this, two things will happen. One is, of course, that you will feel free, you will feel lighter, you will realize you are not defined by conditions. The other is that, if you are willing, you can become an open door whereby I can manifest myself physically through you.

There are many people on earth who have high dreams about Jesus appearing in the sky and proving their Christian beliefs in a way that is undeniable. There are many people who hope that I or another angel will appear in a physical manifestation that no one can deny. This will not happen for a very long time because of free will. There needs to be the ability to deny that God exists because that is what has collectively been desired by a majority of the inhabitants of the earth. Until that dynamic changes, no physical outer proof can be given.

I cannot manifest a physical appearance that all people can see with their physical eyes. I *can* manifest an appearance that those who are open can either see or at least sense, with such a reality that you know what you are sensing in my Presence is more real than what you are seeing through your senses.

Being open doors for the masters

This I can do for those who are open. For you to be open, you need to look beyond these mental images that you might be projecting upon me, so that you do not demand that I should step into a certain form but you are open to experiencing the formless being that I am. When this occurs, then I can manifest myself through you in a manifestation that is as close to the physical, as close to being physical, as I am allowed to do, given the current situation of the collective consciousness. This, of course, will have a much greater impact than when you are invoking my light but still seeing me as a separate or distant being.

We have now for a long time released decrees, and tens of thousands of students have given decrees to Archangel Michael, invoking my Presence. Most of them have seen me as a remote being, existing in a higher realm, who has to come down and do something for you. This decree that you have given before this dictation is a new level of decrees, where it focuses much more on invoking my Presence and you experiencing me as being here with you.

You can give any decree with a sense that I am a distant being and you are invoking me to come closer to earth for a specific purpose, and it will have an effect. You will magnify a certain amount of energy, you will invoke a certain amount of energy, and it will have a positive effect. If you can give a decree with a greater sense of oneness with me, it will have a far greater effect. You can even come to a point where you can invoke and experience my Presence without having to do any outer ritual, but you just feel that I am with you in the situation.

How the masters work

I want to give you some idea of how an archangel works. You have again received an image, going back for a long time, that archangels or angels are doing something very active, almost physical. You have the images of the *Book of Revelation* that there was a war in heaven, and that Archangel Michael fought the dragon, and that I slew the dragon. You are imagining, or many people are imagining, this as a physical battle, like you would see with physical armies, where I would fight the forces of darkness and slay them and kill them. What you do not realize is that this is not how I work at all.

I do not see the forces of darkness as my enemy, as an opponent. I am not fighting them. I do not need to fight them because what they have created, which has a temporary existence, is created out of fear-based energy. I am not a fear-based being. I have no fear in my being. I have no fear-based energy. I am an entirely love-based being, and love recognizes no opposition.

The fallen beings in their pride want to believe that they have misqualified so much energy that they have created all these physical manifestations on earth and all these manifestations in the astral plane, and they want to believe that this can oppose me. It cannot. One form of fear can oppose another form of fear, but no form of fear can oppose love, for love is formless. I do not feel threatened by the devil. I can look at the astral plane without feeling threatened at all.

I cannot manifest myself in the astral plane because of free will, because I work in a very simple way: I manifest my Presence, and the light of love simply makes it impossible for fear to exist where my Presence is manifest to a certain degree. Fear cannot co-exist with love. The devil cannot co-exist in the same space with my Presence. When my Presence is there, fear must go. It can be consumed by me and my angels, by our energy, or it must withdraw if it will not surrender to transcendence. I have no need to fight anything. You have no need to fight any manifestation of anti-love. You have no need to look at earth and think that you have to go out and fight some physical battle to change the current limitations.

We have seen in previous decades how ascended master students got very fired up, as the saying was, about fighting the forces of darkness. They felt they were the avant garde on earth. They were giving their decrees, but they were also, many times, feeling they had to do certain physical things to fight the darkness. What we are calling you to do is to come up higher and realize that it is time to transcend that level, that consciousness, and realize that you are not here to fight the darkness. You are not here to ignore the darkness and deny that it exists and say that everything is good. You are here to realize that there is no need to fight the darkness. You bring the light. You bring the light.

Love that is beyond fear

If you have a dark room, can you take the darkness and remove it? Nay, for it has no substance, no reality. You can bring the light, and the darkness fades away. The real way to "fight" the forces of darkness is to become an open door for the light of love. The real way to vanquish the manifestations of anti-love is to become an open door for love, the love that is not fear-based.

Much of what humans call love is based on fear. It is based on the desire to own, which comes from the fear of loss. True love is beyond that, and that is why, as Mother Mary said, true love can only be unconditional. There is no condition that can hold it. When you become an open door for that love, then you are giving maximum service. I know you may say: "We are so few in numbers. So few people are following the teachings given through this messenger. So few people on a planetary basis are following the teachings of the ascended masters given through any messenger in any organization. How can what we do make a difference?" But it *can* make a difference.

Anything you do makes a difference. Even when you give decrees from a state of separation and see us as separate beings, it still makes a difference. The more you can overcome the separation and step into oneness and experience our Presence, the more of an effect it will have. There are certain things you cannot immediately change on earth, this is what we explained in the latest book about how you can help change the world. Free will does not allow these conditions to be changed until a certain number of people have seen the illusion and transcended the consciousness. What you *can* do is pull up on the collective consciousness because you are part of it when you are in embodiment.

How the fallen beings took the planet down

Do you realize how the fallen beings took this planet to a lower level? They did so by becoming the leaders and making the majority of the people follow them. Well, if a few fallen beings can take the planet down, does it not stand to reason that a few spiritual beings, a few beings who recognize who they are, can also take the planet up? It is perfectly scientific that the few can lead the many. You do not even have to do what the fallen beings do and lead through force and power and make yourself some kind of dictator. You do not need to have physical power over people, because by raising your consciousness you raise the collective.

This is another manifestation of anti-love. The fallen beings as individuals or as a small group have had enormous power over the people. They are doing everything they can to deny the power of the individual because they are really denying the power of the individual to manifest Christhood. What is Christhood? It is that you know you are one with the One Mind. When you know that you are one with the One Mind, then you also know that everything is out of the One Mind. All people come from that One Mind, and therefore you have the authority to raise up the whole. It does make a difference.

I know that you are all facing conditions in your daily lives that make it difficult to span the seemingly two worlds of the spiritual life and your daily life. I know very well that it is one thing to come to a conference and you are raised in consciousness by feeling our Presence, and then you go back to your daily life and the daily grind, as they say. I know this. I understand this.

I still want to give you the vision of what is possible when you find your own personal balance between the spiritual and the daily life. You eventually come to the point where you no longer see any difference, no longer see any conflict, between the two because it all blends together. You realize that you do not always have to be sitting there decreeing in order to invoke my Presence. You can actually invite my Presence to be with you and then you are performing a spiritual service. In your work, when you interact with your children, whatever you do, it can be done with a higher awareness. You endow it with love instead of forcing yourself out of fear to deal with these conditions.

Endowing everything with spiritual light

We want you to come to the point where you are not feeling: "Oh, I have to do something for the ascended masters, so I have to do all these decrees, and this is my only service. But my normal life is just something I am forced to do in order to survive." We want you to come to the point where that separation fades away, and you realize that everything you do can be endowed with the light and the love. It all becomes service. This messenger himself went through a period yesterday of feeling two pulls on him. One was to talk to the people. Another was to focus on being a messenger and taking dictations and leading decrees. He had to make a switch in his consciousness to realize that it is all service. Interacting with other people is also service. It is not just doing something that is seemingly spiritual that is your service to life. It all blends together, my beloved.

Wherever your personal balance is at the moment, we are asking you to step up beyond these outer images of what you are supposed to do as a spiritual person. Instead see that, when you are endowing any activity with love, it is a spiritual service, whatever it may be. There are, of course, certain things you cannot endow with love. I realize that. When you are centered in love, the things that you *can* do, that you *choose* to do, will be a spiritual service.

Seeing beyond older concepts

With this I hope I have given you a slightly different perspective, where again, as Mother Mary said, you can stop imposing the image upon me that really comes from the fallen beings, that I am this remote being in the sky and that I am a dualistic being who has been forced to fight the forces of darkness. They have never forced me to do anything. I have never conformed to their images. It is just that what was given in, for example, the *Book of Revelation* was what people could grasp, given the state of the collective consciousness at the time.

You will see how even the concepts that you have of the Knights of the Round Table were concepts that appealed to people at the time. They had value. We are not denouncing these ideas. We are just saying that, as the consciousness is raised, you will see how certain images fade away and no longer appeal to the people. Then something new needs to come in. New ideas need to be brought forward.

Who can bring them forward other than those who are open to them because they are willing to look beyond the old? We have given teachings through previous messengers that were perfectly valid. They are still valid for people at a certain level of consciousness. We are not asking you to, in any way, look down upon this. We are not asking you to label or judge it. We are just asking you to realize that there have to be some people who are willing to look beyond the old so they can receive the next level, so they are open to the next level of teaching, so they are willing to use it, to embody it. Because otherwise we cannot give more. There is a higher level of teaching we can give than anything we have given previously. It is ready in the etheric octave to be released. We cannot release it right now because not enough people are open to receiving these ideas. Yes, we are giving you hints here and there, but there is still more that could be given, only there are not enough minds that are open to it.

We ask you to consider this, to consider opening your mind by questioning your images: the images of yourself, the images of us, the images of God, the images of how this planet works. That is why we are giving you teachings that can help you do this.

As you do it, you will perform perhaps the highest service that can be performed on a planet like earth, and that is to be the forerunners for bringing forth a new level of spiritual teaching. This is an incredible opportunity. An incredible opportunity. It will not happen by one person being a messenger. There needs to be a critical mass of people who are open, who are willing to look beyond the old images so that they can receive what is given forth.

With these ideas, seeing that your cups are running over and you cannot really contain any more light, then I thank you for your attention, for your love in being willing to come here physically, for your love in wherever you are around the planet of being willing to participate in Mother Mary's vigil and in other ways use the teachings, use the decrees and invocations.

I thank all ascended master students who have used any of the teachings we have given, any of the tools we have given. You are all contributing to the forward movement of the planet, and I thank you in the physical. Even though many will not acknowledge it, it is still important that it is said. We are grateful for the service of all ascended master students. We are grateful, my beloved, and with that I thank you.

2 | AWAKEN PEOPLE TO THE REALITY OF FREE WILL

In the name I AM THAT I AM, Jesus Christ, I call to all representatives of the Divine Father, especially Archangel Michael, to help people overcome all illusions about free will. Help people see the lies and wounds that prevent them from accepting the reality that we have collectively created current conditions on earth, including…

[Make personal calls.]

Part 1

1. Archangel Michael, awaken people to the reality that our physical bodies are not sinful and that we are not sinners because we are in physical bodies.

Archangel Michael, light so blue,
my heart has room for only you.
My mind is one, no longer two,
your love for me is ever true.

**Archangel Michael, you are here,
your light consumes all doubt and fear.
Your Presence is forever near,
you are to me so very dear.**

2. Archangel Michael, awaken people to the reality that we are everywhere in the mind of God and that the barrier that seems to separate us from God is not created by God or the ascended masters. It is an illusion, a veil of energy, that hides the reality that we are everywhere in the mind of God.

Archangel Michael, I will be,
all one with your reality.
No fear can hold me as I see,
this world no power has o'er me.

**Archangel Michael, you are here,
your light consumes all doubt and fear.
Your Presence is forever near,
you are to me so very dear.**

3. Archangel Michael, awaken people to the reality that humankind has created an energy veil that is so dense that we cannot, with the outer senses and the outer mind, sense that there is anything beyond the veil.

> Archangel Michael, hold me tight,
> shatter now the darkest night.
> Clear my chakras with your light,
> restore to me my inner sight.
>
> **Archangel Michael, you are here,
> your light consumes all doubt and fear.
> Your Presence is forever near,
> you are to me so very dear.**

4. Archangel Michael, awaken people to the reality that we cannot see the spiritual world because our minds have formed images based on the material world, and we are subconsciously seeking to project this upon the ascended masters.

> Archangel Michael, now I stand,
> with you the light I do command.
> My heart I ever will expand,
> till highest truth I understand.
>
> **Archangel Michael, you are here,
> your light consumes all doubt and fear.
> Your Presence is forever near,
> you are to me so very dear.**

5. Archangel Michael, awaken people to the reality that the masters would hinder our liberation from form by conforming to the mental images we have. It is the mental images we have of ourselves, of God, of the world that keep us imprisoned in form.

Archangel Michael, in my heart,
from me you never will depart.
Of hierarchy I am a part,
I now accept a fresh new start.

**Archangel Michael, you are here,
your light consumes all doubt and fear.
Your Presence is forever near,
you are to me so very dear.**

6. Archangel Michael, awaken people to the reality that a fallen being is completely identified with an image and has lost touch with reality.

Archangel Michael, sword of blue,
all darkness you are cutting through.
My Christhood I do now pursue,
discernment shows me what is true.

**Archangel Michael, you are here,
your light consumes all doubt and fear.
Your Presence is forever near,
you are to me so very dear.**

7. Archangel Michael, shatter the manifestation of anti-love that makes people see themselves as human, limited, sinful beings who think they are trapped in the form they have right now.

Archangel Michael, in your wings,
I now let go of lesser things.
God's homing call in my heart rings,
my heart with yours forever sings.

**Archangel Michael, you are here,
your light consumes all doubt and fear.
Your Presence is forever near,
you are to me so very dear.**

8. Archangel Michael, awaken people to the reality that form is not inherently sinful when we realize that any form is temporary, is constantly in the process of moving with the River of Life, transcending itself.

Archangel Michael, take me home,
in higher spheres I want to roam.
I am reborn from cosmic foam,
my life is now a sacred poem.

**Archangel Michael, you are here,
your light consumes all doubt and fear.
Your Presence is forever near,
you are to me so very dear.**

9. Archangel Michael, shatter the programming from the dualistic mind that causes people to believe that certain forms are evil and certain forms are good. Awaken people to the reality that form is just form and no form is permanent.

Archangel Michael, light you are,
shining like the bluest star.
You are a cosmic avatar,
with you I will go very far.

Archangel Michael, you are here,
your light consumes all doubt and fear.
Your Presence is forever near,
you are to me so very dear.

Part 2

1. Archangel Michael, awaken people to the reality that every form is in the process of transcending itself. It will either be pulled up by the River of Life, or it will go into a self-destructive spiral. Even a form that is being broken down is transcending itself, so no form can be permanent.

Archangel Michael, light so blue,
my heart has room for only you.
My mind is one, no longer two,
your love for me is ever true.

Archangel Michael, you are here,
your light consumes all doubt and fear.
Your Presence is forever near,
you are to me so very dear.

2. Archangel Michael, awaken people to the reality that we cannot be trapped in form for an indefinite period of time. The idea that suffering could last for all eternity is meaningless when we realize that nothing could be permanent.

Archangel Michael, I will be,
all one with your reality.
No fear can hold me as I see,
this world no power has o'er me.

**Archangel Michael, you are here,
your light consumes all doubt and fear.
Your Presence is forever near,
you are to me so very dear.**

3. Archangel Michael, awaken people to the reality that we are not permanent beings. We are in embodiment to go through the process of transcending ourselves.

Archangel Michael, hold me tight,
shatter now the darkest night.
Clear my chakras with your light,
restore to me my inner sight.

**Archangel Michael, you are here,
your light consumes all doubt and fear.
Your Presence is forever near,
you are to me so very dear.**

4. Archangel Michael, awaken people to the reality that no form can trap us. Liberate people's minds from the illusion created by the dualistic consciousness.

Archangel Michael, now I stand,
with you the light I do command.
My heart I ever will expand,
till highest truth I understand.

> Archangel Michael, you are here,
> your light consumes all doubt and fear.
> Your Presence is forever near,
> you are to me so very dear.

5. Archangel Michael, awaken people to the reality that the challenge of taking embodiment on a dense planet like earth is that it is easy to think we do not have power to change the conditions we face and that we are trapped in them indefinitely.

> Archangel Michael, in my heart,
> from me you never will depart.
> Of hierarchy I am a part,
> I now accept a fresh new start.

> Archangel Michael, you are here,
> your light consumes all doubt and fear.
> Your Presence is forever near,
> you are to me so very dear.

6. Archangel Michael, awaken people to the reality that the fallen beings want us to believe that some of the limitations we see on earth are permanent because they are either created by God or by some immovable laws of nature.

> Archangel Michael, sword of blue,
> all darkness you are cutting through.
> My Christhood I do now pursue,
> discernment shows me what is true.

> **Archangel Michael, you are here,**
> **your light consumes all doubt and fear.**
> **Your Presence is forever near,**
> **you are to me so very dear.**

7. Archangel Michael, awaken people to the reality that history has proven that everything changes. It is not logical to believe that there are some conditions that cannot be changed.

> Archangel Michael, in your wings,
> I now let go of lesser things.
> God's homing call in my heart rings,
> my heart with yours forever sings.

> **Archangel Michael, you are here,**
> **your light consumes all doubt and fear.**
> **Your Presence is forever near,**
> **you are to me so very dear.**

8. Archangel Michael, awaken people to the reality that the fallen beings want us to believe that the conditions that have been co-created by the fallen beings and the inhabitants of earth are permanent and that what we have co-created we cannot uncreate.

> Archangel Michael, take me home,
> in higher spheres I want to roam.
> I am reborn from cosmic foam,
> my life is now a sacred poem.

> Archangel Michael, you are here,
> your light consumes all doubt and fear.
> Your Presence is forever near,
> you are to me so very dear.

9. Archangel Michael, awaken people to the reality that the fallen beings want us to believe that either God has created current conditions or God does not have the power to change them.

> Archangel Michael, light you are,
> shining like the bluest star.
> You are a cosmic avatar,
> with you I will go very far.

> Archangel Michael, you are here,
> your light consumes all doubt and fear.
> Your Presence is forever near,
> you are to me so very dear.

Part 3

1. Archangel Michael, awaken people to the reality that in the distant past, the inhabitants of the earth decided that they wanted to experience what it was like if they did not feel the Presence of God and could create something seemingly on their own.

2 | Awaken People to the Reality of Free Will

Archangel Michael, light so blue,
my heart has room for only you.
My mind is one, no longer two,
your love for me is ever true.

**Archangel Michael, you are here,
your light consumes all doubt and fear.
Your Presence is forever near,
you are to me so very dear.**

2. Archangel Michael, awaken people to the reality that we cannot create anything on our own because we need energy from which to create it, and this energy comes from the ascended masters.

Archangel Michael, I will be,
all one with your reality.
No fear can hold me as I see,
this world no power has o'er me.

**Archangel Michael, you are here,
your light consumes all doubt and fear.
Your Presence is forever near,
you are to me so very dear.**

3. Archangel Michael, awaken people to the reality that we can lower energy in vibration and we can use this fear-based energy to create horizontally. This is what made it possible to create all of the limitations we face.

> Archangel Michael, hold me tight,
> shatter now the darkest night.
> Clear my chakras with your light,
> restore to me my inner sight.
>
> **Archangel Michael, you are here,
> your light consumes all doubt and fear.
> Your Presence is forever near,
> you are to me so very dear.**

4. Archangel Michael, awaken people to the reality when we create from fear-based energy, there will be built-in limitations because fear springs from duality, and duality always has two opposing polarities.

> Archangel Michael, now I stand,
> with you the light I do command.
> My heart I ever will expand,
> till highest truth I understand.
>
> **Archangel Michael, you are here,
> your light consumes all doubt and fear.
> Your Presence is forever near,
> you are to me so very dear.**

5. Archangel Michael, awaken people to the reality that God respects our free will, and when people on earth demanded the opportunity to hide from God, they were allowed to create current limitations.

Archangel Michael, in my heart,
from me you never will depart.
Of hierarchy I am a part,
I now accept a fresh new start.

**Archangel Michael, you are here,
your light consumes all doubt and fear.
Your Presence is forever near,
you are to me so very dear.**

6. Archangel Michael, awaken people to the reality that the ascended masters are always ready to guide us. If we do not ask, you allow us to make any choice we need to make and have the experience we need to have in order to grow in awareness.

Archangel Michael, sword of blue,
all darkness you are cutting through.
My Christhood I do now pursue,
discernment shows me what is true.

**Archangel Michael, you are here,
your light consumes all doubt and fear.
Your Presence is forever near,
you are to me so very dear.**

7. Archangel Michael, awaken people to the reality that the masters allow us to withdraw so that we can feel we have a space on our own. This is part of the path of initiation. It is not evil. It is not sinful. It is just a choice that gave the inhabitants of earth a certain experience.

Archangel Michael, in your wings,
I now let go of lesser things.
God's homing call in my heart rings,
my heart with yours forever sings.

**Archangel Michael, you are here,
your light consumes all doubt and fear.
Your Presence is forever near,
you are to me so very dear.**

8. Archangel Michael, awaken people to the reality that it is not logical to blame God for the conditions that we have co-created by saying we did not want God to interfere.

Archangel Michael, take me home,
in higher spheres I want to roam.
I am reborn from cosmic foam,
my life is now a sacred poem.

**Archangel Michael, you are here,
your light consumes all doubt and fear.
Your Presence is forever near,
you are to me so very dear.**

9. Archangel Michael, awaken people to the reality that it is not logical to expect God to let us create any problem we want, and then when we face consequences we do not like, God is supposed to step in and clean up our mess.

Archangel Michael, light you are,
shining like the bluest star.
You are a cosmic avatar,
with you I will go very far.

> Archangel Michael, you are here,
> your light consumes all doubt and fear.
> Your Presence is forever near,
> you are to me so very dear.

Part 4

1. Archangel Michael, awaken people to the reality that the fallen beings want us to believe that God is responsible for what they have misled us into creating, and that God should then step in and clean up the mess.

> Archangel Michael, light so blue,
> my heart has room for only you.
> My mind is one, no longer two,
> your love for me is ever true.

> Archangel Michael, you are here,
> your light consumes all doubt and fear.
> Your Presence is forever near,
> you are to me so very dear.

2. Archangel Michael, awaken people to the reality that we asked for the learning experience to create in a seemingly separate environment. It would not facilitate our learning if God stepped in to clean up our mess because we no longer like the consequences.

> Archangel Michael, I will be,
> all one with your reality.
> No fear can hold me as I see,
> this world no power has o'er me.
>
> **Archangel Michael, you are here,**
> **your light consumes all doubt and fear.**
> **Your Presence is forever near,**
> **you are to me so very dear.**

3. Archangel Michael, awaken people to the reality that we need to take responsibility and acknowledge that we have co-created the current conditions. If we don't like the consequences, we must undo the choices in our minds by taking back our power to choose.

> Archangel Michael, hold me tight,
> shatter now the darkest night.
> Clear my chakras with your light,
> restore to me my inner sight.
>
> **Archangel Michael, you are here,**
> **your light consumes all doubt and fear.**
> **Your Presence is forever near,**
> **you are to me so very dear.**

4. Archangel Michael, awaken people to the reality that the most subtle manifestation of anti-love, the most subtle abuse of power on earth, is that the fallen ones have made us believe that we are slaves of our own co-creation, that we cannot uncreate what we have created.

Archangel Michael, now I stand,
with you the light I do command.
My heart I ever will expand,
till highest truth I understand.

**Archangel Michael, you are here,
your light consumes all doubt and fear.
Your Presence is forever near,
you are to me so very dear.**

5. Archangel Michael, awaken people to the reality that this is the basic lie on earth. If you can create something, surely you can uncreate it.

Archangel Michael, in my heart,
from me you never will depart.
Of hierarchy I am a part,
I now accept a fresh new start.

**Archangel Michael, you are here,
your light consumes all doubt and fear.
Your Presence is forever near,
you are to me so very dear.**

6. Archangel Michael, awaken people to the reality that there is no condition manifest on earth right now that is not in some way affected by the collective consciousness.

Archangel Michael, sword of blue,
all darkness you are cutting through.
My Christhood I do now pursue,
discernment shows me what is true.

**Archangel Michael, you are here,
your light consumes all doubt and fear.
Your Presence is forever near,
you are to me so very dear.**

7. Archangel Michael, awaken people to the reality that the Elohim did not create the earth with all of the limitations and density we see today. It is all a manifestation of the collective consciousness. Therefore, it can be uncreated by the collective consciousness.

Archangel Michael, in your wings,
I now let go of lesser things.
God's homing call in my heart rings,
my heart with yours forever sings.

**Archangel Michael, you are here,
your light consumes all doubt and fear.
Your Presence is forever near,
you are to me so very dear.**

8. Archangel Michael, awaken people to the reality that currently, there needs to be the ability to deny that God exists because that is what has collectively been desired by a majority of the inhabitants of the earth.

Archangel Michael, take me home,
in higher spheres I want to roam.
I am reborn from cosmic foam,
my life is now a sacred poem.

> **Archangel Michael, you are here,**
> **your light consumes all doubt and fear.**
> **Your Presence is forever near,**
> **you are to me so very dear.**

9. Archangel Michael, awaken people to the reality that the ascended masters cannot act directly on earth, but they can act through us individually when we become the open doors.

> Archangel Michael, light you are,
> shining like the bluest star.
> You are a cosmic avatar,
> with you I will go very far.

> **Archangel Michael, you are here,**
> **your light consumes all doubt and fear.**
> **Your Presence is forever near,**
> **you are to me so very dear.**

Part 5

1. Archangel Michael, awaken people to the reality that for us to be open doors, we need to look beyond the mental images that we are projecting upon the masters.

> Archangel Michael, light so blue,
> my heart has room for only you.
> My mind is one, no longer two,
> your love for me is ever true.

> **Archangel Michael, you are here,**
> **your light consumes all doubt and fear.**
> **Your Presence is forever near,**
> **you are to me so very dear.**

2. Archangel Michael, awaken people to the reality that when we see the formless beings of the masters, they can manifest themselves through us in a manifestation that is as close to being physical as possible, given the current situation of the collective consciousness.

> Archangel Michael, I will be,
> all one with your reality.
> No fear can hold me as I see,
> this world no power has o'er me.

> **Archangel Michael, you are here,**
> **your light consumes all doubt and fear.**
> **Your Presence is forever near,**
> **you are to me so very dear.**

3. Archangel Michael, awaken people to the reality that for us to have maximum impact, we need to establish oneness with the ascended masters by going beyond our mental images.

> Archangel Michael, hold me tight,
> shatter now the darkest night.
> Clear my chakras with your light,
> restore to me my inner sight.

> **Archangel Michael, you are here,**
> **your light consumes all doubt and fear.**
> **Your Presence is forever near,**
> **you are to me so very dear.**

4. Archangel Michael, awaken people to the reality that you are not a fear-based being. You are an entirely love-based being, and love recognizes no opposition.

> Archangel Michael, now I stand,
> with you the light I do command.
> My heart I ever will expand,
> till highest truth I understand.

> **Archangel Michael, you are here,**
> **your light consumes all doubt and fear.**
> **Your Presence is forever near,**
> **you are to me so very dear.**

5. Archangel Michael, awaken people to the reality that the fallen beings want us to believe that they have misqualified so much energy and created all these physical manifestations and all these manifestations in the astral plane so that their creation can oppose you.

> Archangel Michael, in my heart,
> from me you never will depart.
> Of hierarchy I am a part,
> I now accept a fresh new start.

**Archangel Michael, you are here,
your light consumes all doubt and fear.
Your Presence is forever near,
you are to me so very dear.**

6. Archangel Michael, awaken people to the reality that one form of fear can oppose another form of fear, but no form of fear can oppose love, for love is formless. You do not feel threatened by the devil.

Archangel Michael, sword of blue,
all darkness you are cutting through.
My Christhood I do now pursue,
discernment shows me what is true.

**Archangel Michael, you are here,
your light consumes all doubt and fear.
Your Presence is forever near,
you are to me so very dear.**

7. Archangel Michael, awaken people to the reality that you cannot manifest yourself in the astral plane because of free will. The light of love makes it impossible for fear to exist where your Presence is manifest.

Archangel Michael, in your wings,
I now let go of lesser things.
God's homing call in my heart rings,
my heart with yours forever sings.

**Archangel Michael, you are here,
your light consumes all doubt and fear.
Your Presence is forever near,
you are to me so very dear.**

8. Archangel Michael, awaken people to the reality that fear cannot co-exist with love. The devil cannot co-exist in the same space with your Presence. When your Presence is there, fear must go.

Archangel Michael, take me home,
in higher spheres I want to roam.
I am reborn from cosmic foam,
my life is now a sacred poem.

**Archangel Michael, you are here,
your light consumes all doubt and fear.
Your Presence is forever near,
you are to me so very dear.**

9. Archangel Michael, awaken people to the reality that fear can be consumed by you, or it must withdraw if it will not surrender to transcendence. You have no need to fight any manifestation of anti-love.

Archangel Michael, light you are,
shining like the bluest star.
You are a cosmic avatar,
with you I will go very far.

**Archangel Michael, you are here,
your light consumes all doubt and fear.
Your Presence is forever near,
you are to me so very dear.**

Part 6

1. Archangel Michael, awaken people to the reality that as ascended master students we do not need to fight the forces of darkness. Instead, we are here to bring the light that is in contrast to darkness.

> Archangel Michael, light so blue,
> my heart has room for only you.
> My mind is one, no longer two,
> your love for me is ever true.

**Archangel Michael, you are here,
your light consumes all doubt and fear.
Your Presence is forever near,
you are to me so very dear.**

2. Archangel Michael, awaken people to the reality that when we bring the light, darkness fades away. The real way to "fight" the forces of darkness is to become an open door for the light of love.

> Archangel Michael, I will be,
> all one with your reality.
> No fear can hold me as I see,
> this world no power has o'er me.

**Archangel Michael, you are here,
your light consumes all doubt and fear.
Your Presence is forever near,
you are to me so very dear.**

3. Archangel Michael, awaken people to the reality that the real way to vanquish the manifestations of anti-love is to become an open door for love, the love that is not fear-based.

Archangel Michael, hold me tight,
shatter now the darkest night.
Clear my chakras with your light,
restore to me my inner sight.

**Archangel Michael, you are here,
your light consumes all doubt and fear.
Your Presence is forever near,
you are to me so very dear.**

4. Archangel Michael, awaken people to the reality that much of what humans call love is based on fear. It is based on the desire to own, which comes from the fear of loss.

Archangel Michael, now I stand,
with you the light I do command.
My heart I ever will expand,
till highest truth I understand.

**Archangel Michael, you are here,
your light consumes all doubt and fear.
Your Presence is forever near,
you are to me so very dear.**

5. Archangel Michael, awaken people to the reality that true love is beyond fear because it is unconditional. There is no condition that can hold it.

> Archangel Michael, in my heart,
> from me you never will depart.
> Of hierarchy I am a part,
> I now accept a fresh new start.
>
> **Archangel Michael, you are here,**
> **your light consumes all doubt and fear.**
> **Your Presence is forever near,**
> **you are to me so very dear.**

6. Archangel Michael, awaken people to the reality that when we become open doors for true love, we are giving maximum service. Thereby, even a few people can make a difference.

> Archangel Michael, sword of blue,
> all darkness you are cutting through.
> My Christhood I do now pursue,
> discernment shows me what is true.
>
> **Archangel Michael, you are here,**
> **your light consumes all doubt and fear.**
> **Your Presence is forever near,**
> **you are to me so very dear.**

7. Archangel Michael, awaken people to the reality that we can pull up on the collective consciousness because we are part of it when we are in embodiment.

> Archangel Michael, in your wings,
> I now let go of lesser things.
> God's homing call in my heart rings,
> my heart with yours forever sings.
>
> **Archangel Michael, you are here,**
> **your light consumes all doubt and fear.**
> **Your Presence is forever near,**
> **you are to me so very dear.**

8. Archangel Michael, awaken people to the reality of how the fallen beings took this planet to a lower level by becoming the leaders and making the majority of the people follow them.

> Archangel Michael, take me home,
> in higher spheres I want to roam.
> I am reborn from cosmic foam,
> my life is now a sacred poem.
>
> **Archangel Michael, you are here,**
> **your light consumes all doubt and fear.**
> **Your Presence is forever near,**
> **you are to me so very dear.**

9. Archangel Michael, awaken people to the reality that if a few fallen beings can take the planet down, then a few spiritual beings can also take the planet up. It is perfectly scientific that the few can lead the many.

> Archangel Michael, light you are,
> shining like the bluest star.
> You are a cosmic avatar,
> with you I will go very far.

**Archangel Michael, you are here,
your light consumes all doubt and fear.
Your Presence is forever near,
you are to me so very dear.**

Part 7

1. Archangel Michael, awaken people to the reality that the fallen beings as individuals or as a small group have had enormous power over the people, but they are doing everything they can to deny the power of the individual. They are denying the power of the individual to manifest Christhood.

Archangel Michael, light so blue,
my heart has room for only you.
My mind is one, no longer two,
your love for me is ever true.

**Archangel Michael, you are here,
your light consumes all doubt and fear.
Your Presence is forever near,
you are to me so very dear.**

2. Archangel Michael, awaken people to the reality that Christhood is that you know you are one with the One Mind and that everything is out of the One Mind.

Archangel Michael, I will be,
all one with your reality.
No fear can hold me as I see,
this world no power has o'er me.

**Archangel Michael, you are here,
your light consumes all doubt and fear.
Your Presence is forever near,
you are to me so very dear.**

3. Archangel Michael, awaken people to the reality that all people come from the One Mind, and therefore we have the authority to raise up the whole.

Archangel Michael, hold me tight,
shatter now the darkest night.
Clear my chakras with your light,
restore to me my inner sight.

**Archangel Michael, you are here,
your light consumes all doubt and fear.
Your Presence is forever near,
you are to me so very dear.**

4. Archangel Michael, awaken people to the vision of what is possible when we find our own personal balance between the spiritual and the daily life. Help people no longer see any difference or conflict because it all blends together.

Archangel Michael, now I stand,
with you the light I do command.
My heart I ever will expand,
till highest truth I understand.

**Archangel Michael, you are here,
your light consumes all doubt and fear.
Your Presence is forever near,
you are to me so very dear.**

5. Archangel Michael, awaken people to the reality that we do not always have to be decreeing in order to invoke your Presence. We can actually invite your Presence to be with us and then we are performing a spiritual service through all activities.

> Archangel Michael, in my heart,
> from me you never will depart.
> Of hierarchy I am a part,
> I now accept a fresh new start.
>
> **Archangel Michael, you are here,**
> **your light consumes all doubt and fear.**
> **Your Presence is forever near,**
> **you are to me so very dear.**

6. Archangel Michael, awaken people to feel that separation fades away and that everything we do can be endowed with light and love. It all becomes service.

> Archangel Michael, sword of blue,
> all darkness you are cutting through.
> My Christhood I do now pursue,
> discernment shows me what is true.
>
> **Archangel Michael, you are here,**
> **your light consumes all doubt and fear.**
> **Your Presence is forever near,**
> **you are to me so very dear.**

7. Archangel Michael, awaken people to the reality that you are not a remote being in the sky or a dualistic being who has been forced to fight the forces of darkness.

> Archangel Michael, in your wings,
> I now let go of lesser things.
> God's homing call in my heart rings,
> my heart with yours forever sings.
>
> **Archangel Michael, you are here,**
> **your light consumes all doubt and fear.**
> **Your Presence is forever near,**
> **you are to me so very dear.**

8. Archangel Michael, awaken people to the reality that, as the consciousness is raised, certain images fade away and no longer appeal to people. Then something new needs to come in. New ideas need to be brought forward.

> Archangel Michael, take me home,
> in higher spheres I want to roam.
> I am reborn from cosmic foam,
> my life is now a sacred poem.
>
> **Archangel Michael, you are here,**
> **your light consumes all doubt and fear.**
> **Your Presence is forever near,**
> **you are to me so very dear.**

9. Archangel Michael, awaken people to the reality that the only people who can bring forth new ideas are those who are open to them because they are willing to look beyond the old. Help people grasp the opportunity of being part of bringing forth a higher level of ascended master teaching.

Archangel Michael, light you are,
shining like the bluest star.
You are a cosmic avatar,
with you I will go very far.

Archangel Michael, you are here,
your light consumes all doubt and fear.
Your Presence is forever near,
you are to me so very dear.

Sealing

In the name of the Divine Mother, I call to Mother Mary for the sealing of myself and all people in my circle of influence in the creative flow of the Divine Mother, the River of Life. I call for the multiplication of my calls by all representatives of the Divine Mother, so that we form the perfect figure-eight flow of "As Above, so below." Thus, I accept that this is fully manifest, because the mouth of the Lord, the Divine Mother that I AM, has spoken it. Amen.

3 | LOOKING AT EVERYTHING FROM LOVE

I AM the Archeia Charity. I AM the Archeia of the Third Ray of Love. God love, unconditional love, fullness love, the love that flows and raises up all life without seeking to possess.

How do you possess? By holding things back from transcending themselves. By holding people back from transcending themselves so you can keep them in the matrix where you feel comfortable. Is this not what you have seen time and time again on the European continent where there has been, in every society, in every epoch, in every time period, a power elite that wants to hold back the people from transcending themselves?

Is this not the very core of the manifestation of anti-love? You do not want the people to be free. You do not want them to flow with the upward movement of the Spirit that pulls the entire universe up higher. You will not let them flow with that, for you have separated yourself – not you, but you the power elite – have separated yourself from that flow.

You want others to validate your choice to set yourself apart. You have a right to set yourself apart, but you do not have a right to demand that other people should validate your choice and make themselves the slaves of your choice. This is not a right given to you by the Law of Free Will, and thus you cannot take it without taking it by force, deceit and manipulation.

How the power elite uses ideas

You see how this power elite, how the members of it, have used all kinds of ideas, many of them originating on the European continent, in order to manipulate people into not flowing with the River of Life, with the upward movement of life that truly is love. When you truly love, do you not want your beloved to become more? Surely you do.

When you see that individuals want to limit others – be it their spouses, their children, their parents, their significant others – you know they are not coming from divine love. What could you possibly lose by your partner transcending himself or herself and becoming more in the flow of the Spirit?

You can lose nothing. *Your ego* can lose everything. It can lose its sense of being in control, which, of course, is what the ego needs, for it thinks it will die if it is not in control.

Why the power elite is on earth

We have told you that there is a power elite. There is a group of beings who have separated themselves from the flow of the River of Life, and they have been allowed to embody on earth. Surely many people will ask: "Why was this allowed? Why did

3 | Looking at Everything from Love

they come here?" Well, they came here, as we have said, as substitute teachers. When the people had separated themselves from the flow of love, they were trying to make things stand still.

Do you understand, my beloved, that before the fallen beings were allowed to embody on this planet, you did not see many of the wars and conflicts that you see today? But what you saw was standstill. So many societies on this earth were standing still. They had reached a level that was not primitive. It was in many ways sophisticated, compared to the civilizations you see on earth today. The people were satisfied. They were complacent. They felt they had enough. It was so good what they had.

Instead of being willing to transcend it and have more, they became attached to what they had. They wanted to stop the clock. They wanted to stop the forward progression of life. They wanted to hold on to it longer, just a little bit longer, just till the end of this lifetime (which, by the way, at the time was longer than the average lifespan today).

It became clear that the only thing that could shake them out of this, for they would not listen to Spirit anymore, was to allow some beings to embody on earth who could create such conflicts that the people would realize that standstill does not work. There really is no standing still, as we have explained about the second law of thermodynamics and how any closed system will start breaking down and self-destructing. This is what the inhabitants of the earth had not realized, would not realize. The fallen beings were allowed to embody here so they could outplay their consciousness.

It was, of course, inevitable that they would drag many people among the original inhabitants into their conflicts and their wars. It was inevitable that this would create suffering. The thing is, when people close themselves off to the input from Spirit, from the ascended masters, how will they grow unless they see the physical octave outplay in an extreme form the divisions and the conflicts they have in their own consciousness?

The stark reality is that they cannot grow in any other way than through the "School of Hard Knocks." Therefore it was necessary to have someone who could make the knocks harder, for the people at the time had isolated and insulated themselves to some degree from the hard knocks that their own consciousness had created.

It was necessary to allow this to be outplayed. This gave everyone an opportunity. It gave the inhabitants of earth an opportunity to see that the immovability – the standstill, the consciousness that was not transcending itself – did not work. It gave the fallen beings another opportunity to come to a planet and see the contrast between their own warring and conflict and the relative harmony that was on earth at the time. They had the potential to be transformed by this. Some were indeed transformed by it, but as you clearly see, not all were transformed by it.

The warmongers are no longer needed

What you realize, I hope, is the cycles have now turned to the point where those who are the most extreme among the war makers on earth are by cosmic law no longer needed here. The earth has moved to a point – the collective consciousness has moved to a point – where a critical mass of people have seen the fallacy of war. Therefore there is a potential that these warring lifestreams, who will not be transformed, who will not give up their war, can be removed from the earth.

3 | Looking at Everything from Love

For that to happen, a critical mass among the spiritual people must not only see the fallacy of war and the unpleasantness of war and the futility of war. They must also transcend in themselves the very consciousness that generates war. This is indeed what you who are here have started doing. Many of you have completely transcended that consciousness. Therefore we can indeed use you, your chakras, your auras, during this conference to release a certain amount of light that will then bring the judgment of those beings that will not let go of their warring ways.

You understand, as we have explained most recently by Mother Mary in her discourses on war (See the book: *Help the Ascended Masters Stop War*), that the judgment is not some ominous thing. It is actually an opportunity where those who are stuck in a certain state of consciousness are exposed to enough light that they cannot ignore or deny it. Therefore they see that there is something beyond their state of consciousness. Thereby they have a choice that they did not have before, when they were completely blinded by the separate state of consciousness. They can now choose between the light and the darkness.

The judgment is truly a supreme opportunity. Those who will not choose the light, who will not be transformed, will then be taken somewhere else where they can receive another opportunity, depending on their level of consciousness. You are not in any way harming the fallen beings by calling forth their judgment. You are actually giving them an opportunity to get out of the state of consciousness they are in, a state which causes them constant suffering, even though they sometimes ignore the suffering and cover it over by this sense of power that makes them almost drunk, feeling like they are masters of the universe.

As we have already said this morning, those who are embodied, or in other ways attached to a low planet like earth, surely cannot be sophisticated fallen beings, or they would not have manifested what you see manifest on this planet. They are not as high and mighty as they think. They are just so trapped in that state of consciousness that they cannot see anything else. Again, the judgment is an opportunity.

You are not judging. We are not asking you to judge anyone. We are asking you to call forth the judgment of Christ, which will discern between what is real and unreal without applying any kind of value judgment.

Too many wars in Europe

You have given a magnificent service today, both earlier and this evening, by giving this invocation for consuming the records of war. This is again having a double effect. It is giving those who have perpetrated these wars an opportunity to choose an alternative. It is also giving the people an opportunity to choose not to follow these war makers, who have dragged the people into war after war after war on this European continent. When you go home, look up on the Internet and search on wars in Europe, and see how long the list is, going back thousands of years.

You do not need to dwell on them, but I want you to know and realize with the conscious mind how many wars there have been on this continent. You can then have that impetus to look at this long line of wars and ask yourself a simple question: Have you had enough? Do you feel this is enough of wars on this European continent? Has enough blood soaked into the ground on this continent that you can stand up and say: "I will not accept any more wars in Europe"?

3 | Looking at Everything from Love

Then you make that determination. Not with the outer mind; I am not asking you to force your outer mind or to mechanically make this statement. I am asking you to tune in to your heart and reconnect to the love that brought you into embodiment at this time. If you have embodied on the European continent today and you are a spiritual person – certainly a person open to ascended master teachings – it was most likely because you had such a love for Saint Germain and the manifestation of his Golden Age. You wanted to be here to help bring an end to war, which truly has been such a burden on this continent.

I ask you to reconnect to that love and to not force yourself to make the calls about war, but to do it with love, to do it out of love, to be motivated by love, not by anger, my beloved. I do not need you to be angry with those who perpetrate war after war. I do not need you to look back at some of the wars or atrocities that have happened and be angry with these people or even with the dark forces.

Looking at war with love

I ask you to do what very, very few people are able to do: to look at war with love. I am not asking you to love war. I am asking you to look at it from a state of love.

This will require some adjustment. If you are sensitive, you can feel that there is a reaction from you. It is not only a reaction of you personally. It is a reaction from the collective consciousness as I speak these words in the physical. There is an objection. There is a protest that surely one cannot find anything loving about war. One cannot look at it with love.

You *can*, my beloved. It *is* possible. Because if you do not look at it with love, what are you looking at it with? You are looking at it with fear or anger. What is it that reinforces the momentum of war? What is it that so often causes people to feel that they *have* to go to war, that they have no other choice? Is it not fear and anger and hatred? If you hate war, will you not reinforce the very consciousness and the energetic momentums that cause war after war?

How will you be a peacemaker? How will you play a role in removing war from earth? Well, only when you can look at war with love. I know this will require an adjustment from you, but have we not already, in previous dictations during this conference, asked you to make an adjustment, to adjust your vision, to not look at us through the images of the fallen beings? I am now asking you to not look at war through the images of the fallen beings.

They want you to think that war is inevitable, that war is beneficial, that there is something to be gained from war. They want you to think you can only look at it with negative feelings, that you cannot look at it with love. They want you to think that you cannot free yourself from the consciousness of war, the consciousness of anti-love, but you *can,* my beloved. You can indeed. I give you permission to do this.

I AM the Archeia of the Third Ray of Love. I can give you the permission to look at war with love, through the eyes of love. Then you see that no matter how extreme a manifestation war is, it is an outplaying of free will and people's state of consciousness. It is making visible, undeniable at the physical level, that which is in the consciousness at the three higher levels. Thereby you see that, as extreme as war is, it is still possible for people to learn a positive lesson from war. I grant you that we would all like people to learn this without experiencing these extreme manifestations, but given that they cannot learn it in a higher way, they can still learn it through the physical outpicturing of their state of consciousness.

Love people, not war

This is what you realize when you are in love, when you are looking at war through the eyes of love. You are not loving war, but you are loving the people. You are loving them freely by holding the image that they can transcend, that they can rise above it, that they can free themselves from it. When you look at people with love, you do not need to punish other people. You do not need to make them feel bad about what they did in the past.

My beloved, before you can transcend a certain state of consciousness, it is necessary to see the unreality of that state of consciousness. It is *not* necessary to feel bad or guilty about what you have done in the past. In fact, this does not help you transcend the dualistic consciousness. It only ping-pongs you from one extreme, that of *not* seeing what you are doing, to the other dualistic extreme of now feeling guilty for what you did.

Do you understand that the fallen beings want you to be in this consciousness where you look at some people who created war and you feel that they should be made to feel responsible and realize the full manifestation and problem with what they did? You want them to feel bad, to feel guilty.

Think about the big country next to the little country you are in and how many of the nations in Europe have wanted to hold the German people responsible for World War II and Nazism. It was not that they were not responsible, but as we have said before, World War II was not only an expression of the consciousness of the German people, but of all the people in Europe and even the United States and beyond.

You cannot look at World War II and think that you will move the planet forward by making the German people feel bad and feel like they can never rise beyond what was done in the past. You cannot create a more peaceful Europe by wanting to punish the German people for what was done in the past. You can only make a more peaceful Europe by helping the German people transcend the consciousness they had before and during the war.

How will you help them transcend their consciousness? By *you* transcending the consciousness that you had, that your country, that your people had before and during the war. You see, this is looking through the eyes of love. There is no need to punish, to blame, to make other people feel bad. There is a need to make them feel free. Yes, they need to see what they did, but they do not need to see it through the dualistic vision of the fallen beings. They do not need to feel bad and be punished. They need to be liberated. They need to be set free. This is what love wants. This is what love does. It frees everyone from whatever limitations they are trapped in.

You can always be free

You may think that, after something as terrible as the Second World War and the Holocaust, people could never be free of it. This is what the fallen beings want you to believe: Something that happened in the past will define you for all of the future.

As we have said now several times, what do the ascended masters want? We want you to know that there is absolutely nothing that could ever happen on earth that you cannot transcend by making new choices. When you are in love, you can choose to let go of the old, to transcend the old. This is a choice you cannot make when you are in fear, because you would be afraid of losing something.

As Master MORE so eloquently said this morning, you have a wound, and in order to avoid re-experiencing the feeling you had, you are doing everything possible to avoid going into it. You are looking outside yourself and projecting that the problem is out there, that it is these other people that need to change.

Certainly there is a reason why Nazism emerged in Germany and not some other nation, but it doesn't mean that there wasn't a dualistic aspect of the consciousness of France, England and other nations. Do we actually advance the evolution of Europe by making the Germans exclusively responsible for the Second World War? Or do we awaken to the fact that all countries of Europe had a responsibility for this event, that all countries co-created this. Therefore every country has something that they need to transcend.

As Jesus said, once you pull that beam from your own eye, then you can see clearly how to help your brother or sister pull the splinter from his or her eye. Until you have pulled it from your own eye, you will not be able to see it clearly, for you are again blinded by your own wound of what you will not look at in yourself. Therefore you often will not see that the very problem you claim to see in others is actually an illustration of what you have not been willing to see in yourself.

This goes for nations as well. It is not healthy that so many countries are projecting that Nazism or another totalitarian force could never have arisen in their country, for all countries in Europe are to some degree affected by the same consciousness. This continent is not so big that you can separate one part clearly from another.

What will pull Europe up

What is it that will pull Europe up to the next level of evolution? It is a greater degree of oneness and harmony. What is the great victory that you achieved here today with your calls?

It was to come into unison, into harmony. Despite the fact that you do not know each other personally, many of you – you have just come together in this group for the first time – you could still achieve that greater harmony that can only come from love. It cannot be forced, my beloved. Surely you realize this.

You cannot force Europe to come into unison. Was that not what Hitler attempted to do? Was it not what Napoleon attempted to do? Was it not what the Soviets attempted to do? To force union through sameness is the only way that the fallen beings can envision this. You have to destroy differences, then they think there will be union.

There will be union not through force but through love only. It can be no other way because only love can recognize the oneness of all life. What can bring union except the recognition that all life is one? Nothing else, my beloved. That is love: seeing the oneness of all life, regardless of the manifestations that you see with the physical senses on earth. Seeing beyond even war, even the Second World War with all of its suffering. Seeing beyond it to see that this is just an outer manifestation that is not real, and beyond it is still the oneness of all life. This is love. When you can, as was said earlier, love your enemy – because you see that the enemy is also an expression of the One Mind, the one life – then you have transcended separation. Then you are in love. Then you are a force for love.

I wish to congratulate you for coming together, for coming together in that spirit of harmony, oneness and unison. I wish you to extend this unison not only among yourselves horizontally but also vertically with us, as we have made an effort to break down this barrier or distance that you tend to see between you and us. Allow us to step through the veil in your hearts. Allow yourselves and each other to be who you are. As Mother Mary said on the first day, give yourself permission to

3 | Looking at Everything from Love

love yourself. You might repeat this sentence or put it in your own words: Give yourself permission to love yourself.

Surely I do love you. For many of you, saying it will just be words that you have heard before, and many of you may have heard them from people who wanted to control you. So many people think that when you say: "I love you," to another human being, that person is supposed to give you some ownership. You are suddenly entitled to something because you have said that you love that person.

This is not how I say it. I do not desire to own you. How could I possibly be threatened by you exercising the free will given to you by God? I know that I have won my ascension by exercising my free will, and I know that you will eventually win yours by exercising your free will because it cannot be any other way. There will come a point where you begin to see, where all people begin to see, what we have explained to you. It is your own choices that manifest the physical conditions you face, and you can transcend any previous choice by making a higher choice.

I thank you from the core of my being for coming together and being here in this union of hearts that can only come from love.

4 | HELPING PEOPLE LOOK AT EVERYTHING FROM LOVE

In the name I AM THAT I AM, Jesus Christ, I call to all representatives of the Divine Mother, especially Archeia Charity, Maraytaii, Nada, Kuan Yin, Mother Mary, Portia, Liberty, Venus and Omega to help people make the shift in awareness and start to look at everything from love. Help them overcome all illusions of anti-love, including…

[Make personal calls.]

Part 1

1. Beloved Charity, awaken people to the reality that God love, unconditional love, fullness love is the love that flows and raises up all life without seeking to possess.

O Cosmic Mother, sound the gong,
that calls me home where I belong.
I know you love me tenderly,
and in that knowing I am free.

Maraytaii, I resonate
with song that opens cosmic gate.
Your melody makes me vibrate
my sense of self I recreate.

2. Beloved Charity, awaken people to the reality that we seek to possess by holding people back from transcending themselves so we can keep them in the matrix where we feel comfortable.

O Cosmic Mother, hold me tight,
I resonate with your own light.
Your music purifies my heart,
your love to all I do impart.

Maraytaii, I resonate
with song that opens cosmic gate.
Your melody makes me vibrate
my sense of self I recreate.

3. Beloved Charity, awaken people to the reality that in every society, in every epoch, in every time period, there has been a power elite that wants to hold back the people from transcending themselves.

O Cosmic Mother, we are one,
your heart is like a blazing sun.
My being can but amplify,
the sacred sound you magnify.

> **Maraytaii, I resonate
> with song that opens cosmic gate.
> Your melody makes me vibrate
> my sense of self I recreate.**

4. Beloved Charity, awaken people to the reality that the core of the manifestation of anti-love is that you do not want people to be free, you do not want them to flow with the upward movement of the Spirit that pulls the entire universe up higher.

> O Cosmic Mother, I now hear,
> the subtle sound of Sacred Sphere.
> As I attune to Cosmic Hum,
> the lesser self I overcome.

> **Maraytaii, I resonate
> with song that opens cosmic gate.
> Your melody makes me vibrate
> my sense of self I recreate.**

5. Beloved Charity, awaken people to the reality that the members of the power elite have separated themselves from that flow, and they want us to validate their choice to set themselves apart.

> O Cosmic Mother, take me home,
> I am in sync with Sacred OM,
> The sound of sounds will raise me up,
> so only light is in my cup.

**Maraytaii, I resonate
with song that opens cosmic gate.
Your melody makes me vibrate
my sense of self I recreate.**

6. Beloved Charity, awaken people to the reality that you have a right to set yourself apart, but you do not have a right to demand that other people should validate your choice and make themselves the slaves of your choice. That is why the power elite must use force, deceit and manipulation.

O Cosmic Mother, I will be,
a part of cosmic symphony.
All that I AM, an instrument,
for sound that is from heaven sent.

**Maraytaii, I resonate
with song that opens cosmic gate.
Your melody makes me vibrate
my sense of self I recreate.**

7. Beloved Charity, awaken people to the reality that the members of the power elite have used all kinds of ideas in order to manipulate people into not flowing with the River of Life, with the upward movement of life that truly is love.

O Cosmic Mother, I now call,
to enter sacred music hall.
I will be part of life's ascent,
towards the starry firmament.

**Maraytaii, I resonate
with song that opens cosmic gate.
Your melody makes me vibrate
my sense of self I recreate.**

8. Beloved Charity, awaken people to the reality that when you truly love, you want your beloved to become more. When you want to limit others, you are not coming from Divine love.

> O Cosmic Mother, tune my strings,
> my total being with you sings.
> Your song I now reverberate,
> as cosmic love I celebrate.

**Maraytaii, I resonate
with song that opens cosmic gate.
Your melody makes me vibrate
my sense of self I recreate.**

9. Beloved Charity, awaken people to the reality that we cannot lose by our partners transcending themselves and becoming more in the flow of the Spirit. Our egos can lose their sense of being in control, and the ego thinks it will die if it is not in control.

> O Cosmic Mother, I love you,
> your love song keeps me ever true.
> You fill me with your sacred tone,
> and thus I never feel alone.

Maraytaii, I resonate
with song that opens cosmic gate.
Your melody makes me vibrate
my sense of self I recreate.

Part 2

1. Beloved Charity, awaken people to the reality that members of the power elite were allowed to embody on earth as substitute teachers. When the people had separated themselves from the flow of love, they were trying to make things stand still.

> O Nada, blessed cosmic grace,
> filling up my inner space.
> Your song is like a sacred balm,
> my mind a sea of perfect calm.

**With Nada's secret melody,
my mind remains forever free.
Conducting Nada's symphony,
eternal peace I do decree.**

2. Beloved Charity, awaken people to the reality that before the fallen beings were allowed to embody on this planet, there were none of the wars and conflicts we see today.

> O Nada, in your Buddhic mind,
> my inner peace I truly find.
> As I your song reverberate,
> your love I do assimilate.

> With Nada's secret melody,
> my mind remains forever free.
> Conducting Nada's symphony,
> eternal peace I do decree.

3. Beloved Charity, awaken people to the reality that many societies were standing still. They had reached a level that was sophisticated, and the people were satisfied and complacent.

> O Nada, beauty so sublime,
> I follow you beyond all time.
> In soundless sound we do immerse,
> to recreate the universe.

> With Nada's secret melody,
> my mind remains forever free.
> Conducting Nada's symphony,
> eternal peace I do decree.

4. Beloved Charity, awaken people to the reality that people wanted to stop the clock. They wanted to stop the forward progression of life.

> O Nada, future we predict
> where nothing Christhood can restrict.
> With Buddhic mind we do perceive,
> a better future we conceive.

> With Nada's secret melody,
> my mind remains forever free.
> Conducting Nada's symphony,
> eternal peace I do decree.

5. Beloved Charity, awaken people to the reality that the only way to pull those societies out of standstill was to allow some beings to embody on earth who could create such conflicts that the people would realize that standstill does not work.

> O Nada, future we rewrite,
> where might is never, ever right.
> Instead, the mind of Christ is king,
> we see the Christ in every thing.

With Nada's secret melody,
my mind remains forever free.
Conducting Nada's symphony,
eternal peace I do decree.

6. Beloved Charity, awaken people to the reality that there is no standing still because any closed system will start breaking down and self-destructing.

> O Nada, peace is now the norm,
> my Spirit is beyond all form.
> To form I will no more adapt,
> I use potential yet untapped.

With Nada's secret melody,
my mind remains forever free.
Conducting Nada's symphony,
eternal peace I do decree.

7. Beloved Charity, awaken people to the reality that the fallen beings were allowed to embody here so they could outplay their consciousness. It was inevitable that they would drag many people into their conflicts and that this would create suffering.

O Nada, such resplendent joy,
my life I truly can enjoy.
I am allowed to have some fun,
my solar plexus like a sun.

**With Nada's secret melody,
my mind remains forever free.
Conducting Nada's symphony,
eternal peace I do decree.**

8. Beloved Charity, awaken people to the reality that when people close themselves off to input from Spirit, they cannot grow unless they see the physical octave outplay in an extreme form the divisions and the conflicts they have in their own consciousness.

O Nada, service is the key,
to living in reality.
For I see now that life is one,
my highest service has begun.

**With Nada's secret melody,
my mind remains forever free.
Conducting Nada's symphony,
eternal peace I do decree.**

9. Beloved Charity, awaken people to the reality that when people will not listen to Spirit, they can grow only through the "School of Hard Knocks." Therefore, someone had to make the knocks harder.

O Nada, we do now decree,
that life on earth shall be carefree.
With Jesus we complete the quest,
God's kingdom is now manifest.

**With Nada's secret melody,
my mind remains forever free.
Conducting Nada's symphony,
eternal peace I do decree.**

Part 3

1. Beloved Charity, awaken people to the reality that this gave the inhabitants of earth an opportunity to see that the consciousness that was not transcending itself did not work.

O Kuan Yin, what sacred name,
fill me now with Mercy's Flame.
In giving mercy I am free,
forgiving all is magic key.

**In Kuan Yin's sweet melody,
I am set free my Self to be.
In Kuan Yin's vitality,
I claim my immortality.**

2. Beloved Charity, awaken people to the reality that this gave the fallen beings another opportunity to come to a planet and see the contrast between their own warring and conflict and the relative harmony that was on earth at the time.

> O Kuan Yin, I now let go,
> of all attachments here below.
> All pent-up feelings I release,
> free from emotional disease.
>
> **In Kuan Yin's sweet melody,**
> **I am set free my Self to be.**
> **In Kuan Yin's vitality,**
> **I claim my immortality.**

3. Beloved Charity, awaken people to the reality that cycles have now turned to the point where those who are the most extreme among the war makers on earth are by cosmic law no longer needed here.

> O Kuan Yin, why must I feel,
> that life falls short of my ideal?
> All expectations I give up,
> my mind is now an empty cup.
>
> **In Kuan Yin's sweet melody,**
> **I am set free my Self to be.**
> **In Kuan Yin's vitality,**
> **I claim my immortality.**

4. Beloved Charity, awaken people to the reality that the collective consciousness has moved to a point where a critical mass of people have seen the fallacy of war. There is a potential that the warring lifestreams can be removed from the earth.

O Kuan Yin, transcend the past,
as all resentment gone at last.
From future nothing I expect,
eternal now I won't reject.

**In Kuan Yin's sweet melody,
I am set free my Self to be.
In Kuan Yin's vitality,
I claim my immortality.**

5. Beloved Charity, awaken people to the reality that for war to be removed, a critical mass among the spiritual people must see the fallacy of war and transcend in themselves the consciousness that generates war.

O Kuan Yin, uplifting me,
beyond Samsara's raging sea.
All safe inside your Prajna boat,
the farther shore no more remote.

**In Kuan Yin's sweet melody,
I am set free my Self to be.
In Kuan Yin's vitality,
I claim my immortality.**

6. Beloved Charity, awaken people to the reality that the ascended masters can use our chakras to release light that will bring the judgment of those beings that will not let go of their warring ways.

> O Kuan Yin, your alchemy,
> with miracles you set me free.
> As I forgive, I am forgiven,
> by guilt I am no longer driven.
>
> **In Kuan Yin's sweet melody,**
> **I am set free my Self to be.**
> **In Kuan Yin's vitality,**
> **I claim my immortality.**

7. Beloved Charity, awaken people to the reality that the judgment is not some ominous thing. It is an opportunity where those who are stuck in a certain state of consciousness are exposed to enough light that they cannot ignore or deny it.

> O Kuan Yin, all worries gone,
> with nothing done, no thing undone.
> Through separate self I will not do,
> and thus I rest, all one with you.
>
> **In Kuan Yin's sweet melody,**
> **I am set free my Self to be.**
> **In Kuan Yin's vitality,**
> **I claim my immortality.**

8. Beloved Charity, awaken people to the reality that when people receive the judgment, they see that there is something beyond their state of consciousness. They have a choice that they did not have before, when they were completely blinded by the separate state of consciousness. They can now choose between the light and the darkness.

O Kuan Yin, your sanity,
now sets me free from vanity.
For truly, what is that to me;
I just let go and follow thee.

**In Kuan Yin's sweet melody,
I am set free my Self to be.
In Kuan Yin's vitality,
I claim my immortality.**

9. Beloved Charity, awaken people to the reality that the judgment is a supreme opportunity. Those who will not choose the light, who will not be transformed, will then be taken somewhere else where they can receive another opportunity, depending on their level of consciousness.

O Kuan Yin, so sweet the sound,
that emanates from holy ground.
As I let go of ego's chore,
I find myself on farther shore.

**In Kuan Yin's sweet melody,
I am set free my Self to be.
In Kuan Yin's vitality,
I claim my immortality.**

Part 4

1. Beloved Charity, awaken people to the reality that we are not harming the fallen beings by calling forth their judgment. We are giving them an opportunity to get out of the state of consciousness they are in, a state which causes them constant suffering, even though they sometimes feel like they are masters of the universe.

> O Blessed Mary's Song of Life,
> consuming every form of strife.
> As I attune to sound so fair,
> each cell is healthy, I declare.
>
> **O Mother Mary, generate,**
> **the song that does accelerate,**
> **my mind into a peaceful state,**
> **God's perfect love I radiate.**

2. Beloved Charity, awaken people to the reality that we are not judging. We are calling forth the judgment of Christ, which will discern between what is real and unreal without applying any kind of value judgment.

> As life's own song I ever hear,
> it does consume all sense of fear.
> In tune with Mother's symphony,
> from all diseases I AM free.

**O Mother Mary, generate,
the song that does accelerate,
my mind into a peaceful state,
God's perfect love I radiate.**

3. Beloved Charity, give those who have perpetrated war an opportunity to choose an alternative. Give the people an opportunity to choose not to follow these war makers, who have dragged the people into war after war.

In Mother's love I do transcend,
and all my struggles hereby end.
For when with Mother's eye I see,
no imperfection touches me.

**O Mother Mary, generate,
the song that does accelerate,
my mind into a peaceful state,
God's perfect love I radiate.**

4. Beloved Charity, awaken people to the reality that they need to look at the many wars on earth and ask themselves the question: "Have I had enough? Do I feel this is enough of war?" Then people need to take a stand and say: "I will not accept any more wars!"

I see that healing must begin
by finding Living Christ within.
For as I see with single eye,
each cell the light does amplify.

**O Mother Mary, generate,
the song that does accelerate,
my mind into a peaceful state,
God's perfect love I radiate.**

5. Beloved Charity, help people to tune in to their hearts and reconnect to the love that brought them into embodiment at this time. Help people rediscover their love for Saint Germain and the manifestation of his Golden Age and their desire to help bring an end to war.

In Mother's music I am free,
from memories of a lesser me.
My vision in a perfect state,
that all my cells regenerate.

**O Mother Mary, generate,
the song that does accelerate,
my mind into a peaceful state,
God's perfect love I radiate.**

6. Beloved Charity, help people reconnect to that love and to not force themselves to make the calls about war, but to do it with love, to do it out of love, to be motivated by love, not by anger.

O Mother's Love, sweet melody,
from imperfections I AM free.
O Mother Mary, sound of sounds,
within my heart your love abounds.

**O Mother Mary, generate,
the song that does accelerate,
my mind into a peaceful state,
God's perfect love I radiate.**

7. Beloved Charity, awaken people to the reality that we need to look at war with love. You are not asking us to love war but to look at it from a state of love.

> Through Mother's beauty so sublime,
> transcending bounds of space and time.
> All cells beyond the mortal tomb,
> as they are whole in Mother's womb.

**O Mother Mary, generate,
the song that does accelerate,
my mind into a peaceful state,
God's perfect love I radiate.**

8. Beloved Charity, awaken people to the reality that it is possible to look at war with love. If we do not look at it with love, we are looking at it with fear or anger. What reinforces the momentum of war is fear, anger and hatred.

> In resonance with life's own song,
> in life's harmonics I belong.
> The blueprint of my perfect state
> does every cell reconsecrate.

**O Mother Mary, generate,
the song that does accelerate,
my mind into a peaceful state,
God's perfect love I radiate.**

9. Beloved Charity, awaken people to the reality that we can be peacemakers and help remove war from earth only when we can look at war with love. Help us to stop looking at war through the images of the fallen beings.

> The tuning fork in every cell
> is now attuned to Mother's bell.
> From curse of death I AM now free,
> I claim my immortality.
>
> **O Mother Mary, generate,**
> **the song that does accelerate,**
> **my mind into a peaceful state,**
> **God's perfect love I radiate.**

Part 5

1. Beloved Charity, awaken people to the reality that the fallen beings want us to think that war is inevitable, that war is beneficial, that there is something to be gained from war.

> O Portia, in your own retreat,
> with Mother's Love you do me greet.
> As all my tests I now complete,
> old patterns I no more repeat.
>
> **O Portia, opportunity,**
> **I am beyond duality.**
> **I focus now internally,**
> **with you I grow eternally.**

2. Beloved Charity, awaken people to the reality that the fallen beings want us to think we can only look at war with negative feelings, that we cannot look at it with love.

> O Portia, Justice is your name,
> upholding Cosmic Honor Flame,
> No longer will I play the game,
> of seeking to remain the same.
>
> **O Portia, opportunity,**
> **I am beyond duality.**
> **I focus now internally,**
> **with you I grow eternally.**

3. Beloved Charity, awaken people to the reality that the fallen beings want us to think that we cannot free ourselves from the consciousness of war, the consciousness of anti-love, but we *can*, we have your permission to do this.

> O Portia, in the cosmic flow,
> one with you, I ever grow.
> I am the chalice here below,
> of cosmic justice you bestow.
>
> **O Portia, opportunity,**
> **I am beyond duality.**
> **I focus now internally,**
> **with you I grow eternally.**

4. Beloved Charity, awaken people to the reality that no matter how extreme a manifestation war is, it is an outplaying of free will and people's state of consciousness. It is making visible and undeniable at the physical level, that which is in the consciousness at the three higher levels.

> O Portia, cosmic balance bring,
> eternal hope, my heart does sing.
> Protected by your Mother's wing,
> I feel at one with everything.

> **O Portia, opportunity,**
> **I am beyond duality.**
> **I focus now internally,**
> **with you I grow eternally.**

5. Beloved Charity, awaken people to the reality that, as extreme as war is, it is still possible for people to learn a positive lesson from war. If they cannot learn without experiencing these extreme manifestations, they can still learn through the physical outpicturing of their state of consciousness.

> O Portia, bring the Mother Light,
> to set all free from darkest night.
> Your Love Flame shines forever bright,
> with Saint Germain now hold me tight.

> **O Portia, opportunity,**
> **I am beyond duality.**
> **I focus now internally,**
> **with you I grow eternally.**

6. Beloved Charity, awaken people to the reality that when we are in love, when we are looking at war through the eyes of love, we are not loving war, but we are loving the people.

> O Portia, in your mastery,
> I feel transforming chemistry.
> In your light of reality,
> I find the golden alchemy.
>
> **O Portia, opportunity,**
> **I am beyond duality.**
> **I focus now internally,**
> **with you I grow eternally.**

7. Beloved Charity, help people love others freely by holding the image that they can transcend, that they can rise above it, that they can free themselves from it. When we look at people with love, we do not need to punish other people, we do not need to make them feel bad about what they did in the past.

> O Portia, in the cosmic stream,
> I am awake from human dream.
> Removing now the ego's beam,
> I earn my place on cosmic team.
>
> **O Portia, opportunity,**
> **I am beyond duality.**
> **I focus now internally,**
> **with you I grow eternally.**

8. Beloved Charity, awaken people to the reality that before we can transcend a certain state of consciousness, it is necessary to see the unreality of that state of consciousness. It is not necessary to feel bad or guilty about what we have done in the past.

> O Portia, you come from afar,
> you are a cosmic avatar.
> So infinite your repertoire,
> you are for earth a guiding star.
>
> **O Portia, opportunity,**
> **I am beyond duality.**
> **I focus now internally,**
> **with you I grow eternally.**

9. Beloved Charity, awaken people to the reality that feeling shame does not help us transcend the dualistic consciousness. It only ping-pongs us from one extreme, that of not seeing what we are doing, to the other dualistic extreme of now feeling guilty for what we did.

> O Portia, I am confident,
> I am a cosmic instrument.
> I came to earth from heaven sent,
> to help bring forward her ascent.
>
> **O Portia, opportunity,**
> **I am beyond duality.**
> **I focus now internally,**
> **with you I grow eternally.**

Part 6

1. Beloved Charity, awaken people to the reality that the fallen beings want us to look at some people who created war and feel that they should be made to feel responsible and realize the full manifestation and problem with what they did. They should be made to feel bad, to feel guilty.

> O Liberty now set me free
> from devil's curse of poverty.
> I blame not Mother for my lack,
> O Blessed Mother, take me back.

> **O Cosmic Mother Liberty,**
> **conduct Abundance Symphony.**
> **My highest service I now see,**
> **abundance is now real for me.**

2. Beloved Charity, awaken people to the reality that any war is an expression of the consciousness of the people on both sides.

> O Liberty, from distant shore,
> I come with longing to be More.
> I see abundance is a flow,
> abundance consciousness I grow.

> **O Cosmic Mother Liberty,**
> **conduct Abundance Symphony.**
> **My highest service I now see,**
> **abundance is now real for me.**

3. Beloved Charity, awaken people to the reality that the German people were not exclusively responsible for World War II and Nazism. World War II was not only an expression of the consciousness of the German people, but of all the people in the world.

> O Liberty, expose the lie,
> that limitations can me tie.
> The Ma-ter light is not my foe,
> true opulence it does bestow.
>
> **O Cosmic Mother Liberty,**
> **conduct Abundance Symphony.**
> **My highest service I now see,**
> **abundance is now real for me.**

4. Beloved Charity, awaken people to the reality that we cannot look at World War II and think that we will move the planet forward by making the German or Japanese people feel bad and feel like they can never rise beyond what was done in the past.

> O Liberty, expose the plot,
> projected by the fallen lot.
> O Cosmic Mother, I now see,
> that Mother's not my enemy.
>
> **O Cosmic Mother Liberty,**
> **conduct Abundance Symphony.**
> **My highest service I now see,**
> **abundance is now real for me.**

5. Beloved Charity, awaken people to the reality that we cannot create a more peaceful world by wanting to punish certain people for what was done in the past. We can only make a more peaceful world by helping the people transcend the consciousness they had before and during the war.

> O Liberty, with opened eyes,
> I now reject the devil's lies.
> I now embrace the Mother realm,
> for I see Father at the helm.
>
> **O Cosmic Mother Liberty,**
> **conduct Abundance Symphony.**
> **My highest service I now see,**
> **abundance is now real for me.**

6. Beloved Charity, awaken people to the reality that we can help others only when we transcend the consciousness that we had, and that our country and our people had, before and during the war.

> O Liberty, a chalice pure,
> my lower bodies are for sure.
> Release through me your symphony,
> your gift of Cosmic Liberty.
>
> **O Cosmic Mother Liberty,**
> **conduct Abundance Symphony.**
> **My highest service I now see,**
> **abundance is now real for me.**

7. Beloved Charity, awaken people to the reality that when we are looking through the eyes of love, there is no need to punish, to blame, to make other people feel bad. There is a need to make them feel free.

> O Liberty, the open door,
> I am for Symphony of More.
> In chakras mine light you release,
> the flow of love shall never cease.
>
> **O Cosmic Mother Liberty,**
> **conduct Abundance Symphony.**
> **My highest service I now see,**
> **abundance is now real for me.**

8. Beloved Charity, awaken people to the reality that other people need to see what they did, but they do not need to see it through the dualistic vision of the fallen beings. They do not need to feel bad and be punished.

> O Liberty, release the flow,
> of opulence that you bestow.
> For I am willing to receive,
> the Golden Fleece that you now weave.
>
> **O Cosmic Mother Liberty,**
> **conduct Abundance Symphony.**
> **My highest service I now see,**
> **abundance is now real for me.**

9. Beloved Charity, awaken people to the reality that people need to be liberated. They need to be set free. This is what love wants. This is what love does. It frees everyone from whatever limitations they are trapped in.

> O Liberty, release the cure,
> to free the tired and the poor.
> The huddled masses are set free,
> by loving Song of Liberty.
>
> **O Cosmic Mother Liberty,**
> **conduct Abundance Symphony.**
> **My highest service I now see,**
> **abundance is now real for me.**

Part 7

1. Beloved Charity, awaken people to the reality that the fallen beings want us to believe that after something as terrible as the Second World War and the Holocaust, people could never be free of it. Something that happened in the past will define us for all of the future.

> O Venus, show me how to serve,
> your cosmic beauty I observe.
> What love from Venus you now bring,
> our planets do in tandem sing.

**O Venus, service so divine,
you are for earth a cosmic sign.
Your selfless service is now mine,
a life in service I define.**

2. Beloved Charity, awaken people to the reality that the ascended masters want us to know that there is absolutely nothing that could ever happen on earth that we cannot transcend by making new choices.

O Venus, your love is the key,
the hardened hearts on earth are free.
Embracing future bright and bold,
our planet's story is retold.

**O Venus, service so divine,
you are for earth a cosmic sign.
Your selfless service is now mine,
a life in service I define.**

3. Beloved Charity, awaken people to the reality that when we are in love, we can choose to let go of the old, to transcend the old. This is a choice we cannot make when we are in fear because we would be afraid of losing something.

O Venus, loving Mother mine,
my heart your love does now refine.
I am the open door for love,
descending like a Holy Dove.

> **O Venus, service so divine,**
> **you are for earth a cosmic sign.**
> **Your selfless service is now mine,**
> **a life in service I define.**

4. Beloved Charity, awaken people to the reality that when we have a wound, we will do everything possible to avoid going into it. We are looking outside ourselves and projecting that the problem is out there, that it is other people that need to change.

> O Venus, play the secret note,
> that is for hatred antidote.
> All poisoned hearts you gently heal,
> as love's true story you reveal.

> **O Venus, service so divine,**
> **you are for earth a cosmic sign.**
> **Your selfless service is now mine,**
> **a life in service I define.**

5. Beloved Charity, awaken people to the reality that while there was a reason why Nazism emerged in Germany, the consciousness of all other nations also had dualistic aspects.

> O Venus, love fills every need,
> for truly, love is God's first seed.
> O let it blossom, let it grow,
> sweep earth into your loving flow.

> O Venus, service so divine,
> you are for earth a cosmic sign.
> Your selfless service is now mine,
> a life in service I define.

6. Beloved Charity, awaken people to the reality that we do not advance the evolution of the world by making certain people exclusively responsible for the Second World War. Help people awaken to the fact that all countries had a responsibility, and each country has something that it needs to transcend.

> O Venus, music of the spheres,
> heard by those who God reveres.
> Our voices now as one we raise,
> singing in adoring praise.

> O Venus, service so divine,
> you are for earth a cosmic sign.
> Your selfless service is now mine,
> a life in service I define.

7. Beloved Charity, awaken people to the reality that the very problem we claim to see in others is an illustration of what we have not been willing to see in ourselves.

> O Venus, we are joining ranks,
> Sanat Kumara we give thanks.
> Our planet has received new life,
> to lift her out of war and strife.

> O Venus, service so divine,
> you are for earth a cosmic sign.
> Your selfless service is now mine,
> a life in service I define.

8. Beloved Charity, awaken people to the reality that it is not healthy that so many countries are projecting that Nazism or another totalitarian force could never have arisen in their country.

> O Venus, your sweet melody,
> consumes veil of duality.
> Absorbed in tones of Cosmic Love,
> all conflict we now rise above.

> O Venus, service so divine,
> you are for earth a cosmic sign.
> Your selfless service is now mine,
> a life in service I define.

9. Beloved Charity, awaken people to the reality that all countries are to some degree affected by the same consciousness.

> O Venus, shining Morning Star,
> a cosmic herald, that you are.
> The earth set free by sacred sound,
> our planet is now heaven-bound.

> O Venus, service so divine,
> you are for earth a cosmic sign.
> Your selfless service is now mine,
> a life in service I define.

Part 8

1. Beloved Charity, awaken people to the reality that what will pull the world up to the next level of evolution is a greater degree of oneness and harmony.

> Omega, I now meditate,
> upon your throne in cosmic gate.
> I'm born out of the figure-eight,
> that Alpha and you co-create.
>
> **O Song of Life, you vitalize,**
> **all hearts you truly synchronize.**
> **O Sacred Sound, you alchemize,**
> **turn earth into a paradise.**

2. Beloved Charity, awaken people to the reality that we cannot force nations to come into unison. This was what Hitler, Napoleon and the Soviets attempted to do.

> Omega, in your sacred space,
> my cosmic parents I embrace.
> I see that it is such a grace,
> that I take part in cosmic race.
>
> **O Song of Life, you vitalize,**
> **all hearts you truly synchronize.**
> **O Sacred Sound, you alchemize,**
> **turn earth into a paradise.**

3. Beloved Charity, awaken people to the reality that the fallen beings want us to believe that we must force union through sameness, that we have to destroy differences in order to create union.

> Omega in the Central Sun,
> you show me life is cosmic fun.
> And thus a victory is won,
> my homeward journey has begun.
>
> **O Song of Life, you vitalize,**
> **all hearts you truly synchronize.**
> **O Sacred Sound, you alchemize,**
> **turn earth into a paradise.**

4. Beloved Charity, awaken people to the reality that there will be union not through force but through love only. It can be no other way because only love can recognize the oneness of all life.

> Omega, femininity
> is doorway to infinity.
> With you I have affinity,
> to know my own divinity.
>
> **O Song of Life, you vitalize,**
> **all hearts you truly synchronize.**
> **O Sacred Sound, you alchemize,**
> **turn earth into a paradise.**

5. Beloved Charity, awaken people to the reality that nothing can bring union except the recognition that all life is one. Love is seeing the oneness of all life, regardless of the manifestations that you see with the physical senses on earth.

> Omega, in your cosmic flow,
> my plan divine I clearly know.
> My heart is now a lamp aglow,
> as love on all I do bestow.
>
> **O Song of Life, you vitalize,**
> **all hearts you truly synchronize.**
> **O Sacred Sound, you alchemize,**
> **turn earth into a paradise.**

6. Beloved Charity, awaken people to the reality that love means seeing beyond even the Second World War with all of its suffering. Love is seeing that this is just an outer manifestation that is not real, and beyond it is still the oneness of all life.

> Omega, cosmic Mother Flame,
> this is the light from which I came.
> As I take part in cosmic game,
> Christ victory I do proclaim.
>
> **O Song of Life, you vitalize,**
> **all hearts you truly synchronize.**
> **O Sacred Sound, you alchemize,**
> **turn earth into a paradise.**

7. Beloved Charity, awaken people to the reality that love is when we can love our enemy because we see that the enemy is also an expression of the One Mind, the one life. Then we have transcended separation. Then we are in love. Then we are a force for love.

> Omega, I now comprehend,
> why I did to earth descend.
> And thus I fully do intend,
> to help this planet to ascend.
>
> **O Song of Life, you vitalize,**
> **all hearts you truly synchronize.**
> **O Sacred Sound, you alchemize,**
> **turn earth into a paradise.**

8. Beloved Charity, awaken people to the reality that we need to allow ourselves and each other to be who we are. We need to give ourselves permission to love ourselves.

> Omega, I do now aspire,
> to join the ranks of cosmic choir.
> My heart burns with a Christic fire,
> that is this planet's sanctifier.
>
> **O Song of Life, you vitalize,**
> **all hearts you truly synchronize.**
> **O Sacred Sound, you alchemize,**
> **turn earth into a paradise.**

9. Beloved Charity, awaken people to the reality that it is our own choices that manifest the physical conditions we face. Only by acknowledging this, can we transcend any previous choice by making a higher choice.

> Omega, my heart is ablaze,
> my life is in an upward phase.
> Come teach me now the secret phrase,
> so that I can this planet raise.
>
> **O Song of Life, you vitalize,**
> **all hearts you truly synchronize.**
> **O Sacred Sound, you alchemize,**
> **turn earth into a paradise.**

Sealing

In the name of the Divine Mother, I call to Maraytaii, Nada, Kuan Yin and Mother Mary for the sealing of myself and all people in my circle of influence in the creative flow of the Divine Mother, the River of Life. I call for the multiplication of my calls by all representatives of the Divine Mother, so that we form the perfect figure-eight flow of "As Above, so below." Thus, I accept that this is fully manifest, because the mouth of the Lord, the Divine Mother that I AM, has spoken it. Amen.

5 | INTRODUCTION TO SAINT GERMAIN

Kim Michaels: We are now ready for Saint Germain, but Saint Germain wants me to say something, and he doesn't want to tell me what to say, so I am going to start speaking and see what comes up. What is Saint Germain? The natural question is: "Who is Saint Germain?" And that's how we would normally ask it. But do we really know Saint Germain if we ask who? We think: "Well, he must be like a human being. We must be able to define him somehow by comparing him to human beings."

That's, of course, what we can't do, and that's why it's better to ask: "*What* is Saint Germain?" Can we even define him? Can we even put words on it? No, we can't, but we can experience him as a living Presence, and I think that you have probably all experienced Saint Germain in one form or another. I know I have.

I know that, when I first heard about the teachings of the ascended masters, the two masters I responded to the strongest were Mother Mary and Saint Germain. For a very long time I couldn't relate to Jesus as an ascended master because I still had the image the Christian church had put upon Jesus for so long. I knew in my heart that this wasn't right, this wasn't who Jesus is, but I didn't know what else he is. I hadn't experienced it because I couldn't get beyond the image.

I still had the consciousness that Charity was talking about. I felt that it was wrong what the Christians had done, and they somehow needed to be made responsible for it, and somebody darned well needed to feel bad about it. Because of that, I couldn't see Jesus for who he is. I was still seeing that image. I knew the image was wrong, but I could not see Jesus in any other way than through the image.

With Saint Germain I didn't have a preconceived image. There was nothing there. When I first heard about him and saw the picture, I could relate to him more openly. I was open with Saint Germain, I was open with Mother Mary, but not with Jesus.

How to see the masters

I think it's so important for us to grasp that it is like the masters are always here. We think they are way up there, but they are right here. They are just in another dimension, in a higher vibration, but as they were saying in the dictations, we *can* actually see them. We just can't see them if we are imposing a mental image on them or if we are expecting to see them through the physical senses. This is not how we see them, how we experience them.

I have studied perception a little bit. You know that right now your eyes are taking in so many visual impressions that your conscious mind cannot deal with them. That means that all of the light rays that are coming into your eyes—that's not what you are seeing. You are actually not seeing the light that is being reflected back from all of the things in this room. You are not seeing that. The light rays go into your eyes, and your eyes can process them. Then there is some wiring that connects to the visual cortex of the brain, and what you are seeing is an image displayed in your brain. You are not seeing what's *out there*. You are seeing something that's *in here,* but there's a filter imposed by your brain. It's not necessarily an evil filter. It's just to avoid overwhelming your conscious mind with all of the stuff that's coming at you constantly.

It's the same thing with seeing Saint Germain's Presence and Saint Germain's light in this room. Your physical eyes are taking in that light, but your brain is filtering it out because he's so far beyond your normal conception of reality.

There's an old story, which I do not think is true, but that does not matter. You don't have to take it literally. The story is that when Columbus, who was Saint Germain in embodiment, came to the New World and met the inhabitants there, they had never seen any vessel on the sea bigger than a canoe. It's said that they couldn't see the ships, because the ships were so far beyond what they were able to imagine that their brains couldn't accept what their eyes were seeing. It's said that there was one who was the chief of a tribe, and he was the first one who was able to switch and see the ships, and then the others could see them as well.

That ties in with the old fairy tale by Hans Christian Andersen, who was from Denmark like me. That's why I heard it when I was a little child: *The Emperor's New Clothes.* People couldn't see that he was standing there stark naked in front of them because their brains refused to acknowledge what their eyes were seeing. This is what we have to do here. This is our challenge in the physical octave: not to allow these mental images – which have been created by the fallen beings and by people collectively and by ourselves – to block our experience of the reality that's beyond this world, especially the ascended masters.

Seeing beyond images of the masters

When I first heard about Saint Germain, I connected with him, and there was a picture that I really liked of him. You have probably all seen it, and it's a beautiful picture. There's nothing wrong with it, but there also came a point where I realized I had to stop using that image because it was limiting my vision of Saint Germain. It was like I wanted him to conform to this.

Then there were all these stories related to who Saint Germain was in past embodiments and how he was the Wonder Man of Europe. He could walk through solid walls and appear out of nowhere, remove flaws from diamonds and turn lead into gold. He was like this magician. I also came to a point where I realized that this has its place. There are certain points on the path where this has its place because it helps people at a certain level to connect to something that is the Presence of Saint Germain. But it is not the fullness of Saint Germain.

We have to come to the point where we ask ourselves: "What do I want? Do I want this outer image of Saint Germain that has some connection to reality? Or do I want more? Do I want something higher?"

What is Saint Germain? He is the Presence of Freedom, and what's freedom? It can't be trapped anywhere. There is no image you can impose and say: "Now we have defined Saint Germain." We may create this wonderful image: a statue, a beautiful statue, with wonderful eyes, eyes like amethysts, light radiating out. And it is just a most beautiful image, gold all over, jewels and everything. But if we say: "Saint Germain, get in there and stay there," he's going to say, "Sorry, I'm going to have to refuse." It wouldn't help us grow.

It would just limit us by conforming to our images. This is the danger that I have seen both in myself and in many, many ascended master students. They have the best of intentions, the best of intentions, but there comes a point where they have become so comfortable with an image of the ascended masters that it is now stopping their growth instead of enhancing it. That, of course, is the last thing that Saint Germain wants: that we create an image of him that limits our freedom. Why would he want that? He doesn't want that. It's the last thing he would want.

I think that if we really love Saint Germain, if we really honor his Presence, we have to do what they were told to do in Biblical times. We have to take all our idols and destroy them, throw them into the spiritual fire. Saint Germain is the Fire of Freedom. We can take all our images of him and throw them into the fire, and then I think we can experience his Presence in a new way. We can experience this coming dictation in a new way that we may never have experienced him before. It is all a matter of how open we are willing to be to this Presence that cannot be defined.

6 | AN ALCHEMICAL SHIFT IN PEOPLE'S PERCEPTION

Most gracious ladies and gentlemen, I almost do not need to say anything, for you have already heard the core of my message. I am free because I am not defined by anything on earth. You will be free when you do not let anything on earth define you.

What is it that the fallen beings want? They want to be like gods on earth, and how do you become a god on earth? By tricking the people on earth to worship you as a supreme authority because then you can control how they define themselves. What has the Catholic church been doing since its inception? It has been attempting to cause those who thought they were followers of Jesus Christ to define themselves as the opposite kind of being to what Jesus demonstrated.

Original sin is a lie

Look at the concept of original sin: that you are sinners by nature, that God created you as a sinner. Could this idea ever have come from the mind of God? Nay, of course not. Why would God create you as a sinner when you have to make a certain choice in order to overcome that condition?

Do you not see that the fallen beings are not necessarily denying free will? They are saying you are a sinner and, in order to be saved, you have to choose to follow them. If God had created you with a capacity to overcome sin through choice, why would he create you as a sinner?

Why would he not create you as a free being so that sin is a result of choice and therefore can be overcome—not by making the outer choice to follow the fallen beings, but by making the choice to look at yourself and overcome the consciousness that keeps you trapped in a lesser image of yourself.

What is sin, if there is such a thing as sin? Is it not that you are imposing an image upon yourself that is not in alignment with what God created? You are making yourself a god. Instead of accepting the reality that God created you as an extension of its own being, of the one mind, you are imposing an image upon yourself that you are a limited, flawed being. Do you not thereby think you know better than God what God created? Are you not thereby making yourself as a god knowing good and evil, as the serpent said to Eve, and as the serpents indeed have said to every soul, every lifestream in embodiment on earth?

The need for repetition

They have managed to make you believe in this lesser image of yourself that causes you to think that you are defined by conditions on earth, that you are defined by your own past choices, or that you are defined by conditions over which you have no power. This is the essence of the illusion that you are meant to overcome on earth in order to be free to move on. I know, my beloved, we have said this before, but we will continue to say it because every time we say it, we go a step higher on the spiral staircase. Every time we say the same thing again, more people will be awakened by it being said in the physical. You may think that you have heard it before and you understood it the first time, but did you fully grasp it

When you look at the Buddha and how he talked, you will see that he repeated many things. There is a reason for this. It is that there are levels of your consciousness. You are not instantly freed from duality, for it has taken you a long time to create the outer self.

There is a dream perpetrated by the fallen beings, but reinforced and sustained by many spiritual and religious people, even many ascended master students: that of instant deliverance, instant salvation, instant transformation. There are some who believe that, in order to be enlightened, you have to just switch your mind in some magical way, and then you are instantly free. It cannot be done, my beloved. If it could be done, we of the ascended masters would have taught it thousands of years ago, and all human beings would have been free long ago.

Your aura is not confined to time

You are not a static, linear being. You are a spherical being. You have an extension in both space and time. Your consciousness is not confined to this physical body only. We have told you that you have four lower bodies, but what we have not really told you is that the four lower bodies are not confined to time.

You may think of your personal energy field, your aura, as being in existence around your physical body. Many spiritual people even think that the body produces the aura. You know that it does not, but you may still think that it is very much centered around this physical body. Of course, you think that the physical body lives in this time, in this present moment, in this location. This is true of the body, but it is not true of your mind, the totality of your mind.

You know that you can project your mind to a different physical location than where you are right now. You even know that some people have trained themselves to leave the body behind and mentally project themselves to a remote location. You also know that some people can do this by going backwards or forwards in time.

Your energy field, your aura, your total mind, does not exist only in the present moment. It goes as far into the past as you have any wound, any attachment, any unresolved belief or psychology. As Master MORE made you aware of this morning, you all received a trauma when you first came into embodiment on this planet. You have not resolved that trauma fully, or you would not be in embodiment still.

Therefore, your mind, your energy field, reaches all the way back to the first time you came into embodiment on earth. You are constantly being stretched by the fact that your conscious mind is moving on in time, but your subconscious mind is stuck back there. As you keep moving forward in time, you get stretched more and more.

The defense mechanism against trauma

This is what many people feel as an undifferentiated stress, a pressure, a weight, an urge to do something that compels you many times to attack the spiritual path in an unbalanced way because you know that you have to catch up. There is something you have to do, but you don't know what it is so you think you have to work harder. You have to give more decrees. You have to run. You have to choose to do all these spiritual things and not do the unspiritual things.

You become so anxious, so eager. My beloved, I am not finding fault with you here. I love the eager student who is willing to make an effort. I applaud that, but it is, as the old saying goes, good speed, bad sense of direction.

Many of my students have that speed. They have the willingness to try, to T-R-Y, to do something. They have a sense of urgency, but they do not see what is the real goal. The real goal is to start reaching back into the past and resolving what keeps you tied to that distant time, from which the earth and your conscious mind and physical body are moving away at an accelerated rate, my beloved.

The entire universe is expanding at an accelerating rate, as scientists have discovered to their astonishment. They have not made the logical conclusion, which is that this can happen only if there is energy coming from outside the material universe to drive this expansion, but that is another issue for another time.

What you need to realize is that, even though you are on a dense planet that is not keeping pace with the rest of the universe, the earth is still being pulled up at an accelerated rate. This increases the urgency, the stress, that you might feel. Many, many spiritual people feel, in these last few years, overwhelmed, burdened, like there is something they cannot put their finger on that is stressing them out.

I would rather see you being stressed *in,* so that instead of thinking that the cause of your stress is *out there,* you realize it is *in here.* It is because there is some unresolved belief and trauma from your past that you have not seen, that you have not seen for what it is. Therefore, you have not started working on it consciously because you have not recognized it. It has been filtered out, as the messenger said.

The birth trauma, the cosmic birth trauma that you received when you first came into embodiment on earth, is so painful, so overwhelming to you, that there are processes in your subconscious mind that filter it out before it reaches the conscious mind. In the past you felt it would be too overwhelming for you to look at it, too painful. For most of you, my beloved, it is no longer too painful.

I am not saying that all spiritual people are ready to look at this, but most of you who have followed ascended master teachings for a long time, and who have already given a certain amount of decrees and invocations, you are ready to acknowledge this first trauma and to start working on it consciously. I am not saying you are ready to go into it right this second, but you are ready to apply our decrees and invocations to start healing it so that you can start chipping away at it, lessening the energetic pull. Thereby, you will reduce the stress factor that you have felt over these last several years.

The Piscean trauma

There is also another trauma that I would like to make you aware of, and it is the trauma of the Piscean Age. Most of you have been in embodiment, not necessarily continuously, but many times during the Piscean Age. Some of you have been in embodiment almost continuously during these past 2,000 years because you wanted to give the service you could give only by being in embodiment. There were certain initiations that humankind was meant to overcome in those 2,000 years, and there is a certain trauma from having witnessed how the planet has not passed these initiations, how humankind has not passed the initiations of the Piscean Age. There is also a certain trauma of being exposed to the atrocities that most of you have experienced in past lifetimes, be it wars or torture or other forms of suppression.

Right now you are feeling both the pull of your original trauma of coming to the earth and the trauma of the Piscean Age, which you need to resolve before you can fully make it into the Aquarian Age and the Aquarian consciousness. You cannot truly follow me into Aquarius before you have resolved this trauma that you received during Pisces.

Of course, one of the major initiations of Pisces was precisely this: to overcome this idolatry where you think you can create a physical idol, defined based on the current conditions in matter, and then you can confine Spirit to that idol. They have done it with Christ, they have done it with Jesus. They have also attempted to do it with me. I am pointing out to you that there are ascended master students who think they are the faithful followers of Saint Germain, keeping my flame, but they are imposing an idolatrous image upon me. It is keeping them from moving with me into Aquarius, and this is causing stress in them.

They think the only way to overcome it is to give more decrees and more Violet Flame, but this is not going to help. It is not going to be overcome until you look at yourself, recognize that you have an idolatrous image of Saint Germain, and let it go into the fire that I AM.

This is an essential shift in consciousness. You must realize that I am not your image. I AM the fire that is beyond any image and can burn the image. If you worship the image, then you think you have no reason to let that image go into the fire. You may think now: "But what if there is some aspect of my image of Saint Germain that is real? If I put my entire image of Saint Germain into the fire, will it not all be burned? Will Saint

Germain not be burned by his own fire? Will he not be hurt?" Well, of course, I will not be burned by my own fire! You can safely put the totality of your image of Saint Germain into the fire of the Flame of Freedom. Whatever aspects of your image are real, will not be burned by the fire, they will not be consumed by the fire. Dare to let it all go into the fire and allow only what is real to emerge from that fire. If you are attached and unwilling to let it all go into the fire, then you are holding on to what is unreal, and that blocks you from following me into Aquarius. It cannot be any other way.

I cannot, I will not, violate the Law of Free Will. If you say you want to hold on to this wonderful image of Saint Germain that you have created, I will respectfully withdraw my Presence so that it does not impinge upon your consciousness. Then you also will be left behind, for I will not stand still because you are standing still. I am freedom. I am constantly moving.

How to overcome war

How can you overcome war in Europe? Only by moving beyond it, by transcending it, not by holding on to any image. Do you realize that I have talked about an idolatrous image of God, an idolatrous image of me, but you also have idolatrous images of everything that is going on on earth? The fallen beings want you to believe that things have been so bad that they cannot be overcome, or that they require that someone is punished. They think that, because such atrocities have been committed on the European continent, someone needs to burn forever in hell in order to compensate for this.

The infinite God of love has no need for anyone to burn in hell for any length of time. Why would God want a part of its own being to burn forever in hell? God wants all parts of its being to flow with the River of Life and grow towards that point of reunion with Source.

God has never defined any law, any condition, that holds back the self-transcendence of any being with free will. God has never defined such a condition. The fallen beings have attempted to define such conditions and make people believe them. *Believe them not!* It is time, it is high time, that you throw these last shackles off that are holding you trapped in these idolatrous images.

How do you truly love your enemies and forgive those who have hurt you? Not by changing anything on earth. Not by changing what happened in the past, which you cannot change, but by realizing that where you were hurt in the past, there is a part of your being that is attached there, that is stuck there. You need to mentally go back and free that part of your being so it can catch up with the rest of you. Then you are free from that event in the past.

How will you free that part of your being? Only by practicing total forgiveness of those who were the instruments of precipitating the hurt. Only when you have no desire to punish them or make them feel bad, will you be free. I am not asking you to forgive out of some far-flung altruistic motive. I am asking you to forgive for the very practical reason that it is the only way to free yourself.

Non-forgiveness of the German people

As was spoken about before, one of the heaviest burdens on the European continent is indeed the non-forgiveness towards the German people because of the Second World War and the Holocaust. Therefore, I ask you who are here to participate with me in an exercise of spiritual alchemy.

I desire you to center in your hearts. I know you are already there, but still find that point of stillness in your heart. Then from that stillness, from that love, allow yourself to look at whatever images you have in your mind of the Second World War, of the war itself, of what the German people did, of the Holocaust, the concentration camps. Allow yourself to look at these images. Then realize that I am manifesting my Presence with you.

I hold in my right hand a stone that resembles an amethyst but is far more concentrated and powerful. I wish you to visualize that the amethyst is radiating an intense ray of violet flame that is completely consuming the image you are holding of the Second World War and the Holocaust.

Visualize how this violet flame is consuming the image. First it is consuming it in your own consciousness. Then it is consuming it in the collective consciousness of your home country. Then it is consuming it in the collective consciousness of all of Europe.

Then you say with me, as I say the sentence one time, then we repeat it together. I ask you to, as much as possible, stay centered in the heart, in that place of love. Remember what Archeia Charity said about looking at war from love, from the consciousness of love. I will say a sentence, then we repeat it together.

I personally forgive the German people for the Second World War.
Audience: I personally forgive the German people for the Second World War.

On behalf of all people of Europe, I forgive the German people for the Second World War.

Audience: On behalf of all people of Europe, I forgive the German people for the Second World War.

I personally forgive the German people for the Holocaust and the concentration camps.
Audience: I personally forgive the German people for the Holocaust and the concentration camps.

On behalf of all people of Europe, I forgive the German people for the Holocaust and the concentration camps.
Audience: On behalf of all people of Europe, I forgive the German people for the Holocaust and the concentration camps.

I personally forgive all people of Europe for the Second World War.
Audience: I personally forgive all people of Europe for the Second World War.

On behalf of all of the people of Europe, I forgive all people of Europe for the Second World War.
Audience: On behalf of all of the people of Europe, I forgive all people of Europe for the Second World War.

I personally forgive all people of Europe for the Holocaust and the concentration camps.
Audience: I personally forgive all people of Europe for the Holocaust and the concentration camps.

On behalf of all people of Europe, I forgive all people of Europe for the Holocaust and the concentration camps.
Audience: On behalf of all people of Europe, I forgive all people of Europe for the Holocaust and the concentration camps.

I personally forgive Adolf Hitler for the Holocaust and the concentration camps.
Audience: I personally forgive Adolf Hitler for the Holocaust and the concentration camps.

On behalf of all people of Europe, I forgive Adolf Hitler for the Holocaust and the concentration camps.
Audience: On behalf of all people of Europe, I forgive Adolf Hitler for the Holocaust and the concentration camps.

A cosmic service for Europe

My beloved, you have performed a cosmic service that has never been performed on this continent. I am not asking you to be prideful, but I am not asking you to be prideful in the sense that you do not recognize the value of what you have just done. Truly, allow yourselves to recognize that hardly any of the millions of people who are embodying in Europe have been willing to say what you just said. Allow yourself to recognize how necessary it is that people dare to say this, to feel it in their hearts, and to truly thereby set yourselves free from the consciousness of the war and the Holocaust.

This is such a heavy weight hanging over this continent. It is, as they say in America, the 300-pound gorilla that is in the room, but nobody dares to acknowledge that it is in the room. Nobody dares to talk about it. Nobody knows how to talk about this directly and openly, and this is indeed something I desire you to hold in your vision. I desire you to make calls for this: That the people of Europe, and all people who were involved with the Second World War, will be able and willing to openly talk about this and to talk it through so that they can free themselves from it. You are not freeing yourselves by suppressing it.

Truly, I am not saying here that the people of Europe should have talked about this 5 or 20 or 50 years ago. They were not able to do so because the wound was still too painful. What has happened is that – through the efforts of all people who have raised their consciousness, through the efforts of ascended master students who have given the Violet Flame and other decrees – the energies have now been dissipated to a point where it is no longer too painful for people to start talking openly about the Second World War and how it could happen, and about the Holocaust and how this could happen. It is no longer too painful.

Many people are not willing, because the old generation just wants to hold on to its images of how the Germans were the bad guys and they were the heroes for defeating the bad guys. They want to take this image with them to the grave. The young people do not want to even think about the war. It is necessary to have an open dialogue about this before the nations of Europe will be able to free themselves from it.

The danger to European unity

Why do you think the European Union is right now almost on the brink of starting to fracture and fall apart, both through Greece and in other ways? It is because, my beloved, Europe cannot move to the next level until it has shed this heavy burden carried over from the Second World War.

There is only one way to shed the burden, and that is to just forgive. Some people will need to express their feelings before they can forgive. I recognize this. How can they express their feelings when there is no dialogue, when there is no open communication about the issue? I ask you to make the calls for this so that there will be an opening whereby the people in Europe will begin to talk about this, not from the consciousness of wanting to punish and put down, but from the consciousness of wanting to free everyone from the burden of the past.

I AM the ascended master who holds the Flame of Freedom. I want to see everyone on earth free from the past, and I would like to start with you who recognize yourselves as my students. Dare to forgive! It is an act of will, as Master MORE talked about this morning. There comes a point where you need to recognize that you have had enough of being stuck in this non-forgiveness. You will to be free, and the way to be free is to forgive unconditionally, for freedom is unconditional. You will never be free by living up to conditions defined on earth. You will be free only by transcending conditions.

How will you be free? By becoming one with me. How will you become one with me if you hold on to an idolatrous image that is not me? It cannot be done.

I must bow to your free will, but when I have a messenger who is willing to speak the Word and I have students who are willing to hear it, I do not need to step back in silence. I can indeed have my say by speaking it into the collective consciousness.

Do not underestimate the value of this. The fact that certain things have been said by the ascended masters in the physical creates a shift where nothing can remain the same, where there must be change. There *will* be change. I decree it, for I want to see this planet be free from war and all of the other burdens from the past.

I AM Saint Germain. I AM the architect of the Golden Age, and I AM accepting the Golden Age as a fully physically manifest reality on earth. I decree it. I call it forth.

I respect the free will of human beings in embodiment, but I also respect my own free will and the free will of the messengers and the students who will receive the Word. Therefore – by it being spoken, by it being accepted and magnified by you – there is a shift. A new day has begun. A new cycle has been initiated, and it will not be stopped until all are free.

7 | INVOKING AN ALCHEMICAL SHIFT IN PERCEPTION

In the name I AM THAT I AM, Jesus Christ, I call to all representatives of the Divine Father, especially Saint Germain and the Divine Director, to help people shift the way they look at the past. Help people see the mechanisms that prevent them from letting go of the past, including…

[Make personal calls.]

Part 1

1. Saint Germain, awaken people to the reality that we will be free only when we do not let anything on earth define us.

O Saint Germain, you do inspire,
my vision raised forever higher,
with you I form a figure-eight,
your Golden Age I co-create.

**O Saint Germain, what love you bring,
it truly makes all matter sing,
your violet flame does all restore,
with you we are becoming more.**

2. Saint Germain, awaken people to the reality that the fallen beings want to be like gods on earth. You become a god on earth by tricking people to worship you as a supreme authority because then you can control how they define themselves.

O Saint Germain, what Freedom Flame,
released when we recite your name,
acceleration is your gift,
our planet it will surely lift.

**O Saint Germain, what love you bring,
it truly makes all matter sing,
your violet flame does all restore,
with you we are becoming more.**

3. Saint Germain, awaken people to the reality that since its inception the Catholic church has been attempting to cause those who thought they were followers of Jesus to define themselves as the opposite kind of being to what Jesus demonstrated.

7 | *Invoking an Alchemical Shift in perception*

O Saint Germain, in love we claim,
our right to bring your violet flame,
from you Above, to us below,
it is an all-transforming flow.

**O Saint Germain, what love you bring,
it truly makes all matter sing,
your violet flame does all restore,
with you we are becoming more.**

4. Saint Germain, awaken people to the reality that the doctrine of original sin is a lie of the fallen beings. God did not create us as sinners and then say we have to follow the fallen beings in order to overcome that condition.

O Saint Germain, I love you so,
my aura filled with violet glow,
my chakras filled with violet fire,
I am your cosmic amplifier.

**O Saint Germain, what love you bring,
it truly makes all matter sing,
your violet flame does all restore,
with you we are becoming more.**

5. Saint Germain, awaken people to the reality that the fallen beings are not necessarily denying free will. They are saying we are sinners and, in order to be saved, we have to choose to follow them.

O Saint Germain, I am now free,
your violet flame is therapy,
transform all hang-ups in my mind,
as inner peace I surely find.

**O Saint Germain, what love you bring,
it truly makes all matter sing,
your violet flame does all restore,
with you we are becoming more.**

6. Saint Germain, awaken people to the reality that God created us as a free beings so that sin is a result of choice and therefore can be overcome by making the choice to look at ourselves and overcome the consciousness that keeps us trapped in a lesser image of ourselves.

O Saint Germain, my body pure,
your violet flame for all is cure,
consume the cause of all disease,
and therefore I am all at ease.

**O Saint Germain, what love you bring,
it truly makes all matter sing,
your violet flame does all restore,
with you we are becoming more.**

7. Saint Germain, awaken people to the reality that sin is when we are imposing an image upon ourselves that is not in alignment with what God created; we are making yourself gods.

O Saint Germain, I'm karma-free,
the past no longer burdens me,
a brand new opportunity,
I am in Christic unity.

**O Saint Germain, what love you bring,
it truly makes all matter sing,
your violet flame does all restore,
with you we are becoming more.**

8. Saint Germain, awaken people to the reality that instead of accepting that God created us as extensions of its own being, we are imposing an image upon ourselves that we are limited, flawed beings.

O Saint Germain, we are now one,
I am for you a violet sun,
as we transform this planet earth,
your Golden Age is given birth.

**O Saint Germain, what love you bring,
it truly makes all matter sing,
your violet flame does all restore,
with you we are becoming more.**

9. Saint Germain, awaken people to the reality that we thereby think we know better than God what God created. We are making ourselves as gods, knowing good and evil, as the serpents have said to every lifestream in embodiment on earth.

O Saint Germain, the earth is free,
from burden of duality,
in oneness we bring what is best,
your Golden Age is manifest.

**O Saint Germain, what love you bring,
it truly makes all matter sing,
your violet flame does all restore,
with you we are becoming more.**

Part 2

1. Saint Germain, awaken people to the reality that the fallen beings managed to make us believe in this lesser image of ourselves. It causes us to think that we are defined by conditions on earth, that we are defined by our own past choices, or that we are defined by conditions over which we have no power.

Divine Director, I now see,
the world is unreality,
in my heart I now truly feel,
the Spirit is all that is real.

**Divine Director, send the light,
from blindness clear my inner sight,
my vision free, my vision clear,
your guidance is forever here.**

2. Saint Germain, awaken people to the reality that this is the essence of the illusion we are meant to overcome on earth in order to be free to move on.

> Divine Director, vision give,
> in clarity I want to live,
> I now behold my plan Divine,
> the plan that is uniquely mine.
>
> **Divine Director, send the light,**
> **from blindness clear my inner sight,**
> **my vision free, my vision clear,**
> **your guidance is forever here.**

3. Saint Germain, awaken people to the reality that it has taken us a long time to create the outer self, but the fallen beings want us to believe in the dream of instant deliverance, instant salvation, instant transformation.

> Divine Director, show in me,
> the ego games, and set me free,
> help me escape the ego's cage,
> to help bring in the golden age.
>
> **Divine Director, send the light,**
> **from blindness clear my inner sight,**
> **my vision free, my vision clear,**
> **your guidance is forever here.**

4. Saint Germain, awaken people to the reality that we are not static, linear beings. We are spherical beings. We have an extension in both space and time. Our consciousness is not confined to this physical body only. We have four lower bodies, but the four lower bodies are not confined to time.

> Divine Director, I'm with you,
> my vision one, no longer two,
> as karma's veil you do disperse,
> I see a whole new universe.
>
> **Divine Director, send the light,**
> **from blindness clear my inner sight,**
> **my vision free, my vision clear,**
> **your guidance is forever here.**

5. Saint Germain, awaken people to the reality that the mind is not limited in time, as is the physical body. Our energy fields, the totality of our minds, do not exist only in the present moment.

> Divine Director, I go up,
> electric light now fills my cup,
> consume in me all shadows old,
> bestow on me a vision bold.
>
> **Divine Director, send the light,**
> **from blindness clear my inner sight,**
> **my vision free, my vision clear,**
> **your guidance is forever here.**

6. Saint Germain, awaken people to the reality that our minds go as far into the past as we have any wound, any attachment, any unresolved belief or psychology. We all received a trauma when we first came into embodiment on this planet. We have not resolved that trauma fully, or we would not be in embodiment still.

> Divine Director, heart of gold,
> my sacred labor I unfold,
> o blessed Guru, I now see,
> where my own plan is taking me.
>
> **Divine Director, send the light,**
> **from blindness clear my inner sight,**
> **my vision free, my vision clear,**
> **your guidance is forever here.**

7. Saint Germain, awaken people to the reality that our minds, our energy fields, reach all the way back to the first time we came into embodiment on earth.

> Divine Director, by your grace,
> in grander scheme I find my place,
> my individual flame I see,
> uniqueness God has given me.
>
> **Divine Director, send the light,**
> **from blindness clear my inner sight,**
> **my vision free, my vision clear,**
> **your guidance is forever here.**

8. Saint Germain, awaken people to the reality that we are constantly being stretched by the fact that our conscious minds are moving on in time, but our subconscious minds are stuck back there. As we keep moving forward in time, we get stretched more and more.

> Divine Director, vision one,
> I see that I AM God's own Sun,
> with your direction so Divine,
> I am now letting my light shine.
>
> **Divine Director, send the light,**
> **from blindness clear my inner sight,**
> **my vision free, my vision clear,**
> **your guidance is forever here.**

9. Saint Germain, awaken people to the reality that many people feel this as an undifferentiated stress, a pressure, a weight, an urge to do something that compels us to attack the spiritual path in an unbalanced way because we know that we have to catch up.

> Divine Director, what a gift,
> to be a part of Spirit's lift,
> to raise mankind out of the night,
> to bask in Spirit's loving sight.
>
> **Divine Director, send the light,**
> **from blindness clear my inner sight,**
> **my vision free, my vision clear,**
> **your guidance is forever here.**

7 | Invoking an Alchemical Shift in perception

Part 3

1. Saint Germain, awaken people to the reality that the real goal is to start reaching back into the past and resolving what keeps us tied to that distant time, from which the earth and our conscious minds and physical bodies are moving away at an accelerated rate.

> O Saint Germain, you do inspire,
> my vision raised forever higher,
> with you I form a figure-eight,
> your Golden Age I co-create.

> **O Saint Germain, what love you bring,**
> **it truly makes all matter sing,**
> **your violet flame does all restore,**
> **with you we are becoming more.**

2. Saint Germain, awaken people to the reality that the earth is being pulled up at an accelerated rate. This increases the urgency, the stress and makes us feel overwhelmed, and burdened.

> O Saint Germain, what Freedom Flame,
> released when we recite your name,
> acceleration is your gift,
> our planet it will surely lift.

> **O Saint Germain, what love you bring,**
> **it truly makes all matter sing,**
> **your violet flame does all restore,**
> **with you we are becoming more.**

3. Saint Germain, awaken people to the reality that the cause of our stress is not out there, but is in here. It is because there is some unresolved belief and trauma from our past that we have not seen.

> O Saint Germain, in love we claim,
> our right to bring your violet flame,
> from you Above, to us below,
> it is an all-transforming flow.
>
> **O Saint Germain, what love you bring,**
> **it truly makes all matter sing,**
> **your violet flame does all restore,**
> **with you we are becoming more.**

4. Saint Germain, awaken people to the reality that the cosmic birth trauma, that we received when we first came into embodiment on earth, is so painful, so overwhelming to us, that there are processes in our subconscious mind that filter it out before it reaches the conscious mind.

> O Saint Germain, I love you so,
> my aura filled with violet glow,
> my chakras filled with violet fire,
> I am your cosmic amplifier.
>
> **O Saint Germain, what love you bring,**
> **it truly makes all matter sing,**
> **your violet flame does all restore,**
> **with you we are becoming more.**

5. Saint Germain, awaken people to the reality that we need to acknowledge this first trauma and to start working on it consciously. By using decrees and invocations we can lessen the energetic pull and reduce the stress factor.

> O Saint Germain, I am now free,
> your violet flame is therapy,
> transform all hang-ups in my mind,
> as inner peace I surely find.
>
> **O Saint Germain, what love you bring,**
> **it truly makes all matter sing,**
> **your violet flame does all restore,**
> **with you we are becoming more.**

6. Saint Germain, awaken people to the reality that there is also a trauma of the Piscean Age. There were certain initiations that humankind was meant to overcome in those 2,000 years, and there is a certain trauma from having witnessed how humankind has not passed the initiations of the Piscean Age.

> O Saint Germain, my body pure,
> your violet flame for all is cure,
> consume the cause of all disease,
> and therefore I am all at ease.
>
> **O Saint Germain, what love you bring,**
> **it truly makes all matter sing,**
> **your violet flame does all restore,**
> **with you we are becoming more.**

7. Saint Germain, awaken people to the reality that there is also a trauma of being exposed to the atrocities that most of us have experienced in past lifetimes, be it wars or torture or other forms of suppression.

> O Saint Germain, I'm karma-free,
> the past no longer burdens me,
> a brand new opportunity,
> I am in Christic unity.

> **O Saint Germain, what love you bring,**
> **it truly makes all matter sing,**
> **your violet flame does all restore,**
> **with you we are becoming more.**

8. Saint Germain, awaken people to the reality that we are feeling both the pull of our original trauma of coming to the earth and the trauma of the Piscean Age. We need to resolve this before we can fully make it into the Aquarian Age and the Aquarian consciousness.

> O Saint Germain, we are now one,
> I am for you a violet sun,
> as we transform this planet earth,
> your Golden Age is given birth.

> **O Saint Germain, what love you bring,**
> **it truly makes all matter sing,**
> **your violet flame does all restore,**
> **with you we are becoming more.**

9. Saint Germain, awaken people to the reality that one of the major initiations of Pisces was to overcome the idolatry where we think we can create a physical idol, defined based on the current conditions in matter, and then we can confine Spirit to that idol.

> O Saint Germain, the earth is free,
> from burden of duality,
> in oneness we bring what is best,
> your Golden Age is manifest.

> **O Saint Germain, what love you bring,**
> **it truly makes all matter sing,**
> **your violet flame does all restore,**
> **with you we are becoming more.**

Part 4

1. Saint Germain, awaken people to the reality that the fallen beings and many people have made an idol out of Jesus and other ascended masters, including you.

> Divine Director, I now see,
> the world is unreality,
> in my heart I now truly feel,
> the Spirit is all that is real.

> **Divine Director, send the light,**
> **from blindness clear my inner sight,**
> **my vision free, my vision clear,**
> **your guidance is forever here.**

2. Saint Germain, awaken those who think they are the faithful followers of Saint Germain, keeping your flame, but they are imposing an idolatrous image upon you and it is keeping them from moving with you into Aquarius, and this is causing stress in them.

> Divine Director, vision give,
> in clarity I want to live,
> I now behold my plan Divine,
> the plan that is uniquely mine.

> **Divine Director, send the light,**
> **from blindness clear my inner sight,**
> **my vision free, my vision clear,**
> **your guidance is forever here.**

3. Saint Germain, awaken people to the reality that we can overcome stress only by looking at ourselves, recognizing that we have an idolatrous image of you, and letting it go into the fire that you are.

> Divine Director, show in me,
> the ego games, and set me free,
> help me escape the ego's cage,
> to help bring in the golden age.

> **Divine Director, send the light,**
> **from blindness clear my inner sight,**
> **my vision free, my vision clear,**
> **your guidance is forever here.**

4. Saint Germain, awaken people to the reality that we need to go through an essential shift in consciousness. We must realize that you are not our image. You are the fire that is beyond any image and can burn the image.

> Divine Director, I'm with you,
> my vision one, no longer two,
> as karma's veil you do disperse,
> I see a whole new universe.

> **Divine Director, send the light,**
> **from blindness clear my inner sight,**
> **my vision free, my vision clear,**
> **your guidance is forever here.**

5. Saint Germain, awaken people to the reality that if we worship an image, then we think we have no reason to let that image go into the fire. We need to put the totality of our image of Saint Germain into the fire of the Flame of Freedom.

> Divine Director, I go up,
> electric light now fills my cup,
> consume in me all shadows old,
> bestow on me a vision bold.

> **Divine Director, send the light,**
> **from blindness clear my inner sight,**
> **my vision free, my vision clear,**
> **your guidance is forever here.**

6. Saint Germain, awaken people to the reality that if we want to hold on to any image of you, you will withdraw and we will be left behind. You will not stand still because we are standing still. You are freedom and you are constantly moving.

> Divine Director, heart of gold,
> my sacred labor I unfold,
> o blessed Guru, I now see,
> where my own plan is taking me.
>
> **Divine Director, send the light,**
> **from blindness clear my inner sight,**
> **my vision free, my vision clear,**
> **your guidance is forever here.**

7. Saint Germain, awaken people to the reality that there comes a point where we need to recognize that we have had enough of being stuck in this non-forgiveness. We will to be free, and the way to be free is to forgive unconditionally, for freedom is unconditional.

> Divine Director, by your grace,
> in grander scheme I find my place,
> my individual flame I see,
> uniqueness God has given me.
>
> **Divine Director, send the light,**
> **from blindness clear my inner sight,**
> **my vision free, my vision clear,**
> **your guidance is forever here.**

8. Saint Germain, awaken people to the reality that we will never be free by living up to conditions defined on earth. We will be free only by transcending conditions. We will be free only by becoming one with you. We cannot become one with you if you hold on to an idolatrous image that is not you.

> Divine Director, vision one,
> I see that I AM God's own Sun,
> with your direction so Divine,
> I am now letting my light shine.

> **Divine Director, send the light,**
> **from blindness clear my inner sight,**
> **my vision free, my vision clear,**
> **your guidance is forever here.**

9. Saint Germain, I AM accepting the Golden Age as a fully physically manifest reality on earth. I decree it. I call it forth. By it being spoken, by it being accepted and magnified by me, there is a shift. A new day has begun. A new cycle has been initiated, and it will not be stopped until all are free.

> Divine Director, what a gift,
> to be a part of Spirit's lift,
> to raise mankind out of the night,
> to bask in Spirit's loving sight.

> **Divine Director, send the light,**
> **from blindness clear my inner sight,**
> **my vision free, my vision clear,**
> **your guidance is forever here.**

Sealing

In the name of the Divine Mother, I call to Mother Mary for the sealing of myself and all people in my circle of influence in the creative flow of the Divine Mother, the River of Life. I call for the multiplication of my calls by all representatives of the Divine Mother, so that we form the perfect figure-eight flow of "As Above, so below." Thus, I accept that this is fully manifest, because the mouth of the Lord, the Divine Mother that I AM, has spoken it. Amen.

8 | INVOKING FORGIVENESS OF THE GERMAN PEOPLE

In the name I AM THAT I AM, Jesus Christ, I call to all representatives of the Divine Father and the Divine Mother, especially Saint Germain and Portia, to help people overcome all non-forgiveness of the German people. Help people see the lies in their psyches that cause them to hold on to the past, including…

[Make personal calls.]

Part 1

1. Saint Germain, awaken people to the reality that the only way to overcome war is to move beyond it by transcending it, by not by holding on to any image.

O Saint Germain, you do inspire,
my vision raised forever higher,
with you I form a figure-eight,
your Golden Age I co-create.

**O Saint Germain, what love you bring,
it truly makes all matter sing,
your violet flame does all restore,
with you we are becoming more.**

2. Saint Germain, awaken people to the reality that we have idolatrous images of everything that is happening on earth.

O Saint Germain, what Freedom Flame,
released when we recite your name,
acceleration is your gift,
our planet it will surely lift.

**O Saint Germain, what love you bring,
it truly makes all matter sing,
your violet flame does all restore,
with you we are becoming more.**

3. Saint Germain, awaken people to the reality that the fallen beings want us to believe that things have been so bad that they cannot be overcome, or that they require that someone is punished.

O Saint Germain, in love we claim,
our right to bring your violet flame,
from you Above, to us below,
it is an all-transforming flow.

> **O Saint Germain, what love you bring,**
> **it truly makes all matter sing,**
> **your violet flame does all restore,**
> **with you we are becoming more.**

4. Saint Germain, awaken people to the reality that the fallen beings want us to think that, because such atrocities have been committed, someone needs to burn forever in hell in order to compensate for this.

> O Saint Germain, I love you so,
> my aura filled with violet glow,
> my chakras filled with violet fire,
> I am your cosmic amplifier.

> **O Saint Germain, what love you bring,**
> **it truly makes all matter sing,**
> **your violet flame does all restore,**
> **with you we are becoming more.**

5. Saint Germain, awaken people to the reality that the infinite God of love has no need for anyone to burn in hell for any length of time. God wants all parts of its Being to flow with the River of Life and grow towards that point of reunion with Source.

> O Saint Germain, I am now free,
> your violet flame is therapy,
> transform all hang-ups in my mind,
> as inner peace I surely find.

> **O Saint Germain, what love you bring,**
> **it truly makes all matter sing,**
> **your violet flame does all restore,**
> **with you we are becoming more.**

6. Saint Germain, awaken people to the reality that God has never defined any law or condition that holds back the self-transcendence of any being with free will. God has never defined such a condition.

> O Saint Germain, my body pure,
> your violet flame for all is cure,
> consume the cause of all disease,
> and therefore I am all at ease.

> **O Saint Germain, what love you bring,**
> **it truly makes all matter sing,**
> **your violet flame does all restore,**
> **with you we are becoming more.**

7. Saint Germain, awaken people to the reality that the fallen beings have attempted to define such conditions and make people believe them. Help people throw off the last shackles that are holding them trapped in these idolatrous images.

> O Saint Germain, I'm karma-free,
> the past no longer burdens me,
> a brand new opportunity,
> I am in Christic unity.

> **O Saint Germain, what love you bring,**
> **it truly makes all matter sing,**
> **your violet flame does all restore,**
> **with you we are becoming more.**

8. Saint Germain, awaken people to the reality that in order to truly love our enemies and forgive those who have hurt us, we cannot focus on changing anything on earth, we cannot attempt to change what happened in the past, which cannot be changed.

> O Saint Germain, we are now one,
> I am for you a violet sun,
> as we transform this planet earth,
> your Golden Age is given birth.

> **O Saint Germain, what love you bring,**
> **it truly makes all matter sing,**
> **your violet flame does all restore,**
> **with you we are becoming more.**

9. Saint Germain, awaken people to the reality that where we were hurt in the past, there is a part of our beings that is attached and stuck there. We need to mentally go back and free that part of our beings so it can catch up with the rest of us. Then we are free from that event in the past.

> O Saint Germain, the earth is free,
> from burden of duality,
> in oneness we bring what is best,
> your Golden Age is manifest.

> **O Saint Germain, what love you bring,**
> **it truly makes all matter sing,**
> **your violet flame does all restore,**
> **with you we are becoming more.**

Part 2

1. Saint Germain, awaken people to the reality that we can free the trapped parts of our beings only by practicing total forgiveness of those who were the instruments of precipitating the hurt.

> O Portia, in your own retreat,
> with Mother's Love you do me greet.
> As all my tests I now complete,
> old patterns I no more repeat.

> **O Portia, opportunity,**
> **I am beyond duality.**
> **I focus now internally,**
> **with you I grow eternally.**

2. Saint Germain, awaken people to the reality that only when we have no desire to punish others or make them feel bad, will we be free. We need to forgive for the very practical reason that it is the only way to free ourselves.

> O Portia, Justice is your name,
> upholding Cosmic Honor Flame,
> No longer will I play the game,
> of seeking to remain the same.

8 | Invoking Forgiveness of the German People

**O Portia, opportunity,
I am beyond duality.
I focus now internally,
with you I grow eternally.**

3. Saint Germain, awaken people to the reality that one of the heaviest burdens on the European continent is the non-forgiveness towards the German people because of the Second World War and the Holocaust.

O Portia, in the cosmic flow,
one with you, I ever grow.
I am the chalice here below,
of cosmic justice you bestow.

**O Portia, opportunity,
I am beyond duality.
I focus now internally,
with you I grow eternally.**

4. Saint Germain, I am willing to participate with you in an exercise of spiritual alchemy. I am centered in my heart, and from that stillness and love, I allow myself to look at whatever images I have in my mind of the Second World War, of the war itself, of what the German people did, of the Holocaust, the concentration camps.

O Portia, cosmic balance bring,
eternal hope, my heart does sing.
Protected by your Mother's wing,
I feel at one with everything.

> O Portia, opportunity,
> I am beyond duality.
> I focus now internally,
> with you I grow eternally.

5. Saint Germain, I allow myself to look at these images. I now realize that you are manifesting your Presence with me. You hold in your right hand a stone that resembles an amethyst but is far more concentrated and powerful.

> O Portia, bring the Mother Light,
> to set all free from darkest night.
> Your Love Flame shines forever bright,
> with Saint Germain now hold me tight.

> O Portia, opportunity,
> I am beyond duality.
> I focus now internally,
> with you I grow eternally.

6. Saint Germain, I visualize that the amethyst is radiating an intense ray of violet flame that is completely consuming the image I am holding of the Second World War and the Holocaust.

> O Portia, in your mastery,
> I feel transforming chemistry.
> In your light of reality,
> I find the golden alchemy.

> O Portia, opportunity,
> I am beyond duality.
> I focus now internally,
> with you I grow eternally.

7. Saint Germain, I now see that this violet flame is consuming the image. First it is consuming it in my own consciousness. Then it is consuming it in the collective consciousness of my home country. Then it is consuming it in the collective consciousness of all of Europe.

> O Portia, in the cosmic stream,
> I am awake from human dream.
> Removing now the ego's beam,
> I earn my place on cosmic team.

> O Portia, opportunity,
> I am beyond duality.
> I focus now internally,
> with you I grow eternally.

8. Saint Germain, I am joyfully and lovingly releasing all images and feelings I have about the second world war and letting them go into the violet flame that you are radiating to me.

> O Portia, you come from afar,
> you are a cosmic avatar.
> So infinite your repertoire,
> you are for earth a guiding star.

**O Portia, opportunity,
I am beyond duality.
I focus now internally,
with you I grow eternally.**

9. Saint Germain, I am centered in the heart, in that place of love. I am looking at war from love, from the consciousness of love. I say with you: I personally forgive the German people for the Second World War.

O Portia, I am confident,
I am a cosmic instrument.
I came to earth from heaven sent,
to help bring forward her ascent.

**O Portia, opportunity,
I am beyond duality.
I focus now internally,
with you I grow eternally.**

Part 3

1. Saint Germain, on behalf of all people of Europe, I forgive the German people for the Second World War.

O Saint Germain, you do inspire,
my vision raised forever higher,
with you I form a figure-eight,
your Golden Age I co-create.

> **O Saint Germain, what love you bring,**
> **it truly makes all matter sing,**
> **your violet flame does all restore,**
> **with you we are becoming more.**

2. Saint Germain, I personally forgive the German people for the Holocaust and the concentration camps.

> O Saint Germain, what Freedom Flame,
> released when we recite your name,
> acceleration is your gift,
> our planet it will surely lift.

> **O Saint Germain, what love you bring,**
> **it truly makes all matter sing,**
> **your violet flame does all restore,**
> **with you we are becoming more.**

3. Saint Germain, on behalf of all people of Europe, I forgive the German people for the Holocaust and the concentration camps.

> O Saint Germain, in love we claim,
> our right to bring your violet flame,
> from you Above, to us below,
> it is an all-transforming flow.

> **O Saint Germain, what love you bring,**
> **it truly makes all matter sing,**
> **your violet flame does all restore,**
> **with you we are becoming more.**

4. Saint Germain, I personally forgive all people of Europe for the Second World War.

> O Saint Germain, I love you so,
> my aura filled with violet glow,
> my chakras filled with violet fire,
> I am your cosmic amplifier.
>
> **O Saint Germain, what love you bring,**
> **it truly makes all matter sing,**
> **your violet flame does all restore,**
> **with you we are becoming more.**

5. Saint Germain, on behalf of all of the people of Europe, I forgive all people of Europe for the Second World War.

> O Saint Germain, I am now free,
> your violet flame is therapy,
> transform all hang-ups in my mind,
> as inner peace I surely find.
>
> **O Saint Germain, what love you bring,**
> **it truly makes all matter sing,**
> **your violet flame does all restore,**
> **with you we are becoming more.**

6. Saint Germain, I personally forgive all people of Europe for the Holocaust and the concentration camps.

> O Saint Germain, my body pure,
> your violet flame for all is cure,
> consume the cause of all disease,
> and therefore I am all at ease.

8 | Invoking Forgiveness of the German People

**O Saint Germain, what love you bring,
it truly makes all matter sing,
your violet flame does all restore,
with you we are becoming more.**

7. Saint Germain, on behalf of all people of Europe, I forgive all people of Europe for the Holocaust and the concentration camps.

O Saint Germain, I'm karma-free,
the past no longer burdens me,
a brand new opportunity,
I am in Christic unity.

**O Saint Germain, what love you bring,
it truly makes all matter sing,
your violet flame does all restore,
with you we are becoming more.**

8. Saint Germain, I personally forgive Adolf Hitler for the Holocaust and the concentration camps.

O Saint Germain, we are now one,
I am for you a violet sun,
as we transform this planet earth,
your Golden Age is given birth.

**O Saint Germain, what love you bring,
it truly makes all matter sing,
your violet flame does all restore,
with you we are becoming more.**

9. Saint Germain, on behalf of all people of Europe, I forgive Adolf Hitler for the Holocaust and the concentration camps.

> O Saint Germain, the earth is free,
> from burden of duality,
> in oneness we bring what is best,
> your Golden Age is manifest.
>
> **O Saint Germain, what love you bring,**
> **it truly makes all matter sing,**
> **your violet flame does all restore,**
> **with you we are becoming more.**

Part 4

1. Saint Germain, awaken people to the reality that it is absolutely necessary that people dare to say this ritual, to feel it in their hearts, and to thereby set themselves free from the consciousness of the war and the Holocaust.

> O Portia, in your own retreat,
> with Mother's Love you do me greet.
> As all my tests I now complete,
> old patterns I no more repeat.
>
> **O Portia, opportunity,**
> **I am beyond duality.**
> **I focus now internally,**
> **with you I grow eternally.**

8 | Invoking Forgiveness of the German People

2. Saint Germain, awaken people to the reality that this is such a heavy weight hanging over this continent, but nobody dares to acknowledge it. Nobody dares to talk about it.

> O Portia, Justice is your name,
> upholding Cosmic Honor Flame,
> No longer will I play the game,
> of seeking to remain the same.
>
> **O Portia, opportunity,**
> **I am beyond duality.**
> **I focus now internally,**
> **with you I grow eternally.**

3. Saint Germain, awaken people to the reality that the people of Europe, and all people who were involved with the Second World War, must be able and willing to openly talk about this and to talk it through so that they can free themselves from it. We are not freeing ourselves by suppressing it.

> O Portia, in the cosmic flow,
> one with you, I ever grow.
> I am the chalice here below,
> of cosmic justice you bestow.
>
> **O Portia, opportunity,**
> **I am beyond duality.**
> **I focus now internally,**
> **with you I grow eternally.**

4. Saint Germain, awaken people to the reality that the energies have now been dissipated to a point where it is no longer too painful for people to start talking openly about the Second World War and how it could happen, and about the Holocaust and how this could happen.

> O Portia, cosmic balance bring,
> eternal hope, my heart does sing.
> Protected by your Mother's wing,
> I feel at one with everything.
>
> **O Portia, opportunity,**
> **I am beyond duality.**
> **I focus now internally,**
> **with you I grow eternally.**

5. Saint Germain, awaken people to the reality that many people are not willing. The old generation wants to hold on to its images of how the Germans were the bad guys and they were the heroes for defeating the bad guys. They want to take this image with them to the grave.

> O Portia, bring the Mother Light,
> to set all free from darkest night.
> Your Love Flame shines forever bright,
> with Saint Germain now hold me tight.
>
> **O Portia, opportunity,**
> **I am beyond duality.**
> **I focus now internally,**
> **with you I grow eternally.**

6. Saint Germain, awaken people to the reality that the young people do not want to even think about the war. It is necessary to have an open dialogue about this before the nations will be able to free themselves from it.

> O Portia, in your mastery,
> I feel transforming chemistry.
> In your light of reality,
> I find the golden alchemy.
>
> **O Portia, opportunity,**
> **I am beyond duality.**
> **I focus now internally,**
> **with you I grow eternally.**

7. Saint Germain, awaken people to the reality that the European Union is on the brink of starting to fracture and fall apart because Europe cannot move to the next level until it has shed this heavy burden carried over from the Second World War.

> O Portia, in the cosmic stream,
> I am awake from human dream.
> Removing now the ego's beam,
> I earn my place on cosmic team.
>
> **O Portia, opportunity,**
> **I am beyond duality.**
> **I focus now internally,**
> **with you I grow eternally.**

8. Saint Germain, awaken people to the reality that there is only one way to shed the burden, and that is to just forgive. Some people will need to express their feelings before they can forgive, but how can they express their feelings when there is no dialogue, when there is no open communication about the issue?

> O Portia, you come from afar,
> you are a cosmic avatar.
> So infinite your repertoire,
> you are for earth a guiding star.
>
> **O Portia, opportunity,**
> **I am beyond duality.**
> **I focus now internally,**
> **with you I grow eternally.**

9. Saint Germain, awaken people to the reality that the people in Europe need to begin to talk about this, not from the consciousness of wanting to punish and put down, but from the consciousness of wanting to free everyone from the burden of the past.

> O Portia, I am confident,
> I am a cosmic instrument.
> I came to earth from heaven sent,
> to help bring forward her ascent.
>
> **O Portia, opportunity,**
> **I am beyond duality.**
> **I focus now internally,**
> **with you I grow eternally.**

Sealing

In the name of the Divine Mother, I call to Portia and Mother Mary for the sealing of myself and all people in my circle of influence in the creative flow of the Divine Mother, the River of Life. I call for the multiplication of my calls by all representatives of the Divine Mother, so that we form the perfect figure-eight flow of "As Above, so below." Thus, I accept that this is fully manifest, because the mouth of the Lord, the Divine Mother that I AM, has spoken it. Amen.

9 | FREEING PEOPLE FROM THE BURDEN OF CHRISTIANITY

"O Jesus, let the fire of joy consume the devil's subtle ploy." I AM indeed the Ascended Master Jesus Christ, and I carry the Flame of Joy to the earth.

Why is it that the Flame of Joy needs to consume the most subtle ploy of the devil? It is because the most subtle ploy of the devil is that you take everything on earth so seriously that you squeeze out all joy. Look at the history of this European continent, and see how for centuries, in the so-called Dark Ages, all joy was squeezed out of people's lives. They were so concerned about the appalling living conditions they had on earth, but they were even more concerned about what would happen to them after earth, in terms of the fear of burning forever in a fiery hell. How joyful can you be when you are looking at the potential of burning forever in a fiery hell, and you think this is a realistic possibility?

Jesus carries the Flame of Joy

You see my point, do you not? I carry the Flame of Joy for the planet, but has any movement on earth done more to destroy joy than Christianity? The very movement that claims to represent me has come to embody the perversion, the absolute opposition, of the Flame of Joy. Is that not the irony of history if ever I saw it? Indeed it is, indeed it is.

You could look at the Scriptures about my life, and you could see that I did not, at least as recorded in the Scriptures, express a lot of joy in that embodiment. You would even be right, for when I was in physical embodiment, I was facing the entire planetary opposition against the Flame of Joy. I was carrying the weight of this anti-joy, and therefore, even though I had a certain degree of mastery, I was not able to be joyful during the three years of my mission. It was a heavy burden, and therefore I understand that many other people have felt a very heavy burden. I understand that many people today are feeling a heavy burden. I understand that many of the spiritual people, many of the religious people, many ascended master students, are feeling a heavy burden weighing upon them from this weight, this opposition, to the Flame of Joy.

Allow yourselves to be joyful

How can you, when you are facing the potential of the end of the world or some major calamity, be joyful? How can you, when you think that you belong to a small group of people who have to save the world for the ascended masters, feel any joy?

I tell you, my beloved, I am calling you this day to step up higher and allow yourselves to be joyful. Those of you who are here have already attained some mastery of this. Surely, I understand you are not carrying exactly the same weight that I was carrying 2,000 years ago, but you are still carrying a weight that is heavy for you. It is indeed a very good sign of your progress if you can feel joyful about life, joyful about the spiritual path.

I am telling you, as the master who holds the Flame of Joy for the earth, I am giving you permission to be joyful. I am giving you permission to embody the Flame of Joy that I am. Please accept that I, Jesus Christ, am giving you that permission. You do not have to be so serious, my beloved, for even though there are many reasons you can come up with for saying that the earth is in dire straits and it is such a serious situation, I tell you that it is no more serious than you who are in embodiment make it out to be.

Surely, many people want this to be serious, but ask yourselves: Who are the beings who really want human beings to take everything so seriously? Who are the beings who want you, the spiritual beings on earth, to take everything so seriously? When there is a God-Flame of Joy, can it be God who wants you to be so serious? Is it not rather those who want to set themselves up as gods on earth because they do not want to come into oneness with the God-Flame of Joy?

Freeing people from anti-joy

Surely, you can all see this, but the world cannot yet see this. Therefore, I ask you to hold the vision that people will come to see this. I ask you to make the calls that people will come to see that there is a small power elite of fallen beings on earth who have for a very long time been attempting to create this mindset that causes people to take everything so seriously. I ask you especially to see and to make the calls that the spiritual people are awakened to the reality of this, to see the truth that they do not actually further their spiritual growth by being so serious.

There is a point on the path where you need to be, one-pointed, you need to be determined. Do you really think that the Flame of Will and Power held by Master MORE is in opposition to my Flame of Joy? For if you do, you need to reconsider. How can God-Flames be in opposition to each other? Determination is good, but it does not mean that you have to take life seriously. The more seriously you take things, the more of an opposition you are creating. You tend to go into this battle mode of thinking that you are feeling an opposition from without, and you have to battle it by sending out a stronger impulse—by being more determined, by giving more decrees, more Blue Flame decrees. Then you actually abuse Archangel Michael. Instead of the sword of Archangel Michael that is cutting through the energy, you are turning it into a hammer that wants to beat it into the ground, and that is not the highest use of Archangel Michael.

Facing your internal opposition

You need to come to the realization that there is a certain point on the path where there are external forces that are opposing your progress. There are even certain cycles. Certainly when you come together at an event like this, where you are challenging a manifestation of anti-love in Europe, there will be the forces of anti-love that will oppose you. You need to realize that there comes a point on your personal path where it is not external opposition you are feeling. It is your own unbalanced momentums that are sending an impulse into the cosmic mirror. Because you cannot see that you are doing this, the mirror must reflect it back multiplied. This is not opposition from dark forces. It is your own self-created opposition. There will, as we have said before, come a point where you cannot create a strong enough impulse to oppose it, and that is when you experience a breakdown.

I do not desire to see you experience a breakdown. I desire you to go beyond this entire pattern. How do you do it? By not being so serious, by allowing yourself to be joyful on the path, as you have done during this conference. Truly, it is our joy to see you come together and be joyful. We are not sitting up here wanting you to go around with long faces all the time. We want you to have the joy that we have. You see, those who take themselves and their spiritual path so seriously project an image upon the ascended masters that we are sitting up here in the identity realm, or in the lower spiritual realm, and we are as serious up here as you are on earth. But we are not.

We are not even "up here." We are here with you, and we are not serious. Of course, you can say it is easy for us not to be serious. We are not feeling the weight of the energies on earth. This I fully admit. It *is* easier for us not to be serious.

Why you need a sense of humor

How did we get to be ascended? By coming to a point where we no longer took anything on earth seriously. There was nothing on earth that could disturb our peace and our joy and our centeredness in our hearts. There was, as the Buddha demonstrated under the Bo tree, no demon of Mara who could tempt us into a reaction. I tell you: On a planet like earth, my beloved, if you don't have a sense of humor, you can't be non-attached to what is going on on this planet. There comes a point where you have to look at the planet – and you can look at all of the disasters that are going on – but you come to the point of seeing that it is really a game that people are playing. You just have to say: "I just can't take it seriously anymore. I just can't engage myself in it. I just can't be pulled into it." It is the only way. You cannot resolve anything. You cannot say to yourself: "Oh, when the outer conditions change, then I'll be at peace. Then I'll be joyful." Nay, because the outer conditions will not change as long as you take them seriously.

As we have said before, consciousness always comes before the physical manifestation. I am looking to you who are the spiritual people to truly acknowledge this and to truly realize that – regardless of the outer manifestations, regardless of your personal situations, regardless of the planetary situation, regardless of how threatening it may seem – you can be joyful. You can be at peace. You can be non-attached to this. You can look at it and not be so serious about it. It is the only way to be free on the personal level.

Early Christianity was joyful

This is what I came to show 2,000 years ago. Although it is not recorded in the Scriptures, I tell you that there was a joy in the movement I started with my disciples, and the joy came from one very simple thing. It was not so that I went around and cracked jokes all the time. I did not. I don't think I ever told a joke in that lifetime. But when we were in the flow of the Spirit, the Holy Spirit, we felt that joy, because truly there is no greater joy when you are in physical embodiment than feeling the flow of the Holy Spirit through your being. This you have experienced during this conference, both when you give your decrees and invocations and when you are taking in a dictation. This was my original vision for the Christian movement: "I will send you another Comforter that will be with you." It was my vision to have a movement that was entirely directed by the Holy Spirit so that the people who were engaged in that movement, in whatever form – whether they were the preachers on the podium or the congregation receiving it – they were feeling that joy of the flow of the Spirit. It was transforming them so that they could stop taking everything so seriously. There were those in the early centuries that embodied this. There have been a few since who have embodied it. Especially since the formation of the Roman Catholic Church, very few Christians have been able to embody it. You see how, as soon as Christianity became the official religion of the Roman Empire, the fallen beings rushed in to take up the positions of power that were now suddenly created.

Now they saw that this was their potential to set themselves up in the positions they wanted. They were, if not gods on earth, then certainly the people standing between God and the population. Thereby, they would have god-like powers over the people on earth. This has been the scourge of Christianity. Just look at how they have come up with these subtle ideas that have squeezed all joy out of Christianity: the idea of hell, the idea of eternal torment, the idea that you are a sinner by nature.

Removing joy from Christianity

Is it not deliberately designed to squeeze out all joy? They have created a movement that became a tool for controlling the people by making them think that there was no way they could escape the misery on earth. There was no way they could change the misery on earth. They could only look forward to being saved after this lifetime. What did it do? It gave complete control to the fallen beings that were in control of the Christian movement. Nobody could challenge them. Nobody could gainsay them. They had absolute power on earth, and that was, of course, their desire.

It was also the desire of many people to feel that they did not have to take responsibility for themselves. They could just follow the leader, as the old children's game goes. This does not lead to Christhood. You do not manifest Christhood by following a leader on earth.

Listen to what I said: You do not manifest Christhood by following any leader on earth! I do not care whether you consider a certain guru to be enlightened, to be an unascended ascended master, to be in the fullness of his or her Christhood. Whatever authority you claim for a person, whatever idolatrous image you project upon a person, you cannot manifest your Christhood by following a leader on earth.

What is Christhood? It is that you have a personal inner connection to the spiritual realm so that you are following the one leader of the one Holy Spirit.

Christianity needs no leader

There needs to be no supreme leader of the Christian movement as you see in the Pope. This office was not created by me. It is not sponsored from the spiritual realm. It was created by the fallen beings as their own wet dream of what they wanted to accomplish on earth. For almost 17 centuries this matrix of the fallen beings has been upheld in the Christian churches. It has been allowed to be upheld because not enough people had freed themselves from it. They wanted the feeling that they could just be a member of the Christian church and follow the outer rules, and they were guaranteed to be saved. Then they could live their lives any way they wanted. I have allowed this. I have allowed this. It was not that I wanted it, but I respected the free will of the people who claim to be my followers. I have allowed it because of certain cycles that made it necessary for people to have that experience, and also see how far into extremes a movement that claimed to represent Jesus Christ could go when it was not representing Jesus Christ and did not have the flow of the Holy Spirit. You saw it in the Crusades, the Inquisition, the witch hunts, so many other atrocities perpetrated by the Christian movements. You see it even today in the way they are holding people in a state where they see no purpose, they see no path, they see no real future for themselves, other than to mechanically obey and then hope that the promises made by the church are true.

Cycles have turned. They have turned because you and other people have responded not only to our outer teachings but to our inner call. You have lifted yourselves beyond the heavy yoke of the false Christianity that has been promoted now for so long, through not only the Catholic church but certainly also through many Protestant churches and many others, such as the fundamentalists and other groups. Cycles have turned.

The judgment of the false leaders

I, the Ascended Master Jesus Christ, hereby pronounce the judgment of Christ upon the beings who have in the past and who are today upholding the false Christianity. Your day is done on this planet. I pronounce it.

I call upon those who are my true students today to reinforce it through your calls and invocations, and you will see how, in a surprisingly short period of time, certain people will leave embodiment. What you will not see, at least not with your physical senses, is how many fallen beings will be taken out of embodiment in the astral plane, in the mental and in the identity realms. I say out of embodiment because they are in a sense embodying in those realms, as you are embodying in the physical.

I hereby pronounce this judgment, and I pronounce it here in Europe because this is where the Catholic church was formed. Although we are not in Rome, we do not need to be in Rome, for I AM everywhere in the consciousness of God, and this messenger has earlier been in the headquarters of the Catholic church, in the Basilica of Saint Peter's.

I create an arc of light to that previous momentum where I withdrew my light from Christianity. Now I do more than withdrawing my light. I actually send my light, but it is the light of judgment that will not allow this manipulation of the people to go on, that will not allow this idolatry of Christ to continue. Enough is enough!

It is time that people awaken to the reality that what I came to show humankind was that God is in every human being. The kingdom of God is within you. Why do you need an external priesthood and an external church to help you enter the inner kingdom? It can only take your attention away from the inner kingdom, especially when it is designed to do so, instead of being designed to facilitate your connection to the Spirit within.

Organizations in the aquarian age

Surely, it is possible to create an organization that does facilitate people making the inner connection, but it must be designed to do so from the ground up, as they say. So far not very many organizations have managed to do this, partly because they have not been able to pass the initiations of Pisces and overcome the heavy burden of idolatry and elitism that people were meant to transcend in the Piscean Age.

What did I do when I was in physical embodiment? I challenged the power elite. What did they do? They killed me. Look how in the beginning they attempted to physically kill my followers. When they could not do that, when they realized it was not going to work, then they joined the church. They took over the church, and now they killed my example. This is the awareness that needs to spread like rings in the water by you making the calls, by you having transcended this lie, this illusion, then by recognizing that the Christ is in you and you have a Christ potential.

I know that not everyone who hears or reads this dictation will have come to that point of acceptance. I ask you to ponder this, to use the teachings I have given in my books and in other discourses and dictations, so that you can come to the point where you have separated yourself from the lie that causes you to deny your Christhood. You can truly look at yourself and accept: "Yes, I do have the potential to manifest Christhood. I *am* capable. I am worthy to follow the example of Jesus."

Overcoming discrimination

Why have I asked you to give this invocation for removing discrimination from Europe? Because it is only through the Christ mind that you can avoid discrimination. It is only through the Christ mind that you can see the underlying reality that behind all of the outer appearances in the physical octave, all people are one and come from the One Source. This was the message I preached in a veiled form, but what has Christianity become?

It is a movement that preaches the opposite message. How has that been achieved? First of all by elevating me to being fundamentally different from other people: I was "God" from the very beginning. I was of the "same substance" as the Father, therefore fundamentally above all other human beings. Right there, you destroy my example. Who can follow me when I am fundamentally different from the rest of you?

More than that, you have also created the idea that I am the only key to salvation and that there is only one church that represents me and therefore determines whether you can receive my salvation or not. If you are not a member, a mindless member who mechanically accepts the doctrines and follows the practices of the church, then you will go to hell. Right there you have created a fundamental discrimination between Christians and non-Christians.

What did I tell my disciples to do? To go out into all the world and make all people my disciples. This is what so many Christian churches, so many Christian preachers, have used as the justification for thinking that they have – with force if necessary – to make all people members of the Christian religion. Was that what I said? Did I say to go out into all the world and make all people members of a particular Christian religion? Nay. I said to go out and make all people my disciples.

What does it mean to be my disciple? It means you follow my example. You embody the teachings. You open yourself to the Spirit. You allow yourself to accept your potential to manifest Christhood. That is what it means to be my disciple.

What does it mean to manifest Christhood? It means you see beyond all outer manifestations on earth. You see the oneness of all life, and you see that there can be no separation between God and God's creation. It is not possible. It is a lie.

Dividing earth from God's kingdom

Can you see how they took Christianity and they created another division? Instead of seeing beyond outer divisions, they created a new division between Christians and non-Christians, and then between those who were the leaders of the church and those who were the followers.

Now they said that – instead of following Christ within you, instead of being led by the Holy Spirit – you should follow the hierarchy on earth, or they would condemn you to hell. Who gave them the power to condemn anyone to hell? "Certainly not I," said the little red hen, and so do I say. I did not give anyone that power. No one on earth has been given that power by me, and therefore you should know that no one on earth has the power to determine whether you go to hell or to heaven. It is only your state of consciousness that determines this. That is what it means that the kingdom of God is within you. It is the change of consciousness that gives you access to the kingdom, even while you are in physical embodiment.

They created another division that the kingdom of God cannot come here on earth, that you cannot be in the kingdom of God while you are on earth. What they were really saying is: "Well, yes, Jesus slipped by us and manifested Christhood while he was in embodiment, but we are going to make sure that nobody else dares to do that. And we are going to use him as the boogeyman, so to speak, to make you deny your own potential to manifest Christhood."

Daring to be yourself

What did I say when I was in embodiment? The kingdom of God is at hand! That meant you don't have to wait till after this lifetime. You don't have to wait for some date when the world ends before the kingdom of God will be manifest. You can manifest it right here while you are in embodiment.

How do you do it? By daring to be yourself, instead of doing what the fallen beings want you to do: superimposing a mental image upon yourself and thinking you always have to live up to it. Therefore, you don't dare to just flow with life. You don't dare to play. You don't dare to express yourself. What did I say? Unless you receive it as little children, you cannot receive the kingdom. Play with life. Be joyful. Be joyful! Be joyful on your spiritual path.

Do not be so serious, thinking you have to live up to some outer standard. I do not judge you according to the standard created by the fallen beings. In a sense I do not judge you at all. I just look at you and see: Are you being yourself or are you not? If you are not, I try to help you as best I can.

As we have said at this conference, so many times you cannot even hear my help, my direction, because you are superimposing an image upon me, thinking that you have to be so serious in order to hear me. Many times it is actually in the letting go that you open your mind and heart to sensing, experiencing, my direction, my help.

I do not impose upon you. I do not impose upon your free will. If you are attached to a mental image of me and if you are so serious about that image, I do not force you. I do not impose myself upon you. I stand back and allow the universal mirror, the cosmic mirror, to return to you what you are projecting out.

How to hear inner direction

How do you hear me? So many of you ask this. How do you get direction? By surrendering, by letting go of the seriousness, by letting go of the mental images. There must be a space for my direction to enter your mind and heart. So many times you are so preoccupied by so many things that you leave no space. There is no stillness.

How did this messenger start the process of becoming a messenger? Through an act of surrender of his personal ambitions. He has no special abilities that set him apart from any of you. It is not that he has been trained for a hundred embodiments to be a messenger. It is not that he has an attainment that is above yours. He has one thing: the willingness to surrender. Of course, all of you have the ability to surrender. Do you have the willingness? Ask yourself this. Ask yourself this simple question, and then let go.

Then you will start to sense my Presence, for I am with you always. I will not conform to your images, the images created by the Christian religion that many of you have still not freed yourself entirely from. It is true that I have from time to time appeared to people, taking on a certain image, but the test is always to look beyond the image and to sense the Presence behind it. This, of course, is what the fallen beings are not capable of doing, for they do not have the willingness to surrender.

It is not so, my beloved, that, when you go into the duality consciousness or the fallen consciousness, you lose the *ability* to experience that there is something beyond duality. You lose the *willingness* because you are not willing to surrender, to let go, to have that stillness. You are constantly trying to force the universe to fit into your mental image. Thereby, of course, you are constantly forcing yourself to fit into that image. You are creating such a strain that it becomes unbearable, and that is truly what has created hell.

How hell was created

The people there, the beings there, are straining. They are fighting there with such intensity that it is burning up their attention and their lives. Look how many people on earth are doing the same thing while they are in physical embodiment. That is why you can see that there are places that are literally hell on earth because the people are so serious that they will not stand back and say: "Is there another way to look at life? Is there another way to live life?" That is the opening where you can receive an impulse from above – from your higher self, from the ascended masters, from your I AM Presence – that shows you there is an alternative to this state of mind where you are constantly struggling. This is what the Buddha said 2,500 years ago, that life is suffering when you are in this state of consciousness.

The emergence of mystical Christianity

There is a way out of it. That is what I came to give people 2,000 years ago. It has been completely aborted by the official Christian religion. I am, of course, grateful that so many people around the world have begun to restore that mystical Christianity. Not just through the messages I have given through this messenger, or even previous ascended master organizations. There are many other people, some Christian, some not Christian, who are receiving the idea from me that there is a new way to approach Christianity. I ask you who are ascended master students not to set yourselves apart from those, but to reach out to the mystics that are found everywhere. Just connect at a heart level.

My beloved, you do not need to get them to acknowledge the dictations I am giving through this messenger or any other particular teaching or organization. I am asking you to connect at the heart level and to acknowledge that, wherever people are, they have a right to be there. Your role is not to go in and change their minds and make them see what you see. Your role is simple: to demonstrate that you have something that they might not have so that they will be curious and eventually begin to wonder what it is that is different about you, what it is that they recognize, but that they want to have more of.

In order to come to that point, you must connect to them at the heart level. You must make them recognize that you share an inner experience. Even though it might be expressed differently on the outer, you share an inner experience. This is what it truly means to go into all the world and make all people my disciples. It means to help them connect to that flow of the Spirit in the heart.

The flow of the Spirit is the transforming power, but the challenge is that, in order to help people who are in embodiment, the Spirit needs to take on a form that they can recognize. Then it needs to show them that there is more than the form. The challenge you face – and that the fallen beings always fail – is to see beyond the form that the Spirit takes on and realize that the Spirit is always more and therefore cannot be confined to that particular form.

Overcoming the need for validation

My beloved, it truly is a privilege that I have a messenger I can speak through in this way. It is a privilege that I have students who accept that this is the Ascended Master Jesus Christ speaking. I am a formless being, or at least I am beyond form as you conceive of it. The way I speak through this messenger is not the only way I can speak. The way I have appeared to some people is not the only way I can appear. This I ask you to be mindful of so that you can respect other people and not want them to be like you. You recognize that I exist, that I am real, that I am an ascended master. Why do you need recognition and validation from the world?

We have seen this so much in previous ascended master organizations where the students had a need to feel that they were special, that they were doing special work for the ascended masters, that they had the highest teaching, that they were saving the world for Saint Germain, and all of these things. This is nothing but an ego game where you are seeking validation by being special compared to other people, which really means better than other people, more advanced, more spiritual, having greater attainment. Whatever words you want to put on it, it is all the same. It is an ego game. You who recognize me as a real ascended being, why would you need validation by getting other people to accept what you are doing, what you are believing?

It is only your ego that needs this validation. *You* do not! You have access to the kingdom of God within yourselves, and you can connect to me, and through me you will get all of the validation you could ever need. I love you as you truly are, and when you know that you are loved unconditionally by an ascended being, is that not the greatest validation you could have?

Why would you need validation from the world? Why do you need to approach people from the state of mind that you see so many religious people take on, namely that you have to convert them to your beliefs? It is not necessary. Focus on connecting to people at the heart level.

Surely if they ask, you can give them certain teachings, and you are, of course, free to share what you believe with others. There is a difference between sharing freely with others and then having this artificial mind state that you need to somehow get them to accept it. When you are just sharing, you are not concerned about whether they accept it or not and how they react to it. It is not your concern. Set yourself free to be who you are, and share what you believe and what you know. Set others free to react however they want.

Then set yourself free not to stop yourself, not to restrain yourself depending on how they react, but just be yourself, my beloved. *Just be yourself.*

That is truly the greatest gift you can have. The courage, the non-attachment, the surrender, the willingness to be yourself. What does it mean to be yourself? It means to be what God created you to be. What God created you to be is infinitely greater than the outer personality that has been created on earth and been shaped by the conditions on earth.

Freeing yourself from the outer personality

I came to set all free from that outer personality created by the fallen beings. Imagine in the Middle Ages where they had these suits of armor that were very tight, very unpleasant. You know that many of the people who made these suits of armor did not make them to a specific person. They had sort of a model that they used to make them as standard. The people who received those suits of armor, their bodies might not fit the standard, but they had to somehow squeeze themselves into the suits of armor. It was extremely unpleasant, I can assure you.

This is how the outer self is. It has been put upon you from without through many embodiments. You have somehow squeezed your Spirit into it, maybe to the point of being comfortable with it. I came to set all people free so that they could throw off this outer shell and dare to be who they were created to be by God. Dare to be the sons and daughters of God, instead of the sinners and the limited human beings. Naturally I want to see this for all people on earth, but I especially want to see it from you who recognize me as an ascended being.

I will do everything I can to help each one of you personally to throw off this heavy yoke. It does require your surrender, your willingness to look beyond the outer patterns, your willingness to just openly listen. Is there another way to be open to sensing my light, my flame?

Often I cannot help you transcend the outer shell by giving you words. There is a limitation to a dictation because the outer shell, the human personality, the outer self, was not created through words. It uses words, but it was not created, it was not defined, by words. Therefore, you cannot be liberated from it through words. It was created through a total experience of being in the physical octave.

The essence of the birth trauma

Other masters have talked about the cosmic birth trauma of when you first came into embodiment, and you were exposed to this shock of encountering the fallen beings. This was a total experience. It was not words that were put on you. It was something you experienced with the totality of your lower being.

What really happened in that situation was that, when you were in the spiritual realm looking down upon the earth, you still had a clear sense of connection to Source, to God. When you came down here and you were exposed to this shock of the fallen beings, you felt that God was not here with you. You felt that God had abandoned you and left you to the mercy, or rather the non-mercy, of the fallen beings.

The essence of your birth trauma is that you created an image of God and of yourself being separated from God. Since you could not let go of the idea that if God did something to you he must have a reason, you created in your mind a reason why God had left you.

That reason can be described in words, but you cannot be free from it even if you know the words. You can be free from it only by experiencing the Presence of an ascended master or of the Holy Spirit so that you experience that there is a reality beyond this outer self you created. Then you can gradually free yourself from it and heal it.

I am perfectly willing to work with any of you who will apply to me. So are Mother Mary, Master MORE, Saint Germain, any ascended master that is close to your heart. We are willing to help you heal this trauma, but you need to ask, and you need to ask by being open to sensing something that is beyond your normal state of consciousness.

This is what the fallen beings do not want you to achieve, that openness. They will do everything to get you to close your mind and heart and to keep it closed. They will do everything to get you to hold on to some image of the path, of yourself, of me, or whatever it is that you try to superimpose, so that you are not receiving me as the little child.

Resistance to transcendence

If you will observe yourselves, you can feel a certain uneasiness in your physical bodies and in your outer minds. You are beginning to tire. You are beginning, although you will not admit it, to feel I have spoken too long and that you cannot handle it. You need a break. This is the resistance from the physical octave to transcendence.

There is always a resistance to transcendence in the lower energies, the denser energies of the physical octave. I am not blaming you for this. I am just asking you to be aware of it and then to be aware of how many times in your life, in your daily life, that you feel this weight, this opposition to transcendence. Something is pulling you into the old patterns. By being aware of this and the need to do something different, you can perhaps make that switch of consciousness so you can sense my Presence, hear my directions, get a feeling for something else. Even though it is valuable to have these spoken dictations that you can read and hear, the spoken word, the word itself, cannot completely set you free at the level of the analytical mind that understands. There needs to be more than the words. There needs to be the Spirit that may flow through the words, but it needs to be received by you.

This is what the fallen beings have attempted to do: focus on the outer word, the outer teaching, the Bible, the doctrines, the organization, the rituals, the pomp and circumstance. All of these things they have tried to make people focus on so that they cannot receive the Spirit. This is what you can do as service by making the calls on.

Make the calls for people to be free of this entire matrix, this entire mindset, so that the people of Europe can break free from these 17 centuries and even beyond – for more centuries of the Roman Empire – of being forced into this mold that denies Spirit, that squeezes out Spirit. This is truly what needs to happen so that people can at least be free from the effects of Christianity and the way Christianity has been used as a tool to squeeze out the Spirit that is the key to transformation.

This I look forward to seeing people do with the invocations that can be and will be created, based on the dictations given through this conference, even using the invocations we have released before the conference. There is a tremendous potential if enough people will take up this work for transforming Europe. We truly have a much higher vision for the European continent than you can possibly imagine based on the common culture. This, of course, is a topic that is beyond my release. I will leave that to a future dictation.

I will extend to you my gratitude for your willingness to endure this long release where truly I have used the chakras of each and every one of you, and will use the chakras of those who hear or read this, to release the light that brings the judgment. This gives people an opportunity to sense that there is a light beyond the darkness that covers the land.

Well, that darkness has been challenged this day, and by you taking up this call, you can create a momentum that will spread like rings in the water and challenge that darkness. I, from the ascended realm, cannot do this, for I am not allowed to. You who are in embodiment, you can be the open doors for the spreading of the Christ light.

Therefore I say: My gratitude, my joy, for I AM the Flame of Joy, and I AM the Ascended Master Jesus Christ. My joy be with you!

10 | INVOKING THE JUDGMENT OF FALSE CHRISTIANITY

In the name I AM THAT I AM, Jesus Christ, I call to all representatives of the Divine Father, especially Jesus and Lord Maitreya, to bring forth the judgment of the Planetary Christ and the Cosmic Christ upon the false hierarchy behind Christianity. Help people see how the fallen beings have used Christianity in their never-ending power games, including…

[Make personal calls.]

Part 1

1. Beloved Jesus, awaken people to the reality that the most subtle ploy of the devil is to make us take everything on earth so seriously that it squeezes out all joy.

O Jesus, blessed brother mine,
I walk the path that you outline,
a great example to us all,
I follow now your inner call.

**O Jesus, let the Fire of Joy,
consume the devil's subtle ploy,
transfigured is our planet earth,
the golden age is given birth.**

2. Beloved Jesus, awaken people to the reality that you carry the Flame of Joy for the planet, but that no movement on earth has done more to destroy joy than Christianity.

O Jesus, open inner sight,
the ego wants to prove it's right,
but this I will no longer do,
I want to be all one with you.

**O Jesus, let the Fire of Joy,
consume the devil's subtle ploy,
transfigured is our planet earth,
the golden age is given birth.**

3. Beloved Jesus, awaken people to the reality that the movement that claims to represent you has come to embody the absolute opposition of the Flame of Joy.

O Jesus, I now clearly see,
the Key of Knowledge given me,
my Christ self I hereby embrace,
as you fill up my inner space.

> **O Jesus, let the Fire of Joy,**
> **consume the devil's subtle ploy,**
> **transfigured is our planet earth,**
> **the golden age is given birth.**

4. Beloved Jesus, awaken people to the reality that many people are feeling a heavy burden weighing upon them from this opposition to the Flame of Joy.

> O Jesus, show me serpent's lie,
> expose the beam in my own eye,
> as Christ discernment you me give,
> in oneness I forever live.

> **O Jesus, let the Fire of Joy,**
> **consume the devil's subtle ploy,**
> **transfigured is our planet earth,**
> **the golden age is given birth.**

5. Beloved Jesus, awaken people to the reality we need to step up higher and allow ourselves to be joyful. Help people know that you are giving us permission to be joyful, to embody the Flame of Joy that you are.

> O Jesus, I am truly meek,
> and thus I turn the other cheek,
> when the accuser attacks me,
> I go within and merge with thee.

> **O Jesus, let the Fire of Joy,**
> **consume the devil's subtle ploy,**
> **transfigured is our planet earth,**
> **the golden age is given birth.**

6. Beloved Jesus, awaken people to the reality we do not have to be so serious. Even though there are reasons for saying the earth is in a serious situation, it is no more serious than we who are in embodiment make it out to be.

> O Jesus, ego I let die,
> surrender ev'ry earthly tie,
> the dead can bury what is dead,
> I choose to walk with you instead.

> **O Jesus, let the Fire of Joy,**
> **consume the devil's subtle ploy,**
> **transfigured is our planet earth,**
> **the golden age is given birth.**

7. Beloved Jesus, awaken people to the reality that those who want us to take everything so seriously are those who want to set themselves up as gods on earth because they do not want to come into oneness with the God-Flame of Joy.

> O Jesus, help me rise above,
> the devil's test through higher love,
> show me separate self unreal,
> my formless self you do reveal.

> **O Jesus, let the Fire of Joy,**
> **consume the devil's subtle ploy,**
> **transfigured is our planet earth,**
> **the golden age is given birth.**

8. Beloved Jesus, awaken people to the reality that there is a small power elite of fallen beings on earth who have for a very long time been attempting to create the mindset that causes people to take everything so seriously.

> O Jesus, what is that to me,
> I just let go and follow thee,
> with this I do pass ev'ry test,
> to find with you eternal rest.
>
> **O Jesus, let the Fire of Joy,**
> **consume the devil's subtle ploy,**
> **transfigured is our planet earth,**
> **the golden age is given birth.**

9. Beloved Jesus, awaken people to the reality that we do not further our spiritual growth by being so serious. Being determined is not in opposition to being joyful for two God flames do not oppose each other.

> O Jesus, fiery master mine,
> my heart now melting into thine,
> I love with heart and mind and soul,
> the God who is my highest goal.
>
> **O Jesus, let the Fire of Joy,**
> **consume the devil's subtle ploy,**
> **transfigured is our planet earth,**
> **the golden age is given birth.**

Part 2

1. Beloved Jesus, awaken people to the reality that the more seriously we take things, the more of an opposition we are creating. We go into battle mode of thinking that we are feeling an opposition from without, and we have to battle it.

> Maitreya, I am truly meek,
> your counsel wise I humbly seek,
> your vision I so want to see,
> with you in Eden I will be.

> **Maitreya, kindness is the cure,**
> **in fires of kindness I am pure.**
> **Maitreya, now release the fire,**
> **that raises me forever higher.**

2. Beloved Jesus, awaken people to the reality that there is a point on the path where there are external forces that are opposing our progress. There also comes a point where it is not external opposition we are feeling. It is our own unbalanced momentums that are sending an impulse into the cosmic mirror.

> Maitreya, help me to return,
> to learn from you, I truly yearn,
> as oneness is all I desire
> I feel initiation's fire.

> Maitreya, kindness is the cure,
> in fires of kindness I am pure.
> Maitreya, now release the fire,
> that raises me forever higher.

3. Beloved Jesus, awaken people to the reality that when we cannot see that we are doing this, the mirror must reflect it back multiplied. This is not opposition from dark forces. It is our own self-created opposition. There will come a point where we cannot create a strong enough impulse to oppose it, and that is when we experience a breakdown.

> Maitreya, I hereby decide,
> from you I will no longer hide,
> expose to me the very lie
> that caused edenic self to die.

> **Maitreya, kindness is the cure,**
> **in fires of kindness I am pure.**
> **Maitreya, now release the fire,**
> **that raises me forever higher.**

4. Beloved Jesus, awaken people to the reality that we need to go beyond this pattern by not being so serious, by allowing ourselves to be joyful on the path.

> Maitreya, blessed Guru mine,
> my heart of hearts forever thine,
> I vow that I will listen well,
> so we can break the serpent's spell.

> **Maitreya, kindness is the cure,**
> **in fires of kindness I am pure.**
> **Maitreya, now release the fire,**
> **that raises me forever higher.**

5. Beloved Jesus, awaken people to the reality that we ascend by coming to a point where we no longer take anything on earth seriously. There is nothing on earth that can disturb our peace, our joy and the centeredness in our hearts.

> Maitreya, help me see the lie
> whereby the serpent broke the tie,
> the serpent now has naught in me,
> in oneness I am truly free.

> **Maitreya, kindness is the cure,**
> **in fires of kindness I am pure.**
> **Maitreya, now release the fire,**
> **that raises me forever higher.**

6. Beloved Jesus, awaken people to the reality that we need to come to the point where no demon of Mara can tempt us into a reaction. If we don't have a sense of humor, we can't be non-attached to what is happening on this planet.

> Maitreya, truth does set me free
> from falsehoods of duality,
> the fruit of knowledge I let go,
> so your true spirit I do know.

**Maitreya, kindness is the cure,
in fires of kindness I am pure.
Maitreya, now release the fire,
that raises me forever higher.**

7. Beloved Jesus, awaken people to the reality that all of the disasters that are going on are really a game that people are playing. We have to say: "I just can't take it seriously anymore. I just can't engage myself in it. I just can't be pulled into it."

Maitreya, I submit to you,
intentions pure, my heart is true,
from ego I am truly free,
as I am now all one with thee.

**Maitreya, kindness is the cure,
in fires of kindness I am pure.
Maitreya, now release the fire,
that raises me forever higher.**

8. Beloved Jesus, awaken people to the reality that we cannot say: "Oh, when the outer conditions change, then I'll be at peace. Then I'll be joyful." The outer conditions will not change as long as we take them seriously.

Maitreya, kindness is the key,
all shades of kindness teach to me,
for I am now the open door,
the Art of Kindness to restore.

> Maitreya, kindness is the cure,
> in fires of kindness I am pure.
> Maitreya, now release the fire,
> that raises me forever higher.

9. Beloved Jesus, awaken people to the reality that consciousness always comes before the physical manifestation. Regardless of the outer manifestations, regardless of our personal situations, regardless of the planetary situation, we can still be joyful and at peace. It is the only way to be free on the personal level.

> Maitreya, oh sweet mystery,
> immersed in your reality,
> the myst'ry school will now return,
> for this, my heart does truly burn.

> **Maitreya, kindness is the cure,
> in fires of kindness I am pure.
> Maitreya, now release the fire,
> that raises me forever higher.**

Part 3

1. Beloved Jesus, awaken people to the reality that there is no greater joy when we are in physical embodiment than feeling the flow of the Holy Spirit through our beings.

10 | Invoking the Judgment of False Christianity

O Jesus, blessed brother mine,
I walk the path that you outline,
a great example to us all,
I follow now your inner call.

**O Jesus, let the Fire of Joy,
consume the devil's subtle ploy,
transfigured is our planet earth,
the golden age is given birth.**

2. Beloved Jesus, awaken people to the reality that your vision for Christianity was a movement that was entirely directed by the Holy Spirit so that the people were feeling the joy of the flow of the Spirit.

O Jesus, open inner sight,
the ego wants to prove it's right,
but this I will no longer do,
I want to be all one with you.

**O Jesus, let the Fire of Joy,
consume the devil's subtle ploy,
transfigured is our planet earth,
the golden age is given birth.**

3. Beloved Jesus, awaken people to the reality that the flow of the Spirit was transforming them so that they could stop taking everything so seriously.

O Jesus, I now clearly see,
the Key of Knowledge given me,
my Christ self I hereby embrace,
as you fill up my inner space.

**O Jesus, let the Fire of Joy,
consume the devil's subtle ploy,
transfigured is our planet earth,
the golden age is given birth.**

4. Beloved Jesus, awaken people to the reality that since the formation of the Roman Catholic Church, very few Christians have been able to embody this joy. As soon as Christianity became the official religion of the Roman Empire, the fallen beings rushed in to take up the positions of power that were now suddenly created.

> O Jesus, show me serpent's lie,
> expose the beam in my own eye,
> as Christ discernment you me give,
> in oneness I forever live.

**O Jesus, let the Fire of Joy,
consume the devil's subtle ploy,
transfigured is our planet earth,
the golden age is given birth.**

5. Beloved Jesus, awaken people to the reality that the fallen being saw that this was their potential to set themselves up in the positions they wanted. They were, if not gods on earth, then certainly the people standing between the population and God.

> O Jesus, I am truly meek,
> and thus I turn the other cheek,
> when the accuser attacks me,
> I go within and merge with thee.

**O Jesus, let the Fire of Joy,
consume the devil's subtle ploy,
transfigured is our planet earth,
the golden age is given birth.**

6. Beloved Jesus, awaken people to the reality that the fallen beings took god-like powers over the people on earth, coming up with subtle ideas that have squeezed all joy out of Christianity: the idea of hell, eternal torment and that we are sinners by nature.

O Jesus, ego I let die,
surrender ev'ry earthly tie,
the dead can bury what is dead,
I choose to walk with you instead.

**O Jesus, let the Fire of Joy,
consume the devil's subtle ploy,
transfigured is our planet earth,
the golden age is given birth.**

7. Beloved Jesus, awaken people to the reality that the fallen beings have created a movement that became a tool for controlling the people by making them think that there was no way they could escape the misery on earth. There was no way they could change the misery on earth.

O Jesus, help me rise above,
the devil's test through higher love,
show me separate self unreal,
my formless self you do reveal.

**O Jesus, let the Fire of Joy,
consume the devil's subtle ploy,
transfigured is our planet earth,
the golden age is given birth.**

8. Beloved Jesus, awaken people to the reality that when we think we can only look forward to being saved after this lifetime, we give complete control to the fallen beings that are in control of the Christian movement.

> O Jesus, what is that to me,
> I just let go and follow thee,
> with this I do pass ev'ry test,
> to find with you eternal rest.

**O Jesus, let the Fire of Joy,
consume the devil's subtle ploy,
transfigured is our planet earth,
the golden age is given birth.**

9. Beloved Jesus, awaken people to the reality that the fallen beings used Christianity to set themselves up in positions where nobody could challenge them, nobody could gainsay them. They had absolute power on earth.

> O Jesus, fiery master mine,
> my heart now melting into thine,
> I love with heart and mind and soul,
> the God who is my highest goal.

**O Jesus, let the Fire of Joy,
consume the devil's subtle ploy,
transfigured is our planet earth,
the golden age is given birth.**

Part 4

1. Beloved Jesus, awaken people to the reality that many followed the fallen leaders because they did not have to take responsibility for themselves. They wanted to follow the leader, but this does not lead to Christhood.

> Maitreya, I am truly meek,
> your counsel wise I humbly seek,
> your vision I so want to see,
> with you in Eden I will be.

> **Maitreya, kindness is the cure,
> in fires of kindness I am pure.
> Maitreya, now release the fire,
> that raises me forever higher.**

2. Beloved Jesus, awaken people to the reality that we do not manifest Christhood by following any leader on earth. Whatever authority we claim for a person, whatever idolatrous image we project upon a person, we cannot manifest our Christhood by following a leader on earth.

Maitreya, help me to return,
to learn from you, I truly yearn,
as oneness is all I desire
I feel initiation's fire.

Maitreya, kindness is the cure,
in fires of kindness I am pure.
Maitreya, now release the fire,
that raises me forever higher.

3. Beloved Jesus, awaken people to the reality that Christhood means you have a personal inner connection to the spiritual realm so that you are following the one leader of the one Holy Spirit.

Maitreya, I hereby decide,
from you I will no longer hide,
expose to me the very lie
that caused edenic self to die.

Maitreya, kindness is the cure,
in fires of kindness I am pure.
Maitreya, now release the fire,
that raises me forever higher.

4. Beloved Jesus, awaken people to the reality that there needs to be no supreme leader of the Christian movement as we see in the Pope. This office was not created by you. It is not sponsored from the spiritual realm.

Maitreya, blessed Guru mine,
my heart of hearts forever thine,
I vow that I will listen well,
so we can break the serpent's spell.

**Maitreya, kindness is the cure,
in fires of kindness I am pure.
Maitreya, now release the fire,
that raises me forever higher.**

5. Beloved Jesus, awaken people to the reality that the office of the pope was created by the fallen beings, and for almost 17 centuries this matrix of the fallen beings has been upheld in the Christian churches.

Maitreya, help me see the lie
whereby the serpent broke the tie,
the serpent now has naught in me,
in oneness I am truly free.

**Maitreya, kindness is the cure,
in fires of kindness I am pure.
Maitreya, now release the fire,
that raises me forever higher.**

6. Beloved Jesus, awaken people to the reality that this matrix has been upheld because not enough people have freed themselves from it. People wanted the feeling that they could be a member of the Christian church and follow the outer rules, and they were guaranteed to be saved. Then they could live their lives almost any way they wanted.

> Maitreya, truth does set me free
> from falsehoods of duality,
> the fruit of knowledge I let go,
> so your true spirit I do know.
>
> **Maitreya, kindness is the cure,**
> **in fires of kindness I am pure.**
> **Maitreya, now release the fire,**
> **that raises me forever higher.**

7. Beloved Jesus, awaken people to the reality that you have allowed this. It was not what you wanted, but you respected the free will of the people who claim to be your followers.

> Maitreya, I submit to you,
> intentions pure, my heart is true,
> from ego I am truly free,
> as I am now all one with thee.
>
> **Maitreya, kindness is the cure,**
> **in fires of kindness I am pure.**
> **Maitreya, now release the fire,**
> **that raises me forever higher.**

8. Beloved Jesus, awaken people to the reality that you allowed it because of certain cycles that made it necessary for people to have that experience, and also see how far into extremes a movement that claimed to represent Jesus Christ could go when it did not have the flow of the Holy Spirit.

> Maitreya, kindness is the key,
> all shades of kindness teach to me,
> for I am now the open door,
> the Art of Kindness to restore.
>
> **Maitreya, kindness is the cure,**
> **in fires of kindness I am pure.**
> **Maitreya, now release the fire,**
> **that raises me forever higher.**

9. Beloved Jesus, awaken people to the reality that cycles have turned. With you I affirm the judgment of the Ascended Master Jesus Christ upon the beings who have in the past and who are today upholding the false Christianity. Their day is done on this planet. I pronounce it.

> Maitreya, oh sweet mystery,
> immersed in your reality,
> the myst'ry school will now return,
> for this, my heart does truly burn.
>
> **Maitreya, kindness is the cure,**
> **in fires of kindness I am pure.**
> **Maitreya, now release the fire,**
> **that raises me forever higher.**

Part 5

1. Beloved Jesus, I ratify the judgment of Christ upon the false leaders of Christianity, both those in physical embodiment, those in the astral plane, those in the mental realm and those in the identity realm.

> O Jesus, blessed brother mine,
> I walk the path that you outline,
> a great example to us all,
> I follow now your inner call.
>
> **O Jesus, let the Fire of Joy,**
> **consume the devil's subtle ploy,**
> **transfigured is our planet earth,**
> **the golden age is given birth.**

2. Beloved Jesus, with you I hereby pronounce this judgment, and I pronounce it for Europe where the Catholic church was formed.

> O Jesus, open inner sight,
> the ego wants to prove it's right,
> but this I will no longer do,
> I want to be all one with you.
>
> **O Jesus, let the Fire of Joy,**
> **consume the devil's subtle ploy,**
> **transfigured is our planet earth,**
> **the golden age is given birth.**

3. Beloved Jesus, I call into action your arc of light to the previous momentum where you withdrew your light from Christianity. I call into action your light of judgment that will not allow this manipulation of the people to go on, that will not allow this idolatry of Christ to continue. Enough is enough!

> O Jesus, I now clearly see,
> the Key of Knowledge given me,
> my Christ self I hereby embrace,
> as you fill up my inner space.

> **O Jesus, let the Fire of Joy,**
> **consume the devil's subtle ploy,**
> **transfigured is our planet earth,**
> **the golden age is given birth.**

4. Beloved Jesus, awaken people to the reality that you came to show humankind that God is in every human being. The kingdom of God is within us.

> O Jesus, show me serpent's lie,
> expose the beam in my own eye,
> as Christ discernment you me give,
> in oneness I forever live.

> **O Jesus, let the Fire of Joy,**
> **consume the devil's subtle ploy,**
> **transfigured is our planet earth,**
> **the golden age is given birth.**

5. Beloved Jesus, awaken people to the reality that we do not need an external priesthood and an external church to help us enter the inner kingdom.

> O Jesus, I am truly meek,
> and thus I turn the other cheek,
> when the accuser attacks me,
> I go within and merge with thee.
>
> **O Jesus, let the Fire of Joy,**
> **consume the devil's subtle ploy,**
> **transfigured is our planet earth,**
> **the golden age is given birth.**

6. Beloved Jesus, awaken people to the reality that the outer church can only take our attention away from the inner kingdom, especially when it is designed to do so, instead of being designed to facilitate our connection to the Spirit within.

> O Jesus, ego I let die,
> surrender ev'ry earthly tie,
> the dead can bury what is dead,
> I choose to walk with you instead.
>
> **O Jesus, let the Fire of Joy,**
> **consume the devil's subtle ploy,**
> **transfigured is our planet earth,**
> **the golden age is given birth.**

7. Beloved Jesus, awaken people to the reality that it is possible to create an organization that does facilitate people making the inner connection, but it must be designed to do so from the ground up.

O Jesus, help me rise above,
the devil's test through higher love,
show me separate self unreal,
my formless self you do reveal.

**O Jesus, let the Fire of Joy,
consume the devil's subtle ploy,
transfigured is our planet earth,
the golden age is given birth.**

8. Beloved Jesus, awaken people to the reality that not many organizations have managed to do this, partly because they have not been able to pass the initiations of Pisces and overcome the heavy burden of idolatry and elitism that people were meant to transcend in the Piscean Age.

O Jesus, what is that to me,
I just let go and follow thee,
with this I do pass ev'ry test,
to find with you eternal rest.

**O Jesus, let the Fire of Joy,
consume the devil's subtle ploy,
transfigured is our planet earth,
the golden age is given birth.**

9. Beloved Jesus, awaken people to the reality that when you were in physical embodiment, you challenged the power elite. They killed you and then they attempted to kill your followers. When they could not do that, they took over the church and now killed your example.

O Jesus, fiery master mine,
my heart now melting into thine,
I love with heart and mind and soul,
the God who is my highest goal.

**O Jesus, let the Fire of Joy,
consume the devil's subtle ploy,
transfigured is our planet earth,
the golden age is given birth.**

Part 6

1. Beloved Jesus, awaken people to the reality that the Christ is in every human and we all have a Christ potential.

Maitreya, I am truly meek,
your counsel wise I humbly seek,
your vision I so want to see,
with you in Eden I will be.

**Maitreya, kindness is the cure,
in fires of kindness I am pure.
Maitreya, now release the fire,
that raises me forever higher.**

2. Beloved Jesus, awaken people from the lie that causes them to deny their Christhood. Help people look at themselves and accept: "Yes, I do have the potential to manifest Christhood. I am capable. I am worthy to follow the example of Jesus."

Maitreya, help me to return,
to learn from you, I truly yearn,
as oneness is all I desire
I feel initiation's fire.

Maitreya, kindness is the cure,
in fires of kindness I am pure.
Maitreya, now release the fire,
that raises me forever higher.

3. Beloved Jesus, awaken people to the reality that it is only through the Christ mind that we can avoid discrimination. It is only through the Christ mind that we can see the underlying reality that behind all of the outer appearances in the physical octave, all people are one and come from the One Source.

Maitreya, I hereby decide,
from you I will no longer hide,
expose to me the very lie
that caused edenic self to die.

Maitreya, kindness is the cure,
in fires of kindness I am pure.
Maitreya, now release the fire,
that raises me forever higher.

4. Beloved Jesus, awaken people to the reality that this was the message you preached in a veiled form, but Christianity has become a movement that preaches the opposite message.

Maitreya, blessed Guru mine,
my heart of hearts forever thine,
I vow that I will listen well,
so we can break the serpent's spell.

**Maitreya, kindness is the cure,
in fires of kindness I am pure.
Maitreya, now release the fire,
that raises me forever higher.**

5. Beloved Jesus, awaken people to the reality that this has been achieved by elevating you to being fundamentally different from other people, by saying you were "God" from the very beginning and of the "same substance" as the Father.

Maitreya, help me see the lie
whereby the serpent broke the tie,
the serpent now has naught in me,
in oneness I am truly free.

**Maitreya, kindness is the cure,
in fires of kindness I am pure.
Maitreya, now release the fire,
that raises me forever higher.**

6. Beloved Jesus, awaken people to the reality that by making you fundamentally above all other human beings, they destroyed your example. Who can follow you when you are fundamentally different from the rest of us?

Maitreya, truth does set me free
from falsehoods of duality,
the fruit of knowledge I let go,
so your true spirit I do know.

**Maitreya, kindness is the cure,
in fires of kindness I am pure.
Maitreya, now release the fire,
that raises me forever higher.**

7. Beloved Jesus, awaken people to the reality that the fallen beings also created the idea that you are the only key to salvation and that there is only one church that represents you and therefore determines whether we can receive your salvation or not.

Maitreya, I submit to you,
intentions pure, my heart is true,
from ego I am truly free,
as I am now all one with thee.

**Maitreya, kindness is the cure,
in fires of kindness I am pure.
Maitreya, now release the fire,
that raises me forever higher.**

8. Beloved Jesus, awaken people to the reality that the fallen beings have created a fundamental discrimination between Christians and non-Christians. They say that if we are not mindless members who mechanically accept the doctrines and follow the practices of the church, then we will go to hell.

> Maitreya, kindness is the key,
> all shades of kindness teach to me,
> for I am now the open door,
> the Art of Kindness to restore.
>
> **Maitreya, kindness is the cure,**
> **in fires of kindness I am pure.**
> **Maitreya, now release the fire,**
> **that raises me forever higher.**

9. Beloved Jesus, awaken people to the reality that going out into all the world and making all people your disciples means to help people follow your example. We must embody the teachings, open ourselves to the Spirit and allow ourselves to accept our potential to manifest Christhood. That is what it means to be your disciple.

> Maitreya, oh sweet mystery,
> immersed in your reality,
> the myst'ry school will now return,
> for this, my heart does truly burn.
>
> **Maitreya, kindness is the cure,**
> **in fires of kindness I am pure.**
> **Maitreya, now release the fire,**
> **that raises me forever higher.**

Sealing

In the name of the Divine Mother, I call to Mother Mary for the sealing of myself and all people in my circle of influence in the creative flow of the Divine Mother, the River of Life. I call for the multiplication of my calls by all representatives of the Divine Mother, so that we form the perfect figure-eight flow of "As Above, so below." Thus, I accept that this is fully manifest, because the mouth of the Lord, the Divine Mother that I AM, has spoken it. Amen.

11 | SETTING PEOPLE FREE FROM FALSE CHRISTIANITY

In the name I AM THAT I AM, Jesus Christ, I call to all representatives of the Divine Father, especially Jesus and Sanat Kumara to awaken people from the sleep into which their souls have been put by false Christianity. Help people see the lies that the fallen beings have used to keep them loyal to the outer institution instead of the Living Christ, including…

[Make personal calls.]

Part 1

1. Beloved Jesus, awaken people to the reality that manifesting Christhood means we see beyond all outer manifestations on earth. We see the oneness of all life, and we see that there can be no separation between God and God's creation. It is not possible. It is a lie.

> O Jesus, blessed brother mine,
> I walk the path that you outline,
> a great example to us all,
> I follow now your inner call.
>
> **O Jesus, let the Fire of Joy,
> consume the devil's subtle ploy,
> transfigured is our planet earth,
> the golden age is given birth.**

2. Beloved Jesus, awaken people to the reality that the fallen beings used Christianity to create another division. Instead of seeing beyond outer divisions, they created a new division between Christians and non-Christians, and then between those who were the leaders of the church and those who were the followers.

> O Jesus, open inner sight,
> the ego wants to prove it's right,
> but this I will no longer do,
> I want to be all one with you.
>
> **O Jesus, let the Fire of Joy,
> consume the devil's subtle ploy,
> transfigured is our planet earth,
> the golden age is given birth.**

3. Beloved Jesus, awaken people to the reality that the fallen beings said that instead of following Christ within us, instead of being led by the Holy Spirit, we should follow the hierarchy on earth, or they would condemn us to hell.

> O Jesus, I now clearly see,
> the Key of Knowledge given me,
> my Christ self I hereby embrace,
> as you fill up my inner space.
>
> **O Jesus, let the Fire of Joy,
> consume the devil's subtle ploy,
> transfigured is our planet earth,
> the golden age is given birth.**

4. Beloved Jesus, awaken people to the reality that you never gave the fallen beings the power to condemn anyone to hell. No one on earth has been given that power by you, and no one on earth has the power to determine whether we go to hell or to heaven.

> O Jesus, show me serpent's lie,
> expose the beam in my own eye,
> as Christ discernment you me give,
> in oneness I forever live.
>
> **O Jesus, let the Fire of Joy,
> consume the devil's subtle ploy,
> transfigured is our planet earth,
> the golden age is given birth.**

5. Beloved Jesus, awaken people to the reality that it is only our state of consciousness that determines where we go. The kingdom of God is within us. It is a change of consciousness that gives us access to the kingdom, even while we are in physical embodiment.

> O Jesus, I am truly meek,
> and thus I turn the other cheek,
> when the accuser attacks me,
> I go within and merge with thee.
>
> **O Jesus, let the Fire of Joy,**
> **consume the devil's subtle ploy,**
> **transfigured is our planet earth,**
> **the golden age is given birth.**

6. Beloved Jesus, awaken people to the reality that the fallen beings created a division by saying the kingdom of God cannot come here on earth, that we cannot be in the kingdom of God while we are on earth.

> O Jesus, ego I let die,
> surrender ev'ry earthly tie,
> the dead can bury what is dead,
> I choose to walk with you instead.
>
> **O Jesus, let the Fire of Joy,**
> **consume the devil's subtle ploy,**
> **transfigured is our planet earth,**
> **the golden age is given birth.**

7. Beloved Jesus, awaken people to the reality that the fallen beings have said that even though you slipped by them and manifested Christhood while you were in embodiment, they are going to make sure that nobody else dares to do that.

> O Jesus, help me rise above,
> the devil's test through higher love,
> show me separate self unreal,
> my formless self you do reveal.

> **O Jesus, let the Fire of Joy,**
> **consume the devil's subtle ploy,**
> **transfigured is our planet earth,**
> **the golden age is given birth.**

8. Beloved Jesus, awaken people to the reality that the fallen beings have used you as the boogeyman to make us deny our own potential to manifest Christhood.

> O Jesus, what is that to me,
> I just let go and follow thee,
> with this I do pass ev'ry test,
> to find with you eternal rest.

> **O Jesus, let the Fire of Joy,**
> **consume the devil's subtle ploy,**
> **transfigured is our planet earth,**
> **the golden age is given birth.**

9. Beloved Jesus, awaken people to the reality that the kingdom of God is at hand, meaning that we don't have to wait till after this lifetime. We don't have to wait for some date when the world ends before the kingdom of God will be manifest. We can manifest it right here while we are in embodiment.

O Jesus, fiery master mine,
my heart now melting into thine,
I love with heart and mind and soul,
the God who is my highest goal.

**O Jesus, let the Fire of Joy,
consume the devil's subtle ploy,
transfigured is our planet earth,
the golden age is given birth.**

Part 2

1. Beloved Jesus, awaken people to the reality that we manifest the kingdom by daring to be ourselves, instead of doing as the fallen beings and superimposing a mental image upon ourselves and thinking we always have to live up to it.

Sanat Kumara, Ruby Fire,
I seek my place in love's own choir,
with open hearts we sing your praise,
together we the earth do raise.

**Sanat Kumara, Ruby Ray,
bring to earth a higher way,
light this planet with your fire,
clothe her in a new attire.**

2. Beloved Jesus, awaken people to the reality that the fallen beings have caused most people to not dare to flow with life, to play, to express themselves. Yet you said that unless we receive it as little children, we cannot receive the kingdom.

> Sanat Kumara, Ruby Fire,
> initiations I desire,
> I am for you an electrode,
> Shamballa is my true abode.
>
> **Sanat Kumara, Ruby Ray,**
> **bring to earth a higher way,**
> **light this planet with your fire,**
> **clothe her in a new attire.**

3. Beloved Jesus, awaken people to the reality that we need to play with life and be joyful on our spiritual path. We cannot be so serious and think we have to live up to some outer standard.

> Sanat Kumara, Ruby Fire,
> I follow path that you require,
> initiate me with your love,
> the open door for Holy Dove.
>
> **Sanat Kumara, Ruby Ray,**
> **bring to earth a higher way,**
> **light this planet with your fire,**
> **clothe her in a new attire.**

4. Beloved Jesus, awaken people to the reality that you do not judge us according to the standard created by the fallen beings. In a sense you do not judge you at all. You just look at us and see: Are we being ourselves or are we not? If we are not, you try to help us.

Sanat Kumara, Ruby Fire,
your great example all inspire,
with non-attachment and great mirth,
we give the earth a true rebirth.

**Sanat Kumara, Ruby Ray,
bring to earth a higher way,
light this planet with your fire,
clothe her in a new attire.**

5. Beloved Jesus, awaken people to the reality that we cannot hear your help and direction when we are superimposing an image upon you, thinking that we have to be so serious in order to hear you.

Sanat Kumara, Ruby Fire,
you are this planet's purifier,
consume on earth all spirits dark,
reveal the inner Spirit Spark.

**Sanat Kumara, Ruby Ray,
bring to earth a higher way,
light this planet with your fire,
clothe her in a new attire.**

6. Beloved Jesus, awaken people to the reality that it is in the letting go that we open our minds and hearts to sensing, experiencing, your direction, your help.

Sanat Kumara, Ruby Fire,
you are a cosmic amplifier,
the lower forces can't withstand,
vibrations from Venusian band.

**Sanat Kumara, Ruby Ray,
bring to earth a higher way,
light this planet with your fire,
clothe her in a new attire.**

7. Beloved Jesus, awaken people to the reality that if we are attached to a mental image of you and if we are serious about that image, you do not force us. You stand back and allow the cosmic mirror to return to us what we are projecting out.

Sanat Kumara, Ruby Fire,
I am on earth your magnifier,
the flow of love I do restore,
my chakras are your open door.

**Sanat Kumara, Ruby Ray,
bring to earth a higher way,
light this planet with your fire,
clothe her in a new attire.**

8. Beloved Jesus, awaken people to the reality that we hear you by surrendering, by letting go of the seriousness, by letting go of the mental images. There must be a space for your direction to enter our minds and hearts.

Sanat Kumara, Ruby Fire,
Venusian song the multiplier,
as we your love reverberate,
the densest minds we penetrate.

> Sanat Kumara, Ruby Ray,
> bring to earth a higher way,
> light this planet with your fire,
> clothe her in a new attire.

9. Beloved Jesus, awaken people to the reality that we need to surrender personal ambitions and have the willingness to surrender.

> Sanat Kumara, Ruby Fire,
> you are for all the sanctifier,
> the earth is now a holy place,
> purified by cosmic grace.

> Sanat Kumara, Ruby Ray,
> bring to earth a higher way,
> light this planet with your fire,
> clothe her in a new attire.

Part 3

1. Beloved Jesus, awaken people to the reality that you are with us always, but you will not conform to the images created by the Christian religion.

> O Jesus, blessed brother mine,
> I walk the path that you outline,
> a great example to us all,
> I follow now your inner call.

**O Jesus, let the Fire of Joy,
consume the devil's subtle ploy,
transfigured is our planet earth,
the golden age is given birth.**

2. Beloved Jesus, awaken people to the reality that the test is to look beyond the image and to sense the Presence behind it. This is what the fallen beings are not capable of doing, for they do not have the willingness to surrender.

O Jesus, open inner sight,
the ego wants to prove it's right,
but this I will no longer do,
I want to be all one with you.

**O Jesus, let the Fire of Joy,
consume the devil's subtle ploy,
transfigured is our planet earth,
the golden age is given birth.**

3. Beloved Jesus, awaken people to the reality that the fallen beings have not lost the *ability* to experience that there is something beyond duality. They have lost the *willingness* because they are not willing to surrender, to let go, to have that stillness.

O Jesus, I now clearly see,
the Key of Knowledge given me,
my Christ self I hereby embrace,
as you fill up my inner space.

**O Jesus, let the Fire of Joy,
consume the devil's subtle ploy,
transfigured is our planet earth,
the golden age is given birth.**

4. Beloved Jesus, awaken people to the reality that the fallen beings are constantly trying to force the universe to fit into their mental image. They are constantly forcing themselves to fit into that image. They are creating such a strain that it becomes unbearable, and that is truly what has created hell.

O Jesus, show me serpent's lie,
expose the beam in my own eye,
as Christ discernment you me give,
in oneness I forever live.

**O Jesus, let the Fire of Joy,
consume the devil's subtle ploy,
transfigured is our planet earth,
the golden age is given birth.**

5. Beloved Jesus, awaken people to the reality that the beings in hell are straining. They are fighting with such intensity that it is burning up their attention and their lives.

O Jesus, I am truly meek,
and thus I turn the other cheek,
when the accuser attacks me,
I go within and merge with thee.

**O Jesus, let the Fire of Joy,
consume the devil's subtle ploy,
transfigured is our planet earth,
the golden age is given birth.**

6. Beloved Jesus, awaken people to the reality that many people on earth are doing the same thing while they are in physical embodiment. There are places that are literally hell on earth because the people are so serious that they will not stand back and say: "Is there another way to look at life? Is there another way to live life?"

O Jesus, ego I let die,
surrender ev'ry earthly tie,
the dead can bury what is dead,
I choose to walk with you instead.

**O Jesus, let the Fire of Joy,
consume the devil's subtle ploy,
transfigured is our planet earth,
the golden age is given birth.**

7. Beloved Jesus, awaken people to the impulse from above that shows us there is an alternative to the state of mind where we are constantly struggling. Life is suffering when we are in this state of consciousness.

O Jesus, help me rise above,
the devil's test through higher love,
show me separate self unreal,
my formless self you do reveal.

**O Jesus, let the Fire of Joy,
consume the devil's subtle ploy,
transfigured is our planet earth,
the golden age is given birth.**

8. Beloved Jesus, awaken people to the reality that what you came to give people 2,000 years ago was a way out of the struggle. It has been completely aborted by the official Christian religion.

> O Jesus, what is that to me,
> I just let go and follow thee,
> with this I do pass ev'ry test,
> to find with you eternal rest.

**O Jesus, let the Fire of Joy,
consume the devil's subtle ploy,
transfigured is our planet earth,
the golden age is given birth.**

9. Beloved Jesus, awaken people to the reality that you are grateful that so many people around the world have begun to restore mystical Christianity by receiving the idea from you that there is a new way to approach Christianity.

> O Jesus, fiery master mine,
> my heart now melting into thine,
> I love with heart and mind and soul,
> the God who is my highest goal.

11 | Setting People Free from False Christianity

**O Jesus, let the Fire of Joy,
consume the devil's subtle ploy,
transfigured is our planet earth,
the golden age is given birth.**

Part 4

1. Beloved Jesus, awaken people to the reality that all those who strive for a more mystical form of Christianity need to connect at the heart level.

> Sanat Kumara, Ruby Fire,
> I seek my place in love's own choir,
> with open hearts we sing your praise,
> together we the earth do raise.
>
> **Sanat Kumara, Ruby Ray,
> bring to earth a higher way,
> light this planet with your fire,
> clothe her in a new attire.**

2. Beloved Jesus, awaken people to the reality that all mystically inclined people share an inner experience. Even though it might be expressed differently on the outer, we share an inner experience.

> Sanat Kumara, Ruby Fire,
> initiations I desire,
> I am for you an electrode,
> Shamballa is my true abode.

> **Sanat Kumara, Ruby Ray,**
> **bring to earth a higher way,**
> **light this planet with your fire,**
> **clothe her in a new attire.**

3. Beloved Jesus, awaken people to the reality that what it truly means to go into all the world and make all people your disciples is to help them connect to the flow of the Spirit in the heart.

> Sanat Kumara, Ruby Fire,
> I follow path that you require,
> initiate me with your love,
> the open door for Holy Dove.

> **Sanat Kumara, Ruby Ray,**
> **bring to earth a higher way,**
> **light this planet with your fire,**
> **clothe her in a new attire.**

4. Beloved Jesus, awaken people to the reality that the flow of the Spirit is the transforming power. The challenge is that, in order to help people who are in embodiment, the Spirit needs to take on a form that they can recognize. Then it needs to show them that there is more than the form.

> Sanat Kumara, Ruby Fire,
> your great example all inspire,
> with non-attachment and great mirth,
> we give the earth a true rebirth.

> **Sanat Kumara, Ruby Ray,**
> **bring to earth a higher way,**
> **light this planet with your fire,**
> **clothe her in a new attire.**

5. Beloved Jesus, awaken people to the reality that the challenge we face – and that the fallen beings always fail – is to see beyond the form that the Spirit takes on and realize that the Spirit is always more and therefore cannot be confined to that particular form.

> Sanat Kumara, Ruby Fire,
> you are this planet's purifier,
> consume on earth all spirits dark,
> reveal the inner Spirit Spark.

> **Sanat Kumara, Ruby Ray,**
> **bring to earth a higher way,**
> **light this planet with your fire,**
> **clothe her in a new attire.**

6. Beloved Jesus, awaken people to the reality that the One Spirit can take on many forms. We need to respect other people and not want them to be like us. We need no recognition and validation from the world.

> Sanat Kumara, Ruby Fire,
> you are a cosmic amplifier,
> the lower forces can't withstand,
> vibrations from Venusian band.

> **Sanat Kumara, Ruby Ray,**
> **bring to earth a higher way,**
> **light this planet with your fire,**
> **clothe her in a new attire.**

7. Beloved Jesus, awaken people to the reality that we need to overcome the ego game of seeking validation by being special compared to other people, which really means better than other people.

> Sanat Kumara, Ruby Fire,
> I am on earth your magnifier,
> the flow of love I do restore,
> my chakras are your open door.

> **Sanat Kumara, Ruby Ray,**
> **bring to earth a higher way,**
> **light this planet with your fire,**
> **clothe her in a new attire.**

8. Beloved Jesus, awaken people to the reality that it is only the ego that needs this validation. We do not! We have access to the kingdom of God within yourselves, and we can connect to you, and through you get all the validation we need.

> Sanat Kumara, Ruby Fire,
> Venusian song the multiplier,
> as we your love reverberate,
> the densest minds we penetrate.

11 | Setting People Free from False Christianity

> **Sanat Kumara, Ruby Ray,**
> **bring to earth a higher way,**
> **light this planet with your fire,**
> **clothe her in a new attire.**

9. Beloved Jesus, awaken people to the reality that you love all people as we truly are, and when we know that we are loved unconditionally by an ascended being, it is the greatest validation we could have.

> Sanat Kumara, Ruby Fire,
> you are for all the sanctifier,
> the earth is now a holy place,
> purified by cosmic grace.

> **Sanat Kumara, Ruby Ray,**
> **bring to earth a higher way,**
> **light this planet with your fire,**
> **clothe her in a new attire.**

Part 5

1. Beloved Jesus, awaken people to the reality that we do not need to convert other people to our beliefs. We need to focus on connecting to people at the heart level.

> O Jesus, blessed brother mine,
> I walk the path that you outline,
> a great example to us all,
> I follow now your inner call.

> **O Jesus, let the Fire of Joy,**
> **consume the devil's subtle ploy,**
> **transfigured is our planet earth,**
> **the golden age is given birth.**

2. Beloved Jesus, awaken people to the reality that we need to set ourselves free to be who we are, and share what we believe and what we know. We need to set others free to react however they want.

> O Jesus, open inner sight,
> the ego wants to prove it's right,
> but this I will no longer do,
> I want to be all one with you.

> **O Jesus, let the Fire of Joy,**
> **consume the devil's subtle ploy,**
> **transfigured is our planet earth,**
> **the golden age is given birth.**

3. Beloved Jesus, awaken people to the reality that the greatest gift we can have is the courage, the non-attachment, the surrender, the willingness to be ourselves, to be what God created us to be.

> O Jesus, I now clearly see,
> the Key of Knowledge given me,
> my Christ self I hereby embrace,
> as you fill up my inner space.

**O Jesus, let the Fire of Joy,
consume the devil's subtle ploy,
transfigured is our planet earth,
the golden age is given birth.**

4. Beloved Jesus, awaken people to the reality that God created us to be infinitely greater than the outer personality that has been created on earth and been shaped by the conditions on earth.

> O Jesus, show me serpent's lie,
> expose the beam in my own eye,
> as Christ discernment you me give,
> in oneness I forever live.

**O Jesus, let the Fire of Joy,
consume the devil's subtle ploy,
transfigured is our planet earth,
the golden age is given birth.**

5. Beloved Jesus, awaken people to the reality that you came to set all free from the outer personality created by the fallen beings. The outer self has been put upon us from without through many embodiments.

> O Jesus, I am truly meek,
> and thus I turn the other cheek,
> when the accuser attacks me,
> I go within and merge with thee.

**O Jesus, let the Fire of Joy,
consume the devil's subtle ploy,
transfigured is our planet earth,
the golden age is given birth.**

6. Beloved Jesus, awaken people to the reality that you came to set all people free so that they could throw off this outer shell and dare to be who they were created to be by God. We could dare to be the sons and daughters of God, instead of the sinners and the limited human beings.

> O Jesus, ego I let die,
> surrender ev'ry earthly tie,
> the dead can bury what is dead,
> I choose to walk with you instead.

**O Jesus, let the Fire of Joy,
consume the devil's subtle ploy,
transfigured is our planet earth,
the golden age is given birth.**

7. Beloved Jesus, awaken people to the reality that you will do everything you can to help each one of us throw off this heavy yoke. It does require our surrender, our willingness to look beyond the outer patterns, our willingness to openly listen.

> O Jesus, help me rise above,
> the devil's test through higher love,
> show me separate self unreal,
> my formless self you do reveal.

**O Jesus, let the Fire of Joy,
consume the devil's subtle ploy,
transfigured is our planet earth,
the golden age is given birth.**

8. Beloved Jesus, awaken people to the reality that the outer self was created through a total experience of being in the physical octave. The birth trauma of encountering the fallen beings was a total experience. It was not words that were put on us. It was something we experienced with the totality of our lower beings.

> O Jesus, what is that to me,
> I just let go and follow thee,
> with this I do pass ev'ry test,
> to find with you eternal rest.

**O Jesus, let the Fire of Joy,
consume the devil's subtle ploy,
transfigured is our planet earth,
the golden age is given birth.**

9. Beloved Jesus, awaken people to the reality that when we were in the spiritual realm looking down upon the earth, we still had a clear sense of connection to Source, to God. When we came down here and were exposed to this shock of the fallen beings, we felt that God was not here with us. We felt that God had abandoned us and left us to the mercy, or rather the non-mercy, of the fallen beings.

O Jesus, fiery master mine,
my heart now melting into thine,
I love with heart and mind and soul,
the God who is my highest goal.

**O Jesus, let the Fire of Joy,
consume the devil's subtle ploy,
transfigured is our planet earth,
the golden age is given birth.**

Part 6

1. Beloved Jesus, awaken people to the reality that the essence of the birth trauma is that we created an image of God and of ourselves being separated from God. Since we could not let go of the idea that if God did something to us, he must have a reason, we created in our minds a reason why God had left us.

Sanat Kumara, Ruby Fire,
I seek my place in love's own choir,
with open hearts we sing your praise,
together we the earth do raise.

**Sanat Kumara, Ruby Ray,
bring to earth a higher way,
light this planet with your fire,
clothe her in a new attire.**

2. Beloved Jesus, awaken people to the reality that our reason can be described in words, but we cannot be free from it even if we know the words. We can be free from it only by experiencing the Presence of an ascended master or of the Holy Spirit so that we experience that there is a reality beyond the outer self we created. Then we can gradually free yourself from it and heal it.

> Sanat Kumara, Ruby Fire,
> initiations I desire,
> I am for you an electrode,
> Shamballa is my true abode.

> **Sanat Kumara, Ruby Ray,**
> **bring to earth a higher way,**
> **light this planet with your fire,**
> **clothe her in a new attire.**

3. Beloved Jesus, awaken people to the reality that the ascended masters are all willing to work with us personally and help us overcome the birth trauma, but we need to ask, and we need to ask by being open to sensing something that is beyond our normal state of consciousness.

> Sanat Kumara, Ruby Fire,
> I follow path that you require,
> initiate me with your love,
> the open door for Holy Dove.

> **Sanat Kumara, Ruby Ray,**
> **bring to earth a higher way,**
> **light this planet with your fire,**
> **clothe her in a new attire.**

4. Beloved Jesus, awaken people to the reality that the fallen beings do not want us to achieve that openness. They will do everything to get us to close our minds and hearts and to keep them closed. They will do everything to get us to hold on to some image of the path, of ourselves, of you so that we are not receiving you as a little child.

> Sanat Kumara, Ruby Fire,
> your great example all inspire,
> with non-attachment and great mirth,
> we give the earth a true rebirth.
>
> **Sanat Kumara, Ruby Ray,**
> **bring to earth a higher way,**
> **light this planet with your fire,**
> **clothe her in a new attire.**

5. Beloved Jesus, awaken people to the reality that there is always a resistance to transcendence in the lower energies, the denser energies of the physical octave. We need to be aware of how many times in our lives that we feel this weight, this opposition to transcendence.

> Sanat Kumara, Ruby Fire,
> you are this planet's purifier,
> consume on earth all spirits dark,
> reveal the inner Spirit Spark.
>
> **Sanat Kumara, Ruby Ray,**
> **bring to earth a higher way,**
> **light this planet with your fire,**
> **clothe her in a new attire.**

6. Beloved Jesus, awaken people to the reality that we need to see how something is pulling us into the old patterns. Then we can make the switch of consciousness so we can sense your Presence, hear your directions, get a feeling for something else.

> Sanat Kumara, Ruby Fire,
> you are a cosmic amplifier,
> the lower forces can't withstand,
> vibrations from Venusian band.
>
> **Sanat Kumara, Ruby Ray,**
> **bring to earth a higher way,**
> **light this planet with your fire,**
> **clothe her in a new attire.**

7. Beloved Jesus, awaken people to the reality that the fallen beings have attempted to make us focused on the outer word, the outer teaching, the doctrines, the organization, the rituals, the pomp and circumstance. All of these things they have tried to make people focus on so that they cannot receive the Spirit.

> Sanat Kumara, Ruby Fire,
> I am on earth your magnifier,
> the flow of love I do restore,
> my chakras are your open door.
>
> **Sanat Kumara, Ruby Ray,**
> **bring to earth a higher way,**
> **light this planet with your fire,**
> **clothe her in a new attire.**

8. Beloved Jesus, awaken people to the reality that we need to be free of this entire matrix so that the people can break free from this old matrix of being forced into this mold that denies Spirit, that squeezes out Spirit.

> Sanat Kumara, Ruby Fire,
> Venusian song the multiplier,
> as we your love reverberate,
> the densest minds we penetrate.

> **Sanat Kumara, Ruby Ray,**
> **bring to earth a higher way,**
> **light this planet with your fire,**
> **clothe her in a new attire.**

9. Beloved Jesus, awaken people to the reality that people need to be free from the effects of Christianity and the way Christianity has been used as a tool to squeeze out the Spirit that is the key to transformation.

> Sanat Kumara, Ruby Fire,
> you are for all the sanctifier,
> the earth is now a holy place,
> purified by cosmic grace.

> **Sanat Kumara, Ruby Ray,**
> **bring to earth a higher way,**
> **light this planet with your fire,**
> **clothe her in a new attire.**

Sealing

In the name of the Divine Mother, I call to Venus and Mother Mary for the sealing of myself and all people in my circle of influence in the creative flow of the Divine Mother, the River of Life. I call for the multiplication of my calls by all representatives of the Divine Mother, so that we form the perfect figure-eight flow of "As Above, so below." Thus, I accept that this is fully manifest, because the mouth of the Lord, the Divine Mother that I AM, has spoken it. Amen.

12 | A SIGNIFICANT CLEARING OF THE ASTRAL PLANE

I AM the Ascended Master Astrea. I represent the Divine Mother, the White Fire of the Mother light. This light is an unstoppable, unconquerable force. There is no force on earth that can resist or reject or stand against the light of the white Mother.

You have called forth my Presence. You have earned my Presence in this conference by making the calls that few people in Europe are aware they can make or would dare to make, even if they knew about them. Perhaps you do not think about this, my beloved, but there are so many people on earth that would be mortally afraid of doing what you are doing by challenging the forces of darkness. These forces have such a hold on so many people embodied in Europe that the people dare not even stand up and demand their freedom. They cannot even dare to look at Saint Germain, for they are so used to being suppressed by the power elite and the forces of darkness that they dare not even imagine what it means to be truly free.

People are held back by fear

There are so many people in Europe who are held back by fear – fear of this, fear of that, but truly fear of nothing that is real, for nothing real can cause fear. You will say: "Well, was the Second World War not real? Was the Holocaust not real? Are natural disasters and diseases not real?" I would say: "Indeed they are not from the perspective of an Elohim." None of this is real. It has no permanence, but more importantly it was not created based on the vision of Christ, so how can it be real?

It can have a temporary manifestation, but it is no more real than the images you watch on the movie screen. The only difference being that when you are in a movie theater, you know you are watching a movie, but when you are in what you call real life, you do not realize that this is all as unreal as a movie. It is a projection upon the screen of life. There is nothing here that can bind you, that can hold you, for you are a spirit, a free-flowing spirit—if you dare to be free-flowing.

Of course, that is what has happened to so many people. They have been tricked. They have been suppressed. They have been scared into not daring to flow but thinking they have to stay at some station that has been defined for them by the powers that be. For so many centuries the Christian religion defined people's station as sinners, but even materialism or political ideologies have defined the station for people. Did not communism define that most people are workers except the party elite? Does not materialism define that you are no more than an upright-walking animal? Are these not all limitations that cannot in any way hold a spirit when you recognize yourself as a spirit?

12 | A Significant Clearing of the Astral Plane

Astrea clears the astral plane

I have come, magnified by your calls but also by your Presence, by your heart flames, by your conversations, by your willingness to come together. I am here to perform an action unprecedented on the European continent. I am, as I am speaking these words, manifesting my Presence, my flame, in the astral plane that is associated with Europe. I, with legions of angels, am binding the demons that are pulling on the emotional bodies of the people in Europe, pulling them into fear, pulling them into self-destructive patterns, pulling them into addictions, pulling them into self-denial, pulling them into all manner of manifestations of crime and perversions of the true qualities of God, the true activities of God.

How many times on the European continent have you seen war, truly a perversion of the flames and the energies of God? How many crimes have you seen on this continent? How many rapes? How many murders? How many plunderings of villages and towns? How much destruction have you seen that serves no purpose whatsoever, that does not even enrich those who are doing the destruction? It simply destroys and breaks down, shattering people's lives, wounding their souls, thereby making them open, their auras open, to the claws and the psychic hooks of the demons in the astral plane. They are bound now by my legions of angels, by my Circle and Sword of Blue Flame that I hurl into the astral plane.

Cut free the people of Europe! Bind and consume these entities, these demons! Cut free the discarnate souls to move on to other stations! Clear now the astral plane of Europe! Clear it now! Clear it now! Clear it now! Clear it now!

And it is indeed cleared, as much as the law will allow in the present configuration. Do not underestimate what a group, even small in numbers, can accomplish by coming together in unison and making the calls. The call compels the answer. I AM the answer! The Mother Flame is the answer! The Circle and Sword of Astrea is the answer to the cutting free of Europe and Europeans from these astral forces that are pulling them into senseless destruction and self-destruction time and time again.

Let them be bound, and they are bound!
Let them be consumed, and they are consumed!
Let them be no more, and they are no more!

Filling the empty space

Now there is a space. There is an opening. There is a vacuum in the astral plane. As Jesus taught so long ago when he cast out the demons, where there is empty space, other dark forces will rush in to occupy it. But I say: Nay, they shall not rush in. Instead, my angels are rushing in, filling up this space in the astral plane of Europe, and we will hold it for as long as there are people in embodiment who will make the calls to us through our decrees, through our invocations. Then we will occupy. We will occupy until the Christ can come and take up the position that rightfully is the Christ's position to occupy in the emotional body on this planet.

I am not saying that the astral plane of the entire planet is cleared by this action. I am not saying that the astral plane associated with Europe is cleared completely in this action. But there is a very significant clearance, and it is significant that my angels are taking up positions in the astral plane. Every time you make the calls, then they have the authority to claim more territory, so to speak, to bind and consume more forces of darkness, to consume the energies there, and to therefore extend the clearing action of the astral plane further and further.

Truly, you have won a victory. Truly, you have achieved a great action. You have achieved much of the work that we wanted you to achieve at this conference. For this I am grateful. All of us are grateful. All of us congratulate you for this.

There is still some more work to be done by clearing the mental and the identity realms, but the clearing of the astral plane that could be accomplished at this conference has hereby been completed and accomplished fully. Thus you have my gratitude. You have my joy. You have my uplifting, all-conquering joy, the joy that comes when you experience the purity of the white Mother light, when you see this light consuming all darkness, making it disappear as if it never existed. And truly it never existed, for it never had any reality in Christ, so how can it truly have existence?

Elaborate theories

Oh, how the philosophers of earth, many of them born in Europe, have created elaborate theories about what is real, what does it mean to exist and not exist. So many times their minds have been taken over either by forces in the astral plane or those in the mental, even some in the identity realm. Therefore their whole debate about existence and what is real is based on trying to say that one manifestation of the duality consciousness is more real than another manifestation of the duality consciousness.

Truly, nothing that is conceived outside the mind of Christ can ever be real, can ever be said to have existence. It is just a projection upon the screen of life, as fleeting as the images on the movie screen. They will move on, and if you turn off the projector, they instantly disappear. They disappear with the speed of light, for they are projections of light.

I tell you, the manifestations that you see in the physical octave and in the astral plane will not disappear with the speed of light, for they are made of a lower vibration, less quick light rays that therefore will disappear at a somewhat slower rate. Nevertheless, they will disappear in the blink of an eye when enough people stop giving them power, stop projecting them on the screen of life through their own consciousness.

I AM Elohim Astrea, and I AM Purity in action on earth, here, now and forever.

13 | INVOKING THE CLEARING OF THE ASTRAL PLANE

In the name I AM THAT I AM, Jesus Christ, I call to all representatives of the Divine Father, especially Shiva and all representatives of the Divine Mother, especially Mother Mary and Astrea, to clear the astral plane from all demons, discarnates, entities and misqualified energies. Expose all illusions coming from the astral plane and the fallen beings, including...

[Make personal calls.]

Part 1

1. Beloved Astrea, awaken people to the reality that the White Fire of the Mother light is an unstoppable, unconquerable force. There is no force on earth that can resist, reject or stand against the light of the white Mother.

Astrea, loving Being white,
your Presence is my pure delight,
your sword and circle white and blue,
the astral plane is cutting through.

**Astrea, come accelerate,
with purity I do vibrate,
release the fire so blue and white,
my aura filled with vibrant light.**

2. Beloved Astrea, awaken people to the reality that the forces of darkness have such a hold on so many people that the people dare not even stand up and demand their freedom.

Astrea, calm the raging storm,
so purity will be the norm,
my aura filled with blue and white,
with shining armor, like a knight.

**Astrea, come accelerate,
with purity I do vibrate,
release the fire so blue and white,
my aura filled with vibrant light.**

3. Beloved Astrea, awaken people to the reality that many people cannot even dare to look at Saint Germain, for they are so used to being suppressed by the power elite and the forces of darkness that they dare not even imagine what it means to be truly free.

> Astrea, come and cut me free,
> from every binding entity,
> let astral forces all be bound,
> true freedom I have surely found.
>
> **Astrea, come accelerate,**
> **with purity I do vibrate,**
> **release the fire so blue and white,**
> **my aura filled with vibrant light.**

4. Beloved Astrea, awaken people to the reality that there are so many people who are held back by fear, a fear of nothing that is real, for nothing real can cause fear.

> Astrea, I sincerely urge,
> from demons all, do me purge,
> consume them all and take me higher,
> I will endure your cleansing fire.
>
> **Astrea, come accelerate,**
> **with purity I do vibrate,**
> **release the fire so blue and white,**
> **my aura filled with vibrant light.**

5. Beloved Astrea, awaken people to the reality that the Second World War, the Holocaust or natural disasters and diseases are not real from the perspective of an Elohim. None of this has permanence because it was not created based on the vision of Christ.

Astrea, do all spirits bind,
so that I am no longer blind,
I see the spirit and its twin,
the victory of Christ I win.

**Astrea, come accelerate,
with purity I do vibrate,
release the fire so blue and white,
my aura filled with vibrant light.**

6. Beloved Astrea, awaken people to the reality that when we are in so-called "real life," we do not realize that this is all as unreal as a movie. It is a projection upon the screen of life. There is nothing here that can bind us, that can hold us, for we are spirits, free-flowing spirits.

Astrea, clear my every cell,
from energies of death and hell,
my body is now free to grow,
each cell emits an inner glow.

**Astrea, come accelerate,
with purity I do vibrate,
release the fire so blue and white,
my aura filled with vibrant light.**

7. Beloved Astrea, awaken people to the reality that so many people have been tricked, have been suppressed, have been scared into not daring to flow but thinking they have to stay at some station that has been defined for them by the powers that be.

> Astrea, clear my feeling mind,
> in purity my peace I find,
> with higher feeling you release,
> I co-create in perfect peace.
>
> **Astrea, come accelerate,**
> **with purity I do vibrate,**
> **release the fire so blue and white,**
> **my aura filled with vibrant light.**

8. Beloved Astrea, awaken people to the reality that for so many centuries the Christian religion defined people's station as sinners, but even materialism or political ideologies have defined the station for people.

> Astrea, clear my mental realm,
> my Christ self always at the helm,
> I see now how to manifest,
> the matrix that for all is best.
>
> **Astrea, come accelerate,**
> **with purity I do vibrate,**
> **release the fire so blue and white,**
> **my aura filled with vibrant light.**

9. Beloved Astrea, awaken people to the reality that communism defines that most people are workers except the party elite. Materialism defines that we are no more than upright-walking animals. These are limitations that cannot in any way hold a spirit when we recognize ourselves as spirits.

Astrea, with great clarity,
I claim a new identity,
etheric blueprint I now see,
I co-create more consciously.

**Astrea, come accelerate,
with purity I do vibrate,
release the fire so blue and white,
my aura filled with vibrant light.**

Part 2

1. Beloved Astrea, I call you to perform an unprecedented action. I call you to manifest your Presence, your flame, in the astral plane that is associated with ... [Name place].

O Shiva, God of Sacred Fire,
It's time to let the past expire,
I want to rise above the old,
a golden future to unfold.

**O Shiva, clear the energy,
O Shiva, bring the synergy,
O Shiva, make all demons flee,
O Shiva, bring back peace to me.**

2. Beloved Astrea, I call you to come with legions of angels, and bind the demons that are pulling on the emotional bodies of the people.

13 | Invoking the Clearing of the Astral Plane

O Shiva, come and set me free,
from forces that do limit me,
with fire consume all that is less,
paving way for my success.

O Shiva, clear the energy,
O Shiva, bring the synergy,
O Shiva, make all demons flee,
O Shiva, bring back peace to me.

3. Beloved Astrea, I call you to come with legions of angels, and bind the demons that are pulling the people into fear.

O Shiva, Maya's veil disperse,
clear my private universe,
dispel the consciousness of death,
consume it with your Sacred Breath.

O Shiva, clear the energy,
O Shiva, bring the synergy,
O Shiva, make all demons flee,
O Shiva, bring back peace to me.

4. Beloved Astrea, I call you to come with legions of angels, and bind the demons that are pulling the people into self-destructive patterns.

O Shiva, I hereby let go,
of all attachments here below,
addictive entities consume,
the upward path I do resume.

**O Shiva, clear the energy,
O Shiva, bring the synergy,
O Shiva, make all demons flee,
O Shiva, bring back peace to me.**

5. Beloved Astrea, I call you to come with legions of angels, and bind the demons that are pulling the people into addictions.

O Shiva, I recite your name,
come banish fear and doubt and shame,
with fire expose within my mind,
what ego seeks to hide behind.

**O Shiva, clear the energy,
O Shiva, bring the synergy,
O Shiva, make all demons flee,
O Shiva, bring back peace to me.**

6. Beloved Astrea, I call you to come with legions of angels, and bind the demons that are pulling the people into self-denial.

O Shiva, I am not afraid,
my karmic debt hereby is paid,
the past no longer owns my choice,
in breath of Shiva I rejoice.

**O Shiva, clear the energy,
O Shiva, bring the synergy,
O Shiva, make all demons flee,
O Shiva, bring back peace to me.**

7. Beloved Astrea, I call you to come with legions of angels, and bind the demons that are pulling the people into all manner of manifestations of crime and perversions of the true qualities of God, the true activities of God.

> O Shiva, show me spirit pairs,
> that keep me trapped in their affairs,
> I choose to see within my mind,
> the spirits that you surely bind.

> **O Shiva, clear the energy,**
> **O Shiva, bring the synergy,**
> **O Shiva, make all demons flee,**
> **O Shiva, bring back peace to me.**

8. Beloved Astrea, I call you to come with legions of angels, and bind the demons that are pulling the people into war, truly a perversion of the flames and the energies of God.

> O Shiva, naked I now stand,
> my mind in freedom does expand,
> as all my ghosts I do release,
> surrender is the key to peace.

> **O Shiva, clear the energy,**
> **O Shiva, bring the synergy,**
> **O Shiva, make all demons flee,**
> **O Shiva, bring back peace to me.**

9. Beloved Astrea, I call you to come with legions of angels, and bind the demons that are pulling the people into crimes, rapes and murders.

O Shiva, all-consuming fire,
with Parvati raise me higher,
when I am raised your light to see,
all men I will draw onto me.

O Shiva, clear the energy,
O Shiva, bring the synergy,
O Shiva, make all demons flee,
O Shiva, bring back peace to me.

Part 3

1. Beloved Astrea, I call you to come with legions of angels, and bind the demons that are pulling the people into plunderings of villages and towns.

Astrea, loving Being white,
your Presence is my pure delight,
your sword and circle white and blue,
the astral plane is cutting through.

Astrea, come accelerate,
with purity I do vibrate,
release the fire so blue and white,
my aura filled with vibrant light.

2. Beloved Astrea, I call you to come with legions of angels, and bind the demons that are pulling the people into destruction that serves no purpose whatsoever, that does not even enrich those who are doing the destruction.

13 | Invoking the Clearing of the Astral Plane

> Astrea, calm the raging storm,
> so purity will be the norm,
> my aura filled with blue and white,
> with shining armor, like a knight.
>
> **Astrea, come accelerate,**
> **with purity I do vibrate,**
> **release the fire so blue and white,**
> **my aura filled with vibrant light.**

3. Beloved Astrea, I call you to come with legions of angels, and bind the demons that are pulling the people into destruction that destroys and breaks down, shattering people's lives.

> Astrea, come and cut me free,
> from every binding entity,
> let astral forces all be bound,
> true freedom I have surely found.
>
> **Astrea, come accelerate,**
> **with purity I do vibrate,**
> **release the fire so blue and white,**
> **my aura filled with vibrant light.**

4. Beloved Astrea, I call you to come with legions of angels, and bind the demons that are pulling the people into destruction that is wounding people's souls, thereby making their auras open to the claws and the psychic hooks of the demons in the astral plane.

Astrea, I sincerely urge,
from demons all, do me purge,
consume them all and take me higher,
I will endure your cleansing fire.

**Astrea, come accelerate,
with purity I do vibrate,
release the fire so blue and white,
my aura filled with vibrant light.**

5. Beloved Astrea, I call you to come with legions of angels and hurl your Circle and Sword of Blue Flame into the astral plane over … [Name place], binding all demons, discarnates and entities.

Astrea, do all spirits bind,
so that I am no longer blind,
I see the spirit and its twin,
the victory of Christ I win.

**Astrea, come accelerate,
with purity I do vibrate,
release the fire so blue and white,
my aura filled with vibrant light.**

6. Beloved Astrea, I call you to come with legions of angels and cut free the people of … [Name place]!

Astrea, clear my every cell,
from energies of death and hell,
my body is now free to grow,
each cell emits an inner glow.

13 | Invoking the Clearing of the Astral Plane

> **Astrea, come accelerate,**
> **with purity I do vibrate,**
> **release the fire so blue and white,**
> **my aura filled with vibrant light.**

7. Beloved Astrea, I call you to come with legions of angels and bind and consume the entities and demons!

> Astrea, clear my feeling mind,
> in purity my peace I find,
> with higher feeling you release,
> I co-create in perfect peace.

> **Astrea, come accelerate,**
> **with purity I do vibrate,**
> **release the fire so blue and white,**
> **my aura filled with vibrant light.**

8. Beloved Astrea, I call you to come with legions of angels and cut free the discarnate souls to move on to other stations!

> Astrea, clear my mental realm,
> my Christ self always at the helm,
> I see now how to manifest,
> the matrix that for all is best.

> **Astrea, come accelerate,**
> **with purity I do vibrate,**
> **release the fire so blue and white,**
> **my aura filled with vibrant light.**

9. Beloved Astrea, I call you to come with legions of angels and clear now the astral plane of … [Name place]! Clear it now! Clear it now! Clear it now! Clear it now!

> Astrea, with great clarity,
> I claim a new identity,
> etheric blueprint I now see,
> I co-create more consciously.
>
> **Astrea, come accelerate,**
> **with purity I do vibrate,**
> **release the fire so blue and white,**
> **my aura filled with vibrant light.**

Part 4

1. Beloved Astrea, I call you to come with legions of angels and clear the astral plane, as much as the law will allow in the present configuration.

> O Shiva, God of Sacred Fire,
> It's time to let the past expire,
> I want to rise above the old,
> a golden future to unfold.
>
> **O Shiva, clear the energy,**
> **O Shiva, bring the synergy,**
> **O Shiva, make all demons flee,**
> **O Shiva, bring back peace to me.**

2. Beloved Astrea, awaken people to the reality that the call compels the answer. You are the answer! The Mother Flame is the answer! The Circle and Sword of Astrea is the answer to the cutting free of people from these astral forces that are pulling them into senseless destruction and self-destruction time and time again.

> O Shiva, come and set me free,
> from forces that do limit me,
> with fire consume all that is less,
> paving way for my success.
>
> **O Shiva, clear the energy,**
> **O Shiva, bring the synergy,**
> **O Shiva, make all demons flee,**
> **O Shiva, bring back peace to me.**

3. Beloved Astrea, I say with you: Let them be bound. And they *are* bound!

> O Shiva, Maya's veil disperse,
> clear my private universe,
> dispel the consciousness of death,
> consume it with your Sacred Breath.
>
> **O Shiva, clear the energy,**
> **O Shiva, bring the synergy,**
> **O Shiva, make all demons flee,**
> **O Shiva, bring back peace to me.**

4. Beloved Astrea, I say with you: Let them be consumed, and they *are* consumed!

O Shiva, I hereby let go,
of all attachments here below,
addictive entities consume,
the upward path I do resume.

O Shiva, clear the energy,
O Shiva, bring the synergy,
O Shiva, make all demons flee,
O Shiva, bring back peace to me.

5. Beloved Astrea, I say with you: Let them be no more, and they *are* no more!

O Shiva, I recite your name,
come banish fear and doubt and shame,
with fire expose within my mind,
what ego seeks to hide behind.

O Shiva, clear the energy,
O Shiva, bring the synergy,
O Shiva, make all demons flee,
O Shiva, bring back peace to me.

6. Beloved Astrea, I call you to come with legions of angels and fill the space, the opening, the vacuum in the astral plane.

O Shiva, I am not afraid,
my karmic debt hereby is paid,
the past no longer owns my choice,
in breath of Shiva I rejoice.

**O Shiva, clear the energy,
O Shiva, bring the synergy,
O Shiva, make all demons flee,
O Shiva, bring back peace to me.**

7. Beloved Astrea, I say with you: The dark forces shall not rush in. Instead, your angels are rushing in, filling up this space in the astral plane, and you will hold it for as long as there are people in embodiment who will make the calls to you through the decrees and invocations.

> O Shiva, show me spirit pairs,
> that keep me trapped in their affairs,
> I choose to see within my mind,
> the spirits that you surely bind.

**O Shiva, clear the energy,
O Shiva, bring the synergy,
O Shiva, make all demons flee,
O Shiva, bring back peace to me.**

8. Beloved Astrea, I call you to come with legions of angels and occupy until the Christ can come and take up the position that rightfully is the Christ's position to occupy in the emotional body on this planet.

> O Shiva, naked I now stand,
> my mind in freedom does expand,
> as all my ghosts I do release,
> surrender is the key to peace.

> **O Shiva, clear the energy,**
> **O Shiva, bring the synergy,**
> **O Shiva, make all demons flee,**
> **O Shiva, bring back peace to me.**

9. Beloved Astrea, I accept that there is a very significant clearance, and it is significant that your angels are taking up positions in the astral plane.

> O Shiva, all-consuming fire,
> with Parvati raise me higher,
> when I am raised your light to see,
> all men I will draw onto me.

> **O Shiva, clear the energy,**
> **O Shiva, bring the synergy,**
> **O Shiva, make all demons flee,**
> **O Shiva, bring back peace to me.**

Part 5

1. Beloved Astrea, awaken people to the reality that every time we make the calls, then you have the authority to claim more territory, to bind and consume more forces of darkness, to consume the energies and to extend the clearing action of the astral plane further and further.

> Astrea, loving Being white,
> your Presence is my pure delight,
> your sword and circle white and blue,
> the astral plane is cutting through.

13 | Invoking the Clearing of the Astral Plane

Astrea, come accelerate,
with purity I do vibrate,
release the fire so blue and white,
my aura filled with vibrant light.

2. Beloved Astrea, awaken people to the reality that you are the uplifting, all-conquering joy, the joy that comes when we experience the purity of the white Mother light.

Astrea, calm the raging storm,
so purity will be the norm,
my aura filled with blue and white,
with shining armor, like a knight.

Astrea, come accelerate,
with purity I do vibrate,
release the fire so blue and white,
my aura filled with vibrant light.

3. Beloved Astrea, awaken people to the reality that the white Mother light can consume all darkness, making it disappear as if it never existed. And truly it never existed, for it never had any reality in Christ, so how can it truly have existence.

Astrea, come and cut me free,
from every binding entity,
let astral forces all be bound,
true freedom I have surely found.

Astrea, come accelerate,
with purity I do vibrate,
release the fire so blue and white,
my aura filled with vibrant light.

4. Beloved Astrea, awaken people to the reality that the philosophers of earth have created elaborate theories about what is real, what it means to exist and not exist.

> Astrea, I sincerely urge,
> from demons all, do me purge,
> consume them all and take me higher,
> I will endure your cleansing fire.
>
> **Astrea, come accelerate,**
> **with purity I do vibrate,**
> **release the fire so blue and white,**
> **my aura filled with vibrant light.**

5. Beloved Astrea, awaken people to the reality that so many times their minds have been taken over either by forces in the astral plane or those in the mental, even some in the identity realm.

> Astrea, do all spirits bind,
> so that I am no longer blind,
> I see the spirit and its twin,
> the victory of Christ I win.
>
> **Astrea, come accelerate,**
> **with purity I do vibrate,**
> **release the fire so blue and white,**
> **my aura filled with vibrant light.**

6. Beloved Astrea, awaken people to the reality that the whole debate about existence and what is real is based on trying to say that one manifestation of the duality consciousness is more real than another manifestation of the duality consciousness.

that this is fully manifest, because the mouth of the Lord, the Divine Mother that I AM, has spoken it. Amen.

14 | THE MENTAL AND IDENTITY ILLUSIONS OF EUROPE

I AM the ascended master that you have known as the Great Divine Director. I AM, as some of you will know, a cosmic being, which signifies that I hold an office in hierarchy that is beyond one planet. I do represent the Flame of Divine Direction for earth, but I represent the same flame for many, many other planets. Not by any means all planets in the universe, but many more planets than you can truly imagine with the linear human mind and its use of numbers.

This signifies something to you, namely that I am not so concerned about conditions on earth as the ascended masters who work only with earth. I am not thereby saying that I am not interested in earth. I am indeed. But it is not my exclusive area of concern, and therefore I am not as close to earth in vibration as the ascended masters who work specifically with this planet. This signifies that when I do have an opportunity to speak through a messenger in physical embodiment, I come with a higher energy. I release a more powerful energy than you would normally have released in an ascended master dictation. Thus, you may hear that the messenger's voice has trouble carrying the vibration, because it is significantly higher than what he is used to from other masters.

Let not this trouble you, and let it not trouble you if you feel in your own chakras that there is a certain intensity that you do not normally feel. This is a result of the fact that you are being asked to be the intermediaries, the open doors between the much higher vibration of my light and the much lower vibrations of planet earth. This is not an easy task. It is not easy to hold the balance where you are, so to speak, in between two worlds, experiencing both the world you normally experience of earth and the higher vibrations of my Presence. The light that I am is so intense that – were it not stepped down by other ascended masters, by those who are working with the earth – then it would indeed be a force that would burn this planet. This would not be constructive. Even though it certainly would remove darkness, it would also remove people's sense of continuity, and this, of course, is not what we desire.

Saint Germain, my own student, is indeed stepping down this light so that its vibration is not too high to accomplish the purpose that he envisions needs to be accomplished for Europe, as a result of the work you have done at this conference. Truly, I am the one speaking, but the release of the light is stepped down and directed by Saint Germain, who is intimately familiar with the conditions of Europe, having been embodied on this continent several times and having been allowed to step beyond the veil as an ascended master and work with the recalcitrant kings of those past centuries where he attempted to unite the people of Europe.

14 | The mental and identity illusions of Europe

What is Europe?

I therefore, put before you the question: "What is Europe?" It is, more than anything, an idea of unity through diversity, not *in spite of* diversity but *through* diversity.

We have told you that there was a distant past when the inhabitants of the earth had created a downward spiral, because they were so alike, so in conformity, that they reinforced the mindset that prevented them from growing. This was a very distant past, and I do not want you to think that the continents of the earth looked the same then as they do today. Nevertheless, the land mass that is today the European continent was the main land mass at that time where the primary civilization of the earth was located. You have on what is now the European continent these energetic records from that distant time and that distant society.

What do you then see manifest in Europe today? You see so many different groupings of people, based on all of these outer differences and characteristics. Why has Europe become such a melting pot? Because it was necessary to bring so many different people here to break up these old records of conformity. Look at how the fallen beings who have embodied on the European continent – and, of course, the fallen beings who have controlled them in the higher realms – have attempted to create unity through sameness by forcing people into conformity. Back in that distant age when the descent of the planet began, no one was forced into conformity. They came voluntarily into conformity, and those who did not come into conformity ascended from earth. Those that were left were in such conformity that they created the downward spiral, but it was through their own choosing.

Conformity through force

What the fallen beings have attempted to accomplish in Europe is to get people to again come into conformity, but this time through force, by making them the same. This has been counteracted by the fact that so many different people have been embodied on the European continent that trying to force some kind of conformity in Europe is, as the popular saying goes, like herding cats. You will see that all of these different people have been deliberately gathered here in order to prevent the fallen beings from turning Europe into a society so trapped in conformity that the downward spiral could not be turned back.

You have seen some nations in Europe where the people have been willing, at least the majority of them, to come into conformity under some strong leader or some strong ideology. In a sense you could say that most of Europe in the Catholic era was in conformity around the church, but even greater conformity was achieved in Germany during Nazism and in Russia during Soviet times. Still, there was not total conformity, and this was indeed because there were so many different peoples embodied on this continent.

"Why then was this necessary?" you might ask. Because it was necessary, in this age, that those lifestreams who were embodied when the descent of the earth began were given a similar initiation as the one that led them into the downward spiral. It was similar but not the same, in the sense that this time they were brought together from many different backgrounds. They had so many different characteristics that they were not as uniform as they were back then. The other difference was that this time they were allowed to be affected by the fallen beings, both to give them an opportunity and to give the fallen beings an opportunity to overcome their past momentums of conformity.

Europe as a process of initiation

You may look at Europe during the past 2,000 years as a giant initiation process for a certain group of lifestreams. They are being given the same opportunity again, only it is not the same because the universe and even planet earth have moved into other spirals. Therefore, nothing can ever be the same, even though the people and their state of consciousness have not changed very much since that previous age. Still, cycles have changed, and therefore the initiation is slightly different.

What you saw Saint Germain attempt to do was to get the kings, the leaders of the time, to see beyond their own personal differences and come into a form of cooperation that could have united the nations of Europe, not under one physical leader but under a higher form of leadership. Had these kings responded – and not all of them were fallen beings – it would have been possible for Saint Germain to guide the leaders of the European nation for the last several centuries.

This, of course, did not come to pass. The plan has now shifted to where Saint Germain is no longer addressing the leaders. He is addressing the so-called common people, who after all are not so common because you are spiritual beings in embodiment. You have considerable attainment in freeing yourselves from your own egos and thus becoming the open doors for that which is more. The plan then is still to unite Europe, not by making everyone the same but by making you embrace and accept your differences.

Seeing beyond outer differences

Do you perhaps see, those of you who have been here physically for this conference, that even though you have all selected yourselves to come here because you resonate with the teachings of the ascended masters, you still have outer differences from your nations, from your families, from your culture? Despite these outer differences, you have come together here, and you have not been threatened by each other's differences. You have not gone into the oh-so-common ego game of seeking to force other people to come into conformity with your way of looking at life, so that you can feel validated and not threatened. Instead, you have looked to a higher vision, to a higher principle, a higher purpose, namely the ascended masters, who are truly your own older brothers and sisters, or we might say that you are the extensions of the ascended masters.

When you recognize this, you can see beyond the outer differences. They are still there. You recognize the differences. You can also come to value the differences because they give different perspectives, but you also see beyond them to see the higher unity behind the outer differences. This is, of course, a microcosm of what is the highest potential for Europe.

The European Union

This is the true purpose of the European Union, which is a grand experiment of whether people can come into union. So far, of course, it has been the fallen beings who have attempted to take control and force some kind of sameness by creating a forced uniformity through the economy and through the political process.

14 | The mental and identity illusions of Europe

You are beginning to see how this is no longer quite working as they had hoped. The union is, so to speak, being stretched almost to the breaking point in some areas. This is not because there is anything wrong or unsustainable about having a European Union, but it is because it has not yet reached the point, the level of consciousness, where true union can be sustainable. It is still based on the considerations of this world, the duality consciousness, the desire for control through conformity, and not on the higher vision of Saint Germain and the ascended masters.

Who can bring that higher vision? Well, many people. You yourselves can, of course, be part of bringing this vision by raising your consciousness, by making the calls and invocations, by sharing your presence and speaking to other people. You can also be part of it by holding the vision and making the calls on behalf of the many, many people who can bring forth a piece of the puzzle of Saint Germain's vision for Europe, but who are not, and who do not need to be, familiar with ascended master teachings. You are, my beloved, the forerunners for Saint Germain's Golden Age.

Do not fall into the trap of thinking that you alone will bring it forth. You have the expertise in one field, spirituality. Some of you also have expertise in a particular field in your occupation, but you cannot have the expertise in every field that is necessary in order to bring forth the Golden Age. This is a big undertaking, a very complex endeavor, so there must be many, many people all throughout Europe who each receive a piece of that vision. Many of them are not openly spiritual. Some of them are not spiritual at all. But they still have the opening in their consciousness to receive one idea in a lifetime that can help bring society forward. It will be very helpful to us of the ascended masters if you will hold the vision and make the calls for these people to be free to receive their contribution.

Seeing the overall picture that is Europe

You may have seen some of the images that have been created, where they have taken a large number of individual photographs, and when you look at some of these pictures close up, you see the individual photographs clearly. And you see only the individual pictures. But if you then zoom out and see it from a greater distance, you see that the individual pictures form a mosaic, and the mosaic has a larger picture in it. This is how we see Europe.

We are not focused on the differences that divide people. We are able to look from a greater distance and therefore see the overall picture formed by the mosaic of the individual picture tiles. This is how you can come to see Europe as well. By holding this vision, by asking us to give you a clearer vision of the greater picture, you can become open doors for anchoring it in the collective consciousness. This truly is a great service of what Saint Germain has called "eye magic" where you use the power of vision to create a magic effect so that other people can begin to see the larger mosaic formed by the individual pictures of the millions of people who embody in Europe. They can even begin then to see beyond some of these outer divisions that divide people so much.

There has already been significant progress in seeing beyond race. This was brought about by the very hard lesson of the Holocaust and the racial hatred, which many nations in Europe have made a determined effort to raise themselves above. It is far better that the collective consciousness is pulled up by those who are the spiritual people acting as the magnet so that they do not have to have these hard lessons. For I tell you that if every division in Europe had to be overcome through such dramatic events, then it would be devastating and create such wounds in the souls of the people of Europe that it would prevent the manifestation of the Golden Age. It would also take a very long time, and Saint Germain does not envision that it will take so long to manifest a Golden Age in Europe.

Find freedom from judging others

The only real solution here is that those who are the spiritual people hold the vision, make the calls, overcome the consciousness that you alone have to take credit for bringing in the Golden Age, but instead reach that level where you are seeking to raise the whole. You are seeking to raise the all. You are truly only wanting people to be raised up and liberated so they can bring forth their individual gifts. Truly, we have seen students of the ascended masters fall into this trap of wanting to feel that they were so special that they had a – mostly subconscious and unrecognized – desire to hold other people down so that they could stand out as the ones who did the important work. They sometimes envisioned that in some future time there would be this grand ceremony, and they would be recognized as the ones who saved the earth.

This, of course, is not the way we work, we of the ascended masters, for we see the oneness of all life. We see and we acknowledge how important you are as the forerunners, but we do not see you through a value judgment that makes you better or more important than other people. We see a reflection of ourselves in all people on earth, so we value each one infinitely, in a way that cannot be measured by the dualistic mind and therefore cannot be subjected to a value judgment. Find that inner freedom where you do not evaluate and judge others and therefore do not evaluate and judge yourselves. This is a great freedom to have, for then you are truly open to Divine Direction. You do not place a preconceived image on what form that Divine Direction should take. You are not wanting the Great Divine Director to come in and validate your human vision, fulfill your human needs to be greater than others. Of course, I will not play that game with anyone on earth. I AM a cosmic being. If anyone in embodiment on earth imagines that I will validate their fantasies, they are out of touch with the reality of who I AM, and thus they are not in contact with the Great Divine Director. Perhaps they are in contact with an imposter, and they think they are receiving genuine direction, but it cannot be so if you think you are more important than other people. Truly we seek only to raise up all.

I do not want you to think that I do not care about each individual, but I do want you to realize that I look at the earth from a greater distance than even Saint Germain. Therefore, I see a greater picture than he sees from his vantage point, and certainly a much greater picture than you see while you are in embodiment. I simply want you to have the sense of realism that if you are to receive my Divine Direction, you need to be willing to look beyond your human desires and imaginations.

Clearing the mental and identity realms

This, of course, brings me to the topic of the clearing out of the mental and the identity realms on earth, an action that I have been performing as I have been speaking, inasmuch as I have been able to do so based on the work you have been doing at this conference: the – I will say magnificent – work you have

14 | The mental and identity illusions of Europe

been doing, not only through invocations and decrees but by being together, by talking to each other, by talking in a group, by clarifying your vision and your ideas. This has value because, whatever you do at such a conference, we of the masters are constantly using your chakras to send out light to the planet, or in this case to Europe and to the collective consciousness.

If you have been feeling an intensity during this dictation, it is because I have been using your chakras to release light into the identity realm, into the mental realm. I have large numbers of angels who have come with me. I have angels that are normally working under Saint Germain and the other Chohans who have come into the identity and the mental realms over Europe. They have performed both a clearing action and also the binding of certain of the demons that are existing there – the taking, the bringing forth of the judgment, of some of the fallen beings embodied there – so that we can clear out what can be cleared out in this cycle.

This is partly based on the statement of Jesus Christ that he no longer accepts the falsity of Christianity and the presence of these false teachers who have used him and his example to enslave the people on earth, whereas he truly came to set them free. It is time that they be removed from the earth because certainly when the Christ who has been in embodiment on earth and has vowed to still work with the earth makes the decision that this is enough, then I as a cosmic being can only reinforce and validate that decision. I am not making those kinds of decisions, for I have not been in embodiment on earth. I truly support those who have ascended from such a dense planet and who have now decided that enough is enough.

Thereby I count you all. Although you have not ascended yet, you have also come to that point of deciding that enough is enough, that it is time to bring in a new cycle. This must mean that those who will not let go of the old – who will not embrace the new, who have had opportunity after opportunity and turned it down – they must be removed to some other realm so that the majority of the people on earth can be freed from the heavy weight and the illusions perpetrated by these beings.

Europe as the cradle for ideas

You can look at planet earth and its recent history, and you could ask yourself: "Has any bad idea that has influenced this planet not come out of Europe?" You would indeed see that most of the ideas that have influenced this planet in a negative way have come out of someone who was embodied, or had been embodied, on the European continent. Europe has been a cradle for so many ideas, both good and false, both constructive and non-constructive. It is the potential for Europe to play its part in the bringing forth of the Golden Age by being a cradle for ideas that are received from the ascended masters.

What the fallen beings have attempted to do in Europe is indeed to bring forth their own conceived ideas, ideas based on the duality consciousness, ideas designed to validate them and give them greater control and put themselves up as gods on earth. No more shall this be allowed, for these beings are removed. The records of their imaginations and their energies are removed from the identity and mental octaves, and therefore these realms are cleared.

Again, the angels of the Chohans will take up positions in the mental and identity realms, so that there cannot be other dark beings from other places that can rush in and fill the empty spaces. The spaces are not empty, for they are filled with light. When you make the calls that reinforce this action, then they can expand that sphere of light in the mental and

14 | The mental and identity illusions of Europe

identity realms. Thus we can together – you in embodiment, us in the ascended realm, and those of us who have taken up positions in the identity and mental realms – we can form that figure-eight flow whereby we create an upward spiral that will very, very quickly begin to clear out these false ideas from the collective consciousness of Europe.

People will wake up, and they will just feel a new freedom. Some will just let the old ideas fall away, as they let go of a heavy overcoat in the spring when they feel the warming rays of the sun. They do not need to analyze. They do not need to look at it. They just throw it off and walk away from it. Others will need to take a look. They will need to analyze. They will see, all of a sudden: "How could we ever believe in these ideas? How could we ever believe in such nonsense? How could we ever take it seriously and think that this had some kind of power over us? Truly the emperor has nothing on."

What a freedom people will feel when they come to that point individually. What a freedom many have already felt by having some ideas fall away over the last decades. Many people during the '70s and '80s were truly ensnared by the utopian dream created through communism and Marxism and socialism. Many have since been awakened from this dream and seen the unreality of it. Many have not yet been awakened but can and will be awakened in the coming times, as the mental and identity realms are cleared and as more light can stream through from the ascended octave. More and more people can then tune in to and consciously receive the ideas that the Chohans and the archangels and the Elohim are constantly releasing from their realm into the four levels of the material universe of earth and of Europe. Europe can again become a cradle for innovation and new ideas and new thinking. Europe can become a cradle for looking at the past and clearly seeing the falsity and the unreality of some ideas and practices.

The vision of a new money system

Truly I perform an action now aimed at bringing forth a new, sustainable money system, a new way to look at the economy, a way that is beyond what any economist has been able to envision so far. It is so far beyond that this messenger cannot bring forth a message on it because he does not have enough knowledge of the economy. There are people in embodiment who have that knowledge, and who will be able to begin receiving pieces of Saint Germain's vision for a Golden Age sustainable economy in Europe. When I say sustainable, I do not mean static. I mean an economy that forms an upward spiral and brings forth more and more wealth, without at the same time creating more and more debt and more and more inflation. It brings growth without the negative effects that you see in the artificially created economy of the fallen beings.

I hereby pronounce the judgment of Christ and the judgment of the Great Divine Director upon the money system of the fallen angels here in Europe. Let those beings that have brought forth this false money system receive their judgment this day. Let them receive the opportunity to choose whether they will embrace the light or reject the light, and let those who reject the light be removed from the earth now and forevermore.

This is a dispensation. This is a gift from my heart. It is not one that was scheduled, or at least not guaranteed, for this conference, but it is a gift that I bring forth because I see that you have done your part. You have been willing to come up higher, to multiply the opportunity. I provide the increase by taking one jewel from my belt of many jewels and depositing it in the mental realm over Europe, taking another jewel and depositing it in the identity realm.

This then is my gift of a momentum of energy of Divine Direction that I give to the people of Europe because of what you have been willing to overcome and transcend in yourselves, and because of the service you have been willing to perform. I do not here count only you who are physically present at this conference, but all of those who have taken up the teachings of the ascended masters and used our decrees and invocations. It is a gift that you have earned. You have my gift. You have my gratitude. You have my joy.

Divine Direction I AM.

15 | CLEARING THE MENTAL AND IDENTITY REALMS

In the name I AM THAT I AM, Jesus Christ, I call to all representatives of the Divine Father, especially the Divine Director and to all representatives of the Divine Mother, especially the Goddess of Liberty, for a total clearance of the mental and identity realms. Help people see the many false mental beliefs and the false sense of identity, including…

[Make personal calls.]

Part 1

1. Divine Director, I am willing to be an intermediary between the higher vibration of your light and the lower vibrations of planet earth. I am willing to hold the balance, experiencing both the world I normally experience of earth and the higher vibrations of your Presence.

Divine Director, I now see,
the world is unreality,
in my heart I now truly feel,
the Spirit is all that is real.

**Divine Director, send the light,
from blindness clear my inner sight,
my vision free, my vision clear,
your guidance is forever here.**

2. Divine Director, awaken people to the reality that [Europe] is, more than anything, an idea of unity through diversity, not in spite of diversity but through diversity.

Divine Director, vision give,
in clarity I want to live,
I now behold my plan Divine,
the plan that is uniquely mine.

**Divine Director, send the light,
from blindness clear my inner sight,
my vision free, my vision clear,
your guidance is forever here.**

3. Divine Director, consume the energetic records from a distant time when societies had started a downward spiral through sameness and conformity.

Divine Director, show in me,
the ego games, and set me free,
help me escape the ego's cage,
to help bring in the golden age.

> Divine Director, send the light,
> from blindness clear my inner sight,
> my vision free, my vision clear,
> your guidance is forever here.

4. Divine Director, awaken people to the reality that it was necessary to bring so many different people together in order to break up these old records of conformity.

> Divine Director, I'm with you,
> my vision one, no longer two,
> as karma's veil you do disperse,
> I see a whole new universe.

> Divine Director, send the light,
> from blindness clear my inner sight,
> my vision free, my vision clear,
> your guidance is forever here.

5. Divine Director, awaken people to the reality that the fallen beings who have embodied on earth, and the fallen beings who have controlled them in the higher realms, have attempted to create unity through sameness by forcing people into conformity.

> Divine Director, I go up,
> electric light now fills my cup,
> consume in me all shadows old,
> bestow on me a vision bold.

**Divine Director, send the light,
from blindness clear my inner sight,
my vision free, my vision clear,
your guidance is forever here.**

6. Divine Director, awaken people to the reality that what the fallen beings have attempted to accomplish is to get people to again come into conformity, but this time through force, by making them the same.

Divine Director, heart of gold,
my sacred labor I unfold,
o blessed Guru, I now see,
where my own plan is taking me.

**Divine Director, send the light,
from blindness clear my inner sight,
my vision free, my vision clear,
your guidance is forever here.**

7. Divine Director, awaken people to the reality that many different people have been deliberately gathered in order to prevent the fallen beings from creating a society so trapped in conformity that the downward spiral could not be turned back.

Divine Director, by your grace,
in grander scheme I find my place,
my individual flame I see,
uniqueness God has given me.

> **Divine Director, send the light,
> from blindness clear my inner sight,
> my vision free, my vision clear,
> your guidance is forever here.**

8. Divine Director, awaken people to the reality that in some nations the people have been willing to come into conformity under some strong leader or some strong ideology. Still, there is not total conformity, and this is because there are so many different peoples embodied together.

> Divine Director, vision one,
> I see that I AM God's own Sun,
> with your direction so Divine,
> I am now letting my light shine.

> **Divine Director, send the light,
> from blindness clear my inner sight,
> my vision free, my vision clear,
> your guidance is forever here.**

9. Divine Director, awaken people to the reality that it was necessary, in this age, that those lifestreams who were embodied when the descent of the earth began were given a similar initiation as the one that led them into the downward spiral.

> Divine Director, what a gift,
> to be a part of Spirit's lift,
> to raise mankind out of the night,
> to bask in Spirit's loving sight.

> **Divine Director, send the light,**
> **from blindness clear my inner sight,**
> **my vision free, my vision clear,**
> **your guidance is forever here.**

Part 2

1. Divine Director, awaken people to the reality that in this age the people have been affected by the fallen beings, both in order to give them an opportunity and to give the fallen beings an opportunity to overcome their past momentums of conformity.

> O Liberty now set me free
> from devil's curse of poverty.
> I blame not Mother for my lack,
> O Blessed Mother, take me back.
>
> **O Cosmic Mother Liberty,**
> **conduct Abundance Symphony.**
> **My highest service I now see,**
> **abundance is now real for me.**

2. Divine Director, awaken people to the reality that during the past 2,000 years, there has been a giant initiation process for a certain group of lifestreams.

> O Liberty, from distant shore,
> I come with longing to be More.
> I see abundance is a flow,
> abundance consciousness I grow.

> O Cosmic Mother Liberty,
> conduct Abundance Symphony.
> My highest service I now see,
> abundance is now real for me.

3. Divine Director, awaken people to the reality that Saint Germain attempted to get the kings to see beyond their own personal differences and come into a form of cooperation that could have united the nations, not under one physical leader but under a higher form of leadership.

> O Liberty, expose the lie,
> that limitations can me tie.
> The Ma-ter light is not my foe,
> true opulence it does bestow.

> O Cosmic Mother Liberty,
> conduct Abundance Symphony.
> My highest service I now see,
> abundance is now real for me.

4. Divine Director, awaken people to the reality that these kings responded, it would have been possible for Saint Germain to guide the leaders for the last several centuries.

> O Liberty, expose the plot,
> projected by the fallen lot.
> O Cosmic Mother, I now see,
> that Mother's not my enemy.

> **O Cosmic Mother Liberty,**
> **conduct Abundance Symphony.**
> **My highest service I now see,**
> **abundance is now real for me.**

5. Divine Director, awaken people to the reality that today Saint Germain is no longer addressing the leaders. He is addressing the people, and the plan is still to unite people, not by making everyone the same but by making us embrace and accept our differences.

> O Liberty, with opened eyes,
> I now reject the devil's lies.
> I now embrace the Mother realm,
> for I see Father at the helm.

> **O Cosmic Mother Liberty,**
> **conduct Abundance Symphony.**
> **My highest service I now see,**
> **abundance is now real for me.**

6. Divine Director, awaken people to the reality that people need to overcome the ego game of seeking to force other people to come into conformity with their way of looking at life, so they you can feel validated and not threatened.

> O Liberty, a chalice pure,
> my lower bodies are for sure.
> Release through me your symphony,
> your gift of Cosmic Liberty.

> O Cosmic Mother Liberty,
> conduct Abundance Symphony.
> My highest service I now see,
> abundance is now real for me.

7. Divine Director, awaken people to the reality that we need to look for a higher vision and principle, a higher purpose, namely the ascended masters, who are truly our older brothers and sisters.

> O Liberty, the open door,
> I am for Symphony of More.
> In chakras mine light you release,
> the flow of love shall never cease.

> O Cosmic Mother Liberty,
> conduct Abundance Symphony.
> My highest service I now see,
> abundance is now real for me.

8. Divine Director, awaken people to the reality that when we recognize that we are the extensions of the ascended masters, we can see beyond the outer differences.

> O Liberty, release the flow,
> of opulence that you bestow.
> For I am willing to receive,
> the Golden Fleece that you now weave.

> O Cosmic Mother Liberty,
> conduct Abundance Symphony.
> My highest service I now see,
> abundance is now real for me.

9. Divine Director, awaken people to the reality that we need to value the differences because they give different perspectives, but we also see beyond them to see the higher unity behind the outer differences.

> O Liberty, release the cure,
> to free the tired and the poor.
> The huddled masses are set free,
> by loving Song of Liberty.
>
> **O Cosmic Mother Liberty,**
> **conduct Abundance Symphony.**
> **My highest service I now see,**
> **abundance is now real for me.**

Part 3

1. Divine Director, awaken people to the reality that the European Union is a grand experiment of whether people can come into union. So far, the fallen beings have attempted to take control and force some kind of sameness by creating a forced uniformity through the economy and the political process.

> Divine Director, I now see,
> the world is unreality,
> in my heart I now truly feel,
> the Spirit is all that is real.

> **Divine Director, send the light,**
> **from blindness clear my inner sight,**
> **my vision free, my vision clear,**
> **your guidance is forever here.**

2. Divine Director, awaken people to the reality that this is no longer working as they had hoped. The union is not working in some areas.

> Divine Director, vision give,
> in clarity I want to live,
> I now behold my plan Divine,
> the plan that is uniquely mine.

> **Divine Director, send the light,**
> **from blindness clear my inner sight,**
> **my vision free, my vision clear,**
> **your guidance is forever here.**

3. Divine Director, awaken people to the reality that this is not because there is anything wrong or unsustainable about having a European Union, but it is because it has not yet reached the level of consciousness where true union can be sustainable.

> Divine Director, show in me,
> the ego games, and set me free,
> help me escape the ego's cage,
> to help bring in the golden age.

> **Divine Director, send the light,**
> **from blindness clear my inner sight,**
> **my vision free, my vision clear,**
> **your guidance is forever here.**

4. Divine Director, awaken people to the reality that we need to look beyond the considerations of this world, the duality consciousness, the desire for control through conformity, and grasp the higher vision of Saint Germain and the ascended masters.

> Divine Director, I'm with you,
> my vision one, no longer two,
> as karma's veil you do disperse,
> I see a whole new universe.
>
> **Divine Director, send the light,**
> **from blindness clear my inner sight,**
> **my vision free, my vision clear,**
> **your guidance is forever here.**

5. Divine Director, awaken the people who have the potential to bring forth a piece of the puzzle of Saint Germain's vision. Awaken those who are the forerunners for Saint Germain's Golden Age.

> Divine Director, I go up,
> electric light now fills my cup,
> consume in me all shadows old,
> bestow on me a vision bold.
>
> **Divine Director, send the light,**
> **from blindness clear my inner sight,**
> **my vision free, my vision clear,**
> **your guidance is forever here.**

6. Divine Director, awaken the many people throughout the world who can each receive a piece of that vision, those who have the opening in their consciousness to receive one idea in a lifetime that can help bring society forward.

> Divine Director, heart of gold,
> my sacred labor I unfold,
> o blessed Guru, I now see,
> where my own plan is taking me.
>
> **Divine Director, send the light,**
> **from blindness clear my inner sight,**
> **my vision free, my vision clear,**
> **your guidance is forever here.**

7. Divine Director, awaken people to the need to look beyond the differences that divide people and see the overall picture. Give people a clearer vision of the greater picture and anchor it in the collective consciousness.

> Divine Director, by your grace,
> in grander scheme I find my place,
> my individual flame I see,
> uniqueness God has given me.
>
> **Divine Director, send the light,**
> **from blindness clear my inner sight,**
> **my vision free, my vision clear,**
> **your guidance is forever here.**

8. Divine Director, awaken the spiritual people to our potential to pull up the collective consciousness, so that people do not have to have these hard lessons. Help us overcome the consciousness that we alone have to take credit for bringing in the Golden Age, but instead reach the level where we are seeking to raise the whole.

> Divine Director, vision one,
> I see that I AM God's own Sun,
> with your direction so Divine,
> I am now letting my light shine.
>
> **Divine Director, send the light,**
> **from blindness clear my inner sight,**
> **my vision free, my vision clear,**
> **your guidance is forever here.**

9. Divine Director, awaken the spiritual people from the trap of wanting to feel that we were so special, and any desire to hold other people down so that we can stand out as the ones who did the important work.

> Divine Director, what a gift,
> to be a part of Spirit's lift,
> to raise mankind out of the night,
> to bask in Spirit's loving sight.
>
> **Divine Director, send the light,**
> **from blindness clear my inner sight,**
> **my vision free, my vision clear,**
> **your guidance is forever here.**

Part 4

1. Divine Director, awaken people to the reality that the ascended masters see the oneness of all life. You see a reflection of yourselves in all people on earth, so you value each one infinitely, in a way that cannot be measured by the dualistic mind and therefore cannot be subjected to a value judgment.

> O Liberty now set me free
> from devil's curse of poverty.
> I blame not Mother for my lack,
> O Blessed Mother, take me back.
>
> **O Cosmic Mother Liberty,**
> **conduct Abundance Symphony.**
> **My highest service I now see,**
> **abundance is now real for me.**

2. Divine Director, awaken people to the inner freedom where we do not evaluate and judge others and therefore do not evaluate and judge ourselves.

> O Liberty, from distant shore,
> I come with longing to be More.
> I see abundance is a flow,
> abundance consciousness I grow.
>
> **O Cosmic Mother Liberty,**
> **conduct Abundance Symphony.**
> **My highest service I now see,**
> **abundance is now real for me.**

3. Divine Director, awaken people to Divine Direction without projecting a preconceived image on what form that Divine Direction should take or wanting you to validate our human vision or fulfill our human needs.

> O Liberty, expose the lie,
> that limitations can me tie.
> The Ma-ter light is not my foe,
> true opulence it does bestow.
>
> **O Cosmic Mother Liberty,**
> **conduct Abundance Symphony.**
> **My highest service I now see,**
> **abundance is now real for me.**

4. Divine Director, awaken people to the sense of realism that if we are to receive your Divine Direction, we need to be willing to look beyond our human desires and imaginations.

> O Liberty, expose the plot,
> projected by the fallen lot.
> O Cosmic Mother, I now see,
> that Mother's not my enemy.
>
> **O Cosmic Mother Liberty,**
> **conduct Abundance Symphony.**
> **My highest service I now see,**
> **abundance is now real for me.**

5. Divine Director, awaken people to the reality that the ascended masters can use our chakras to send out light to the planet and to the collective consciousness.

15 | Clearing the Mental and Identity Realms

> O Liberty, with opened eyes,
> I now reject the devil's lies.
> I now embrace the Mother realm,
> for I see Father at the helm.
>
> **O Cosmic Mother Liberty,**
> **conduct Abundance Symphony.**
> **My highest service I now see,**
> **abundance is now real for me.**

6. Divine Director, send your angels and the angels of Saint Germain and the other Chohans into the identity and the mental realms over … [Name place].

> O Liberty, a chalice pure,
> my lower bodies are for sure.
> Release through me your symphony,
> your gift of Cosmic Liberty.
>
> **O Cosmic Mother Liberty,**
> **conduct Abundance Symphony.**
> **My highest service I now see,**
> **abundance is now real for me.**

7. Divine Director, I call the angels to perform both a clearing action and also the binding of the demons.

> O Liberty, the open door,
> I am for Symphony of More.
> In chakras mine light you release,
> the flow of love shall never cease.

**O Cosmic Mother Liberty,
conduct Abundance Symphony.
My highest service I now see,
abundance is now real for me.**

8. Divine Director, I call the angels to bring forth of the judgment of some of the fallen beings embodied in … [Name place], so that they clear out what can be cleared out in this cycle.

> O Liberty, release the flow,
> of opulence that you bestow.
> For I am willing to receive,
> the Golden Fleece that you now weave.

**O Cosmic Mother Liberty,
conduct Abundance Symphony.
My highest service I now see,
abundance is now real for me.**

9. Divine Director, I ratify the statement of Jesus Christ that he no longer accepts the falsity of Christianity and the presence of these false teachers who have used him and his example to enslave the people on earth. I say with Jesus that it is time that they be removed from the earth.

> O Liberty, release the cure,
> to free the tired and the poor.
> The huddled masses are set free,
> by loving Song of Liberty.

> O Cosmic Mother Liberty,
> conduct Abundance Symphony.
> My highest service I now see,
> abundance is now real for me.

Part 5

1. Divine Director, awaken all spiritual people to the fact that we have come to that point of deciding that enough is enough, that it is time to bring in a new cycle. Those who will not let go of the old must be removed to some other realm so that the majority of the people on earth can be freed from the heavy weight and the illusions perpetrated by these beings.

> Divine Director, I now see,
> the world is unreality,
> in my heart I now truly feel,
> the Spirit is all that is real.

> **Divine Director, send the light,**
> **from blindness clear my inner sight,**
> **my vision free, my vision clear,**
> **your guidance is forever here.**

2. Divine Director, awaken people to the reality that most of the ideas that have influenced this planet in a negative way have come out of someone who was embodied, or had been embodied, on the European continent.

Divine Director, vision give,
in clarity I want to live,
I now behold my plan Divine,
the plan that is uniquely mine.

**Divine Director, send the light,
from blindness clear my inner sight,
my vision free, my vision clear,
your guidance is forever here.**

3. Divine Director, awaken people to the reality that Europe has been a cradle for many ideas, both good and false, both constructive and non-constructive. Europe's part in the bringing forth of the Golden Age is to be a cradle for ideas that are received from the ascended masters.

Divine Director, show in me,
the ego games, and set me free,
help me escape the ego's cage,
to help bring in the golden age.

**Divine Director, send the light,
from blindness clear my inner sight,
my vision free, my vision clear,
your guidance is forever here.**

4. Divine Director, awaken people to the reality that the fallen beings have attempted to bring forth their own ideas based on the duality consciousness, ideas designed to validate them and give them greater control and put themselves up as gods on earth.

Divine Director, I'm with you,
my vision one, no longer two,
as karma's veil you do disperse,
I see a whole new universe.

**Divine Director, send the light,
from blindness clear my inner sight,
my vision free, my vision clear,
your guidance is forever here.**

5. Divine Director, I affirm with you that this shall no longer be allowed, for these beings are removed. The records of their imaginations and their energies are removed from the identity and mental octaves, and therefore these realms are cleared.

Divine Director, I go up,
electric light now fills my cup,
consume in me all shadows old,
bestow on me a vision bold.

**Divine Director, send the light,
from blindness clear my inner sight,
my vision free, my vision clear,
your guidance is forever here.**

6. Divine Director, I call forth the angels of the Chohans to take up positions in the mental and identity realms, so that there cannot be other dark beings from other places that can rush in and fill the empty spaces. The spaces are not empty, for they are filled with light.

Divine Director, heart of gold,
my sacred labor I unfold,
o blessed Guru, I now see,
where my own plan is taking me.

Divine Director, send the light,
from blindness clear my inner sight,
my vision free, my vision clear,
your guidance is forever here.

7. Divine Director, I call for the angels of the Chohans to reinforce this action and expand the sphere of light in the mental and identity realms. We who are in embodiment and you in the ascended realm form a figure-eight flow whereby we create an upward spiral that will quickly clear out these false ideas from the collective consciousness.

Divine Director, by your grace,
in grander scheme I find my place,
my individual flame I see,
uniqueness God has given me.

Divine Director, send the light,
from blindness clear my inner sight,
my vision free, my vision clear,
your guidance is forever here.

8. Divine Director, I call for people to wake up, feel a new freedom and let the old ideas fall away. They do not need to analyze. They do not need to look at it. They just throw it off and walk away from it.

Divine Director, vision one,
I see that I AM God's own Sun,
with your direction so Divine,
I am now letting my light shine.

**Divine Director, send the light,
from blindness clear my inner sight,
my vision free, my vision clear,
your guidance is forever here.**

9. Divine Director, I call for you to help those who need to take a look and analyze. Help them reach the realization: "How could we ever believe in these ideas? How could we ever believe in such nonsense? How could we ever take it seriously and think that this had some kind of power over us? Truly, the emperor has nothing on."

Divine Director, what a gift,
to be a part of Spirit's lift,
to raise mankind out of the night,
to bask in Spirit's loving sight.

**Divine Director, send the light,
from blindness clear my inner sight,
my vision free, my vision clear,
your guidance is forever here.**

Part 6

1. Divine Director, awaken people from the utopian dream created through communism, Marxism and socialism. Clear the mental and identity realms from these ideas so that more light can stream through from the ascended octave.

> O Liberty now set me free
> from devil's curse of poverty.
> I blame not Mother for my lack,
> O Blessed Mother, take me back.
>
> **O Cosmic Mother Liberty,**
> **conduct Abundance Symphony.**
> **My highest service I now see,**
> **abundance is now real for me.**

2. Divine Director, awaken people so they can tune in to and consciously receive the ideas that the Chohans, the archangels and the Elohim are constantly releasing from your realm into the four levels of the material universe of earth.

> O Liberty, from distant shore,
> I come with longing to be More.
> I see abundance is a flow,
> abundance consciousness I grow.
>
> **O Cosmic Mother Liberty,**
> **conduct Abundance Symphony.**
> **My highest service I now see,**
> **abundance is now real for me.**

3. Divine Director, awaken people so that Europe can again become a cradle for innovation and new ideas and new thinking. Europe can become a cradle for looking at the past and clearly seeing the falsity and the unreality of some ideas and practices.

> O Liberty, expose the lie,
> that limitations can me tie.
> The Ma-ter light is not my foe,
> true opulence it does bestow.

> **O Cosmic Mother Liberty,**
> **conduct Abundance Symphony.**
> **My highest service I now see,**
> **abundance is now real for me.**

4. Divine Director, I call you to perform an action to bring forth a new, sustainable money system, a new way to look at the economy, a way that is beyond what any economist has been able to envision so far.

> O Liberty, expose the plot,
> projected by the fallen lot.
> O Cosmic Mother, I now see,
> that Mother's not my enemy.

> **O Cosmic Mother Liberty,**
> **conduct Abundance Symphony.**
> **My highest service I now see,**
> **abundance is now real for me.**

5. Divine Director, awaken those people in embodiment who have the knowledge, and who will be able to begin receiving pieces of Saint Germain's vision for a Golden Age sustainable economy.

> O Liberty, with opened eyes,
> I now reject the devil's lies.
> I now embrace the Mother realm,
> for I see Father at the helm.
>
> **O Cosmic Mother Liberty,**
> **conduct Abundance Symphony.**
> **My highest service I now see,**
> **abundance is now real for me.**

6. Divine Director, I call forth a sustainable economy that is not static. I call forth an economy that forms an upward spiral and brings forth more and more wealth, without at the same time creating more and more debt and more and more inflation.

> O Liberty, a chalice pure,
> my lower bodies are for sure.
> Release through me your symphony,
> your gift of Cosmic Liberty.
>
> **O Cosmic Mother Liberty,**
> **conduct Abundance Symphony.**
> **My highest service I now see,**
> **abundance is now real for me.**

7. Divine Director, I call forth an economy that brings growth without the negative effects that we see in the artificially created economy of the fallen beings.

> O Liberty, the open door,
> I am for Symphony of More.
> In chakras mine light you release,
> the flow of love shall never cease.
>
> **O Cosmic Mother Liberty,**
> **conduct Abundance Symphony.**
> **My highest service I now see,**
> **abundance is now real for me.**

8. Divine Director, with you I pronounce the judgment of Christ and the judgment of the Great Divine Director upon the money system of the fallen angels. Let those beings that have brought forth this false money system receive their judgment this day. Let them receive the opportunity to choose whether they will embrace the light or reject the light, and let those who reject the light be removed from the earth now and forevermore.

> O Liberty, release the flow,
> of opulence that you bestow.
> For I am willing to receive,
> the Golden Fleece that you now weave.
>
> **O Cosmic Mother Liberty,**
> **conduct Abundance Symphony.**
> **My highest service I now see,**
> **abundance is now real for me.**

9. Divine Director, I call forth a multiplied release of light from the jewels you have deposited in the mental and identity realms over Europe. I call for the light to shatter and expose the plans that the fallen beings have for preventing the manifestation of Saint Germain's Golden Age.

> O Liberty, release the cure,
> to free the tired and the poor.
> The huddled masses are set free,
> by loving Song of Liberty.
>
> **O Cosmic Mother Liberty,**
> **conduct Abundance Symphony.**
> **My highest service I now see,**
> **abundance is now real for me.**

Sealing

In the name of the Divine Mother, I call to Liberty and Mother Mary for the sealing of myself and all people in my circle of influence in the creative flow of the Divine Mother, the River of Life. I call for the multiplication of my calls by all representatives of the Divine Mother, so that we form the perfect figure-eight flow of "As Above, so below." Thus, I accept that this is fully manifest, because the mouth of the Lord, the Divine Mother that I AM, has spoken it. Amen.

16 | HOW YOU CAN BE FREE FROM YOUR PAST

(Mother Mary:) My beloved hearts, you have now seen a very practical demonstration of the challenges you all face in the physical octave. Things do not always go in the ideal way. There are things that disturb you, that disturb your sense of what should or should not happen. This ties in with the dictation you have heard now again of what I want to say at this conference.

There are times where you cannot fix what went wrong in the physical octave, so you just have to forgive and move on as if it had never happened. Look at the continent of Europe. Look at the many wars and conflicts. Look at the many people who have been hurt. As we have said, their souls stretch back in time to when they received that original hurt, or another trauma in some war or as the result of whatever they have been exposed to. Whatever happened in the past cannot be fixed. It cannot be changed. It cannot be repaired. It cannot be undone.

How the past can be undone

Ah, but it *can* be undone! Not in the physical. But, you see, the physical moment of when something happened to you in the past no longer exists. It has been undone by the passage of time. Many of you have come to look at time as something that is controlling your life because your daily life so much revolves around being certain places at certain times. But have you ever considered that in an unascended sphere time is a gift? For no situation, however pleasurable or unpleasurable, can be fixed in space, because time moves on. There is no need to go back and repair what happened during the Second World War. Time has moved on.

They say that time is the great healer, but it is not true. Time moves on, but healing comes from releasing, from forgiving the scars that are in your soul. You cannot undo the physical thing that happened – for example, during the Second World War on the European continent – but you can undo the scar in your own soul from being in embodiment at that time. When you undo it for yourself, you can then begin to help other people heal themselves also. You cannot heal these people for them. You can, however, free them from some of the energy. You can pull on their consciousness so that they can come to see what you see, and therefore see the value of letting go, and finally let go.

How to forgive

No amount of changes, no amount of actions, no amount of punishing those who harmed you, will ever heal you. The ultimate healer is the act of surrender, the act of forgiving. What does it mean to forgive? It means that you put the act of giving before the act of holding on. What does it mean to give? It means to let go and release it. Ownership means holding on, so only by forgiving – by giving up, by releasing the hurt, by releasing the desire to punish, by releasing the sense that this should not have happened – only by doing this, by releasing, can you be free from the past.

The past truly is not the past. You look at it with the linear mind, and you have created a linear time line. You say that in 1942 so and so many people were killed in this or that battle, and you think that this happened in the past. It *did* in the linear time line. The real effect that is lingering is the effect in people's minds, in their souls, and that is not truly in the past, in the sense that it is separated from you. It truly is a part of that stretch of your soul that Saint Germain talked about. The importance of this is to realize that you can heal in the present anything that happened in the past—when you stop being unwilling to go into the feelings, to go into the hurt. And you can do this on behalf of other people.

During this conference you have, without perhaps consciously realizing it, gone into much of the pain that is in the collective consciousness on this continent of Europe. You have not been overwhelmed by it. You may have touched it. You may have sensed it. But you have come to that point of going through it, and when you go through it and come out on the other side and realize: "I am still here," then you can release, and you can feel that release.

Some of you know that you have been killed in both the First and the Second World Wars or in other wars, and you have experienced that release. All of you can experience it personally, and all of you can actually experience the release on behalf of others. This does not mean that they release it in their own individual minds, but it does mean that there is a release in the collective mind. Therefore, by going through these exercises, you can indeed help the collective mind progress. You can help heal the collective mind.

A powerful matrix

Now this matrix that we have given you here, of playing part of a dictation and then giving a decree to the master who gave the dictation, is a very powerful matrix. [The participants had played part of Mother Mary's previous dictation, then stopped the recording and given a section of her decree.] You can, of course, do it with a written dictation, but it is more powerful when you play the audio dictation and stop it and give the decree, play a little more and stop it and give another verse of the decree, and so on. This is a powerful matrix that you can repeat individually or in groups. You could even do it over the Internet if someone was willing to organize this.

It is a way of you forming the Omega polarity to the Alpha action of our releases whereby you anchor it in the physical in a different way. You form, you close, the figure-eight flow and send it back up to us whereby we can multiply it and send more. Truly, what you have done with this exercise is a very powerful, a very significant healing for many people who embody in Europe today, and who have been hurt by the many wars on this continent.

The feminine wisdom

You may look at Europe and wonder what is going to solve the present problems. Well, there are two things that will bring forth a solution to the present problems in Europe. One is a healing of the individual and the collective psyche. Many of the problems you see in Europe are born from the fact that people have been scarred in past lives or in this life, and therefore they cannot overcome that sense of being hurt, of being incomplete, of being somehow flawed, and upholding some kind of animosity against another group of people. Many times they do not know why, but it is because these people hurt them in a past life. Although they do not have the conscious memory, it still lingers in their four lower bodies that these people cannot be trusted, that these people should somehow be punished. This is a major conflict in many of the problems. It is a major reason for many of the problems that you see in Europe.

The other one, the other factor that could bring forth a solution, is something we have not, until now, talked much about, but which we will talk about more in the future. That is the feminine wisdom, the wisdom of the Mother. You have the concept in Christianity of the divine Sophia, which represents the wisdom of the feminine. The problem with this concept, both in Christian context and in other contexts, is that people tend to mix up the Divine Feminine, the Divine Feminine wisdom, with women in physical embodiment. They tend to think that feminine wisdom is restricted to women, those who are in a physical body.

Of course, as we have taught you, the Conscious You is beyond male and female. You can embody as a male in one embodiment and as a female in another. You need to step up to a higher concept and realize that the feminine wisdom of which I speak is not confined to the sex of the body. It is a condition of the Conscious You and the I AM Presence. We may say that the I AM Presence stores the divine blueprint for your individual being, and that blueprint is the Divine Father, the Divine Masculine, the Alpha aspect. What then is the Divine Mother, the Divine Feminine wisdom? What is the Omega aspect? It is what we have called your causal body.

Your causal body stores all of your positive experiences from your embodiments on earth, and therefore it contains this database of experiences of knowing how the material universe works, how the Mother realm works.

Many people on earth have forgotten this wisdom and are not using it, primarily because the fallen beings, after they started embodying on earth, have done everything they could to put down not only women but also the feminine aspect of wisdom. Why have they done this? Well, they have done it partly because they always do this, because they hate the Mother realm, the physical octave. They feel they are in the unascended sphere, where the Mother realm is dense, as a punishment from God because they were thrown out of heaven, as they see it. As we have explained, they were simply making choices and could not follow the ascending spiral of the universe, so they confined themselves to the unascended sphere. As a result of this, they hate the material realm, they hate the Mother, and they put her down.

Feminine wisdom without spirit

But it should also be understood that, as we have said, there was a previous age when the inhabitants of the earth had created a downward spiral. And how had they created that downward spiral? They had done so by embracing the wisdom of the feminine aspect while ignoring or denying the masculine, the Alpha aspect.

You understand that, in the material universe of an unascended sphere, the density is such that the divine wisdom can help you move around in a circle. The feminine wisdom can help you move around in a circle, and you can create a very comfortable state. But when you do not have the divine Alpha, the Divine Father, there will be no upward spiral. Your movement becomes the closed circle, which will then, by the force of the Divine Feminine, become a downward spiral that will lead to a breakdown of the comfortable state you have created. You need both the masculine wisdom and the feminine wisdom to work in harmony. What the fallen beings have done is that they have done all that they could do to separate the two.

They, of course, do not have the masculine wisdom – they have a perverted form of it – but they have done everything they could to raise up that perverted wisdom as the absolute truth, as the only form of wisdom, and thereby put down the feminine wisdom. The fallen beings are attempting to set themselves up as gods on earth, and they think they have the power to force the material universe to conform to their ideas. They think they can create an ideology or a belief system and force the universe to conform. It is only the Divine Feminine that can break this illusion when the Mother realm, when the material world, refuses to conform to man-made ideas. This is the force that is built into the matter realm. It is not the feminine wisdom. It is what I have called the contracting force, and the result of this force is that nothing in the material universe can stand still. It must swing, it must vibrate, it must oscillate.

Why nothing can stand still

You can see a visual illustration of this in a pendulum that must swing from side to side. It cannot stand still in any of the extreme positions. Now you know, of course, that if you have a pendulum and you let it swing, then it will eventually come to rest in the center, but this is because of the gravity and the friction of the physical octave. What I am talking about is beyond a physical pendulum. There is literally a force built into the matter realm that will allow nothing to stand still. It must swing unless it is in perfect harmony with the Father aspect of wisdom, with the Christ mind.

Of course, even when you are in perfect harmony with the Christ mind, you are not standing still. You are going up in the ascending spiral. But when you are out of alignment with the Christ mind, the force built into the Mother makes sure that you must go from one extreme towards the other. The further you go out towards one extreme, the more you generate the force that will pull the pendulum back towards the other extreme. Your life becomes this oscillating movement from one extreme to the other, and it is this fact and force, this seesaw motion, that eventually breaks down the structures you have created and seek to maintain.

When you then align yourself with the Christ, there is still an oscillating movement. Now, instead of swinging just from side to side, it actually takes you into an upward spiral that is still somewhat circular but has a clear direction going up. There is still an oscillating movement from one side of the spiral to the other, but there is a general upward movement, and this is the ascending spiral.

You need spiritual and practical wisdom

This, of course, cannot be achieved by the Father aspect of wisdom alone. It can only be achieved when Father and Mother are in unison. You cannot as a spiritual person actually walk the spiritual path by only looking for the Alpha aspect of wisdom. You cannot walk the spiritual path only by having an idea of how you should be as a spiritual person and then forcing yourself to conform to it. You must also, on the spiritual path, tune in to the feminine aspect of wisdom and start looking at how the material universe actually works. There are many spiritual people throughout the ages who have thought that the only way to be spiritual was to withdraw from normal life, withdraw from society, and live in some monastic setting. There are many today who think they have to withdraw and not really concern themselves about the physical realities of life. This is not balance, and this will not give you maximum growth.

There is a need to step up to that level where you recognize you are a spiritual person, but you look at the physical realm, the material realm, and say: "How do things actually work here?" Many spiritual people have not really asked themselves that question: "How does life work? What are the principles for how matter works?" You tend to look at the world as imperfect or even as opposing your spiritual growth. You look for some spiritual teaching or ideas of how the world should work, and then you want to force the matter realm to conform to the ideas. There is a built-in force of the Mother that creates this oscillating movement from one extreme to another.

You may think that this is a breaking down of the structures, and it *is* a breaking down of the physical structures. But it is truly a liberation of the being, the Conscious You, the Spirit that has embodied and been entrapped in matter. It is a liberating force, and that means that it is a changing wisdom.

Masculine and feminine wisdom always change

Many tend to look at the Father aspect of wisdom as unchanging. You look for some absolute truth, and if it is absolute, then it should not have to change. Even the Father aspect of wisdom is constantly changing. Because the wisdom that we see from the ascended realm is very different from what you can see from the unascended realm, and that means that when a sphere ascends, even the Divine Father aspect of wisdom changes.

The Divine Mother aspect of wisdom is constantly changing also because it is not seeking to live up to some absolute standard. It is looking at what is actually manifest right now and what needs to happen for people to become free of the structures that are existing right now. It is not attempting to create an ideal state. It is simply attempting to always shatter the imbalances, or to accentuate the imbalances, in order to set people free, in order to set the lifestreams free from their entrapment in the Mother realm.

Putting down feminine wisdom

What can truly liberate Europe from many of the problems you see today is the raising up of this feminine aspect of wisdom in both men and women on the European continent. You will see, of course, that Christianity was a major factor in putting down this feminine wisdom. Not only did it put down women and say that women were responsible for the fall, but it also put down the idea that human beings, that so-called *ordinary* human beings, could have any form of wisdom. It was only the elite who could have wisdom. Wisdom had to come from above.

The movement that you saw during what has become known as the witch hunts was a movement where a great number of women were waking up to their ability to observe how the material universe works and apply it, in order to heal diseases or many other conditions. This is an example where wisdom can come from below, so to speak, from the internalization from lifetimes of how the matter universe works. It is in the uniting of these two forms of wisdom that you can transcend the problems.

Right now Europe is attempting to solve many problems through the perverted version of the Father aspect of wisdom generated by the fallen beings. This will not work, as you are clearly beginning to see. There needs to be an upsurge in the use and the recognition of the feminine wisdom. Right now this is mostly coming from women, although many women who have taken up leadership positions have been seduced into thinking that, in order to get along in a male-dominated world, they have to become like men, at least when they are dealing with business or politics. It is not truly women alone who can bring this change. Men also need to do so—many of the men who are more intuitive, who are more of the softer men, as the saying goes. They are not soft in the sense of being weak. They are just not aggressive because they do not have the unbalanced masculine wisdom of the fallen beings.

Calling forth change

This is a change that you can visualize. This is a change you can call forth by doing with this dictation what you have done with the previous one. You can indeed perform a mighty service even by holding the vision of this uniting of the feminine and the masculine wisdom to form that Christ discernment, that Christ vision, that does not swing towards either of the dualistic extremes but stays on the middle way. This does not mean that it does not see the swings because it acknowledges that, as long as you are in embodiment, there will be that oscillating movement. This is the characteristic of an unascended sphere, and it will be there until the sphere ascends. It is not a matter of stopping the oscillating movement. It is a matter of pulling it into an upward spiral. It is the oscillations that, in a sense, give you the kind of experiences that you need to have in an unascended sphere, and you do not seek to stop that which is the key to growth. You make sure that is does not become the source of standstill or the downward spiral.

My beloved, you have performed a mighty service here. I realize that your bodies and minds are somewhat tired of this. You have carried a lot of weight in the opposition from the European continent to this release of my dictation and this healing, this uniting of the male and feminine wisdom. There is no greater manifestation of anti-love than this perversion, this separation of the masculine and feminine wisdom. Therefore, there is nothing that the fallen beings and the dark forces oppose more than the uniting of the two.

Even though you have performed a mighty work, as the Great Divine Director said, of fulfilling the goals we had for this conference, this knowledge of the Divine Feminine and the Divine Masculine and the two forms of wisdom is the service we have given you on top of what was scheduled. Because you have already completed the other assignment, and as you have heard before, the reward for service is more service. This has indeed been our joy to give you that service, and we hope that you too can look beyond the burdens of the physical octave and find that joy in yourselves.

My release is complete. My joy is full. May your joy be full also!

17 | HELPING PEOPLE LET GO OF THE PAST

In the name I AM THAT I AM, Jesus Christ, I call to all representatives of the Divine Mother, especially Mother Mary, to help people grasp the value of surrender so they can let go of the past. Help people see the conditions that prevent them from forgiving unconditionally, including…

[Make personal calls.]

Part 1

1. Mother Mary, awaken people to the reality that the challenge we face in the physical octave is that things do not always work in an ideal way. There are things that disturb our sense of what should or should not happen.

O Blessed Mary's Song of Life,
consuming every form of strife.
As I attune to sound so fair,
each cell is healthy, I declare.

**O Mother Mary, generate,
the song that does accelerate,
my mind into a peaceful state,
God's perfect love I radiate.**

2. Mother Mary, awaken people to the reality that there are times where we cannot fix what went wrong in the physical octave, so we just have to forgive and move on as if it had never happened.

As life's own song I ever hear,
it does consume all sense of fear.
In tune with Mother's symphony,
from all diseases I AM free.

**O Mother Mary, generate,
the song that does accelerate,
my mind into a peaceful state,
God's perfect love I radiate.**

3. Mother Mary, awaken people to the reality that when people have been hurt in a past life, their souls stretch back in time to when they received that original hurt.

In Mother's love I do transcend,
and all my struggles hereby end.
For when with Mother's eye I see,
no imperfection touches me.

17 | Helping People Let Go of the Past

O Mother Mary, generate,
the song that does accelerate,
my mind into a peaceful state,
God's perfect love I radiate.

4. Mother Mary, awaken people to the reality that whatever happened in the past cannot be fixed. It cannot be changed. It cannot be repaired. It cannot be undone in the physical.

I see that healing must begin
by finding Living Christ within.
For as I see with single eye,
each cell the light does amplify.

O Mother Mary, generate,
the song that does accelerate,
my mind into a peaceful state,
God's perfect love I radiate.

5. Mother Mary, awaken people to the reality that the physical moment when something happened to us in the past no longer exists. It has been undone by the passage of time.

In Mother's music I am free,
from memories of a lesser me.
My vision in a perfect state,
that all my cells regenerate.

O Mother Mary, generate,
the song that does accelerate,
my mind into a peaceful state,
God's perfect love I radiate.

6. Mother Mary, awaken people to the reality that in an unascended sphere time is a gift. No situation, however pleasurable or unpleasurable, can be fixed in space because time moves on. There is no need to go back and repair what happened in the past. Time has moved on.

> O Mother's Love, sweet melody,
> from imperfections I AM free.
> O Mother Mary, sound of sounds,
> within my heart your love abounds.
>
> **O Mother Mary, generate,**
> **the song that does accelerate,**
> **my mind into a peaceful state,**
> **God's perfect love I radiate.**

7. Mother Mary, awaken people to the reality that time is not the great healer. Time moves on, but healing comes from releasing, from forgiving the scars that are in our souls.

> Through Mother's beauty so sublime,
> transcending bounds of space and time.
> All cells beyond the mortal tomb,
> as they are whole in Mother's womb.
>
> **O Mother Mary, generate,**
> **the song that does accelerate,**
> **my mind into a peaceful state,**
> **God's perfect love I radiate.**

8. Mother Mary, awaken people to the reality that we cannot undo the physical things that happened, but we *can* undo the scars in our own souls from being in embodiment at that time.

17 | Helping People Let Go of the Past

> In resonance with life's own song,
> in life's harmonics I belong.
> The blueprint of my perfect state
> does every cell reconsecrate.
>
> **O Mother Mary, generate,**
> **the song that does accelerate,**
> **my mind into a peaceful state,**
> **God's perfect love I radiate.**

9. Mother Mary, awaken people to the reality that when we undo it for ourselves, we can begin to help other people heal themselves also. We cannot heal these people for them. We can free them from some of the energy. We can pull on their consciousness so that they can come to see what we see, and therefore see the value of letting go.

> The tuning fork in every cell
> is now attuned to Mother's bell.
> From curse of death I AM now free,
> I claim my immortality.
>
> **O Mother Mary, generate,**
> **the song that does accelerate,**
> **my mind into a peaceful state,**
> **God's perfect love I radiate.**

Part 2

1. Mother Mary, awaken people to the reality that no amount of changes, no amount of actions, no amount of punishing those who harmed us, will ever heal us. The ultimate healer is the act of surrender, the act of forgiving.

> O blessed Mary, Mother mine,
> there is no greater love than thine,
> as we are one in heart and mind,
> my place in hierarchy I find.
>
> **O Mother Mary, generate,**
> **the song that does accelerate,**
> **the earth into a higher state,**
> **all matter does now scintillate.**

2. Mother Mary, awaken people to the reality that forgiving means that we put the act of giving before the act of holding on. Giving means to let go and release. Ownership means holding on.

> I came to earth from heaven sent,
> as I am in embodiment,
> I use Divine authority,
> commanding you to set earth free.
>
> **O Mother Mary, generate,**
> **the song that does accelerate,**
> **the earth into a higher state,**
> **all matter does now scintillate.**

3. Mother Mary, awaken people to the reality that only by forgiving – by giving up, by releasing the hurt, by releasing the desire to punish, by releasing the sense that this should not have happened – only by releasing can we be free from the past.

> I call now in God's sacred name,
> for you to use your Mother Flame,
> to burn all fear-based energy,
> restoring sacred harmony.
>
> **O Mother Mary, generate,**
> **the song that does accelerate,**
> **the earth into a higher state,**
> **all matter does now scintillate.**

4. Mother Mary, awaken people to the reality that the past truly is not the past. An event happened in a linear time line, but the real effect that is lingering is the effect in our minds, and that is not in the past in the sense that it is separated from us.

> Your sacred name I hereby praise,
> collective consciousness you raise,
> no more of fear and doubt and shame,
> consume it with your Mother Flame.
>
> **O Mother Mary, generate,**
> **the song that does accelerate,**
> **the earth into a higher state,**
> **all matter does now scintillate.**

5. Mother Mary, awaken people to the reality that we can heal in the present anything that happened in the past—when we stop being unwilling to go into the feelings, to go into the hurt. We can do this on behalf of other people.

> All darkness from the earth you purge,
> your light moves as a mighty surge,
> no force of darkness can now stop,
> the spiral that goes only up.

> **O Mother Mary, generate,**
> **the song that does accelerate,**
> **the earth into a higher state,**
> **all matter does now scintillate.**

6. Mother Mary, awaken people to the reality that when we go into the hurt and pain, we can come out on the other side and realize: "I am still here." Then we can release, and we can even experience the release on behalf of others so there is a release in the collective mind.

> All elemental life you bless,
> removing from them man-made stress,
> the nature spirits are now free,
> outpicturing Divine decree.

> **O Mother Mary, generate,**
> **the song that does accelerate,**
> **the earth into a higher state,**
> **all matter does now scintillate.**

7. Mother Mary, awaken people to the reality that when we invoke your light, we are forming the Omega polarity to the Alpha action of your releases whereby we anchor it in the physical. We close the figure-eight flow and send it back up to you whereby you can multiply it and send more.

> I raise my voice and take my stand,
> a stop to war I do command,
> no more shall warring scar the earth,
> a golden age is given birth.

O Mother Mary, generate,
the song that does accelerate,
the earth into a higher state,
all matter does now scintillate.

8. Mother Mary, awaken people to the reality that what is going to solve the present problems is a healing of the individual and the collective psyche. Many of the problems we see are born from the fact that people have been scarred in past lives or in this life, and therefore they cannot overcome that sense of being hurt, of being incomplete, of being somehow flawed.

> As Mother Earth is free at last,
> disasters belong to the past,
> your Mother Light is so intense,
> that matter is now far less dense.

O Mother Mary, generate,
the song that does accelerate,
the earth into a higher state,
all matter does now scintillate.

9. Mother Mary, awaken people to the reality that we are often upholding some kind of animosity against another group of people because these people hurt us in a past life. This still lingers in our four lower bodies and it is a major reason for many of the problems we see in the world.

> In Mother Light the earth is pure,
> the upward spiral will endure,
> prosperity is now the norm,
> God's vision manifest as form.
>
> **O Mother Mary, generate,**
> **the song that does accelerate,**
> **the earth into a higher state,**
> **all matter does now scintillate.**

Part 3

1. Mother Mary, awaken people to the reality that the other factor that could bring forth a solution, is the feminine wisdom, the wisdom of the Mother.

> O Blessed Mary's Song of Life,
> consuming every form of strife.
> As I attune to sound so fair,
> each cell is healthy, I declare.
>
> **O Mother Mary, generate,**
> **the song that does accelerate,**
> **my mind into a peaceful state,**
> **God's perfect love I radiate.**

2. Mother Mary, awaken people to the reality that people tend to mix up the Divine Feminine, the Divine Feminine wisdom, with women in physical embodiment. They tend to think that feminine wisdom is restricted to women.

> As life's own song I ever hear,
> it does consume all sense of fear.
> In tune with Mother's symphony,
> from all diseases I AM free.
>
> **O Mother Mary, generate,**
> **the song that does accelerate,**
> **my mind into a peaceful state,**
> **God's perfect love I radiate.**

3. Mother Mary, awaken people to the reality that the Conscious You is beyond male and female. Feminine wisdom is not confined to the sex of the body. It is a condition of the Conscious You and the I AM Presence.

> In Mother's love I do transcend,
> and all my struggles hereby end.
> For when with Mother's eye I see,
> no imperfection touches me.
>
> **O Mother Mary, generate,**
> **the song that does accelerate,**
> **my mind into a peaceful state,**
> **God's perfect love I radiate.**

4. Mother Mary, awaken people to the reality that the I AM Presence stores the divine blueprint for our individual being, which is the Alpha aspect. The Omega aspect is the causal body, which stores all of our positive experiences from our embodiments on earth, giving us knowledge of how the material universe works.

> I see that healing must begin
> by finding Living Christ within.
> For as I see with single eye,
> each cell the light does amplify.

> **O Mother Mary, generate,**
> **the song that does accelerate,**
> **my mind into a peaceful state,**
> **God's perfect love I radiate.**

5. Mother Mary, awaken people to the reality that many people have forgotten this wisdom, primarily because the fallen beings have done everything they could to put down not only women but also the feminine aspect of wisdom.

> In Mother's music I am free,
> from memories of a lesser me.
> My vision in a perfect state,
> that all my cells regenerate.

> **O Mother Mary, generate,**
> **the song that does accelerate,**
> **my mind into a peaceful state,**
> **God's perfect love I radiate.**

6. Mother Mary, awaken people to the reality that the fallen beings hate the Mother realm, the physical octave. They feel they are in the unascended sphere, where the Mother realm is dense, as a punishment from God.

> O Mother's Love, sweet melody,
> from imperfections I AM free.
> O Mother Mary, sound of sounds,
> within my heart your love abounds.
>
> **O Mother Mary, generate,**
> **the song that does accelerate,**
> **my mind into a peaceful state,**
> **God's perfect love I radiate.**

7. Mother Mary, awaken people to the reality that it is unbalanced to embrace the wisdom of the feminine aspect while ignoring or denying the masculine, the Alpha aspect.

> Through Mother's beauty so sublime,
> transcending bounds of space and time.
> All cells beyond the mortal tomb,
> as they are whole in Mother's womb.
>
> **O Mother Mary, generate,**
> **the song that does accelerate,**
> **my mind into a peaceful state,**
> **God's perfect love I radiate.**

8. Mother Mary, awaken people to the reality that the density of the material universe of an unascended sphere is such that the feminine wisdom can help us move around in a circle, and we can create a very comfortable state.

In resonance with life's own song,
in life's harmonics I belong.
The blueprint of my perfect state
does every cell reconsecrate.

O Mother Mary, generate,
the song that does accelerate,
my mind into a peaceful state,
God's perfect love I radiate.

9. Mother Mary, awaken people to the reality that when we do not have the divine Alpha, there will be no upward spiral. Our movement becomes the closed circle, which will become a downward spiral that will lead to a breakdown of the comfortable state we have created.

The tuning fork in every cell
is now attuned to Mother's bell.
From curse of death I AM now free,
I claim my immortality.

O Mother Mary, generate,
the song that does accelerate,
my mind into a peaceful state,
God's perfect love I radiate.

Part 4

1. Mother Mary, awaken people to the reality that we need both the masculine wisdom and the feminine wisdom to work in harmony. The fallen beings have done everything they could to separate the two.

> O blessed Mary, Mother mine,
> there is no greater love than thine,
> as we are one in heart and mind,
> my place in hierarchy I find.
>
> **O Mother Mary, generate,**
> **the song that does accelerate,**
> **the earth into a higher state,**
> **all matter does now scintillate.**

2. Mother Mary, awaken people to the reality that the fallen beings do not have the masculine wisdom, but only a perverted form of it. They have done everything they could to raise up that perverted wisdom as the absolute truth, as the only form of wisdom, and thereby put down the feminine wisdom.

> I came to earth from heaven sent,
> as I am in embodiment,
> I use Divine authority,
> commanding you to set earth free.
>
> **O Mother Mary, generate,**
> **the song that does accelerate,**
> **the earth into a higher state,**
> **all matter does now scintillate.**

3. Mother Mary, awaken people to the reality that the fallen beings are attempting to set themselves up as gods on earth, and they think they have the power to force the material universe to conform to their ideas. They think they can create an ideology or a belief system and force the universe to conform.

> I call now in God's sacred name,
> for you to use your Mother Flame,
> to burn all fear-based energy,
> restoring sacred harmony.
>
> **O Mother Mary, generate,**
> **the song that does accelerate,**
> **the earth into a higher state,**
> **all matter does now scintillate.**

4. Mother Mary, awaken people to the reality that it is only the Divine Feminine that can break the illusion. It does so when the Mother realm, the material world, refuses to conform to man-made ideas. This is the force that is built into the matter realm.

> Your sacred name I hereby praise,
> collective consciousness you raise,
> no more of fear and doubt and shame,
> consume it with your Mother Flame.
>
> **O Mother Mary, generate,**
> **the song that does accelerate,**
> **the earth into a higher state,**
> **all matter does now scintillate.**

5. Mother Mary, awaken people to the reality that this force is not the feminine wisdom. It is the contracting force, and the result is that nothing in the material universe can stand still. It must swing, it must vibrate, it must oscillate.

> All darkness from the earth you purge,
> your light moves as a mighty surge,
> no force of darkness can now stop,
> the spiral that goes only up.

**O Mother Mary, generate,
the song that does accelerate,
the earth into a higher state,
all matter does now scintillate.**

6. Mother Mary, awaken people to the reality that there is a force built into the matter realm that will allow nothing to stand still. It must swing unless it is in perfect harmony with the Father aspect of wisdom, with the Christ mind.

> All elemental life you bless,
> removing from them man-made stress,
> the nature spirits are now free,
> outpicturing Divine decree.

**O Mother Mary, generate,
the song that does accelerate,
the earth into a higher state,
all matter does now scintillate.**

7. Mother Mary, awaken people to the reality that when we are in perfect harmony with the Christ mind, we are not standing still. We are going up in the ascending spiral.

> I raise my voice and take my stand,
> a stop to war I do command,
> no more shall warring scar the earth,
> a golden age is given birth.
>
> **O Mother Mary, generate,**
> **the song that does accelerate,**
> **the earth into a higher state,**
> **all matter does now scintillate.**

8. Mother Mary, awaken people to the reality that when we are out of alignment with the Christ mind, the force built into the Mother makes sure that we must go from one extreme towards the other.

> As Mother Earth is free at last,
> disasters belong to the past,
> your Mother Light is so intense,
> that matter is now far less dense.
>
> **O Mother Mary, generate,**
> **the song that does accelerate,**
> **the earth into a higher state,**
> **all matter does now scintillate.**

9. Mother Mary, awaken people to the reality that the further we go out towards one extreme, the more we generate the force that will pull the pendulum back towards the other extreme. Our lives become this oscillating movement from one extreme to the other. It is this force, this seesaw motion, that eventually breaks down the structures we have created and seek to maintain.

> In Mother Light the earth is pure,
> the upward spiral will endure,
> prosperity is now the norm,
> God's vision manifest as form.
>
> **O Mother Mary, generate,**
> **the song that does accelerate,**
> **the earth into a higher state,**
> **all matter does now scintillate.**

Part 5

1. Mother Mary, awaken people to the reality that when we align ourselves with the Christ, there is still an oscillating movement. Instead of swinging from side to side, it takes us into an upward spiral.

> O Blessed Mary's Song of Life,
> consuming every form of strife.
> As I attune to sound so fair,
> each cell is healthy, I declare.
>
> **O Mother Mary, generate,**
> **the song that does accelerate,**
> **my mind into a peaceful state,**
> **God's perfect love I radiate.**

2. Mother Mary, awaken people to the reality that this cannot be achieved by the Father aspect of wisdom alone. It can only be achieved when Father and Mother are in unison.

As life's own song I ever hear,
it does consume all sense of fear.
In tune with Mother's symphony,
from all diseases I AM free.

**O Mother Mary, generate,
the song that does accelerate,
my mind into a peaceful state,
God's perfect love I radiate.**

3. Mother Mary, awaken people to the reality that we cannot walk the spiritual path by only looking for the Alpha aspect of wisdom. We must tune in to the feminine aspect of wisdom and start looking at how the material universe actually works.

In Mother's love I do transcend,
and all my struggles hereby end.
For when with Mother's eye I see,
no imperfection touches me.

**O Mother Mary, generate,
the song that does accelerate,
my mind into a peaceful state,
God's perfect love I radiate.**

4. Mother Mary, awaken people to the reality that in order to be spiritual, we do not have to withdraw from normal life and not really concern ourselves about the physical realities of life. This is not balance, and this will not give us maximum growth.

17 | Helping People Let Go of the Past

I see that healing must begin
by finding Living Christ within.
For as I see with single eye,
each cell the light does amplify.

**O Mother Mary, generate,
the song that does accelerate,
my mind into a peaceful state,
God's perfect love I radiate.**

5. Mother Mary, awaken people to the reality that we need to look at the material realm and say: "How do things actually work here? How does life work? What are the principles for how matter works?"

In Mother's music I am free,
from memories of a lesser me.
My vision in a perfect state,
that all my cells regenerate.

**O Mother Mary, generate,
the song that does accelerate,
my mind into a peaccful state,
God's perfect love I radiate.**

6. Mother Mary, awaken people to the reality that we tend to look at the world as imperfect or even as opposing our spiritual growth. We look for some spiritual teaching of how the world should work, and then we want to force the matter realm to conform to these ideas.

O Mother's Love, sweet melody,
from imperfections I AM free.
O Mother Mary, sound of sounds,
within my heart your love abounds.

**O Mother Mary, generate,
the song that does accelerate,
my mind into a peaceful state,
God's perfect love I radiate.**

7. Mother Mary, awaken people to the reality that the built-in force of the Mother that creates the oscillating movement from one extreme to another is truly a liberation of the being, the Conscious You, the Spirit that has embodied and been entrapped in matter. It is a liberating force, and that means that it is a changing wisdom.

Through Mother's beauty so sublime,
transcending bounds of space and time.
All cells beyond the mortal tomb,
as they are whole in Mother's womb.

**O Mother Mary, generate,
the song that does accelerate,
my mind into a peaceful state,
God's perfect love I radiate.**

8. Mother Mary, awaken people to the reality that we tend to look at the Father aspect of wisdom as unchanging. We look for some absolute truth, and if it is absolute, then it should not have to change.

In resonance with life's own song,
in life's harmonics I belong.
The blueprint of my perfect state
does every cell reconsecrate.

**O Mother Mary, generate,
the song that does accelerate,
my mind into a peaceful state,
God's perfect love I radiate.**

9. Mother Mary, awaken people to the reality that the Father aspect of wisdom is constantly changing. The wisdom in the ascended realm is very different from what we can see from the unascended realm.

The tuning fork in every cell
is now attuned to Mother's bell.
From curse of death I AM now free,
I claim my immortality.

**O Mother Mary, generate,
the song that does accelerate,
my mind into a peaceful state,
God's perfect love I radiate.**

Part 6

1. Mother Mary, awaken people to the reality that the Divine Mother aspect of wisdom is constantly changing because it is not seeking to live up to some absolute standard. It is looking at what is actually manifest right now and what needs to happen for people to become free of the structures that are existing right now.

> O blessed Mary, Mother mine,
> there is no greater love than thine,
> as we are one in heart and mind,
> my place in hierarchy I find.
>
> **O Mother Mary, generate,**
> **the song that does accelerate,**
> **the earth into a higher state,**
> **all matter does now scintillate.**

2. Mother Mary, awaken people to the reality that feminine wisdom is not attempting to create an ideal state. It is attempting to always shatter the imbalances, or to accentuate the imbalances, in order to set people free from their entrapment in the Mother realm.

> I came to earth from heaven sent,
> as I am in embodiment,
> I use Divine authority,
> commanding you to set earth free.

17 | Helping People Let Go of the Past

**O Mother Mary, generate,
the song that does accelerate,
the earth into a higher state,
all matter does now scintillate.**

3. Mother Mary, awaken people to the reality that what can truly liberate the world from many of the problems we see today is the raising up of this feminine aspect of wisdom in both men and women.

I call now in God's sacred name,
for you to use your Mother Flame,
to burn all fear-based energy,
restoring sacred harmony.

**O Mother Mary, generate,
the song that does accelerate,
the earth into a higher state,
all matter does now scintillate.**

4. Mother Mary, awaken people to the reality that Christianity was a major factor in putting down this feminine wisdom. It put down the idea that ordinary human beings could have any form of wisdom. It was only the elite who could have wisdom. Wisdom had to come from above.

Your sacred name I hereby praise,
collective consciousness you raise,
no more of fear and doubt and shame,
consume it with your Mother Flame.

**O Mother Mary, generate,
the song that does accelerate,
the earth into a higher state,
all matter does now scintillate.**

5. Mother Mary, awaken people to the reality that wisdom can come from "below," from the internalization from lifetimes of how the matter universe works. It is in the uniting of these two forms of wisdom that we can transcend the problems.

All darkness from the earth you purge,
your light moves as a mighty surge,
no force of darkness can now stop,
the spiral that goes only up.

**O Mother Mary, generate,
the song that does accelerate,
the earth into a higher state,
all matter does now scintillate.**

6. Mother Mary, awaken people to the reality that people are attempting to solve many problems through the perverted version of the Father aspect of wisdom generated by the fallen beings. This will not work.

All elemental life you bless,
removing from them man-made stress,
the nature spirits are now free,
outpicturing Divine decree.

**O Mother Mary, generate,
the song that does accelerate,
the earth into a higher state,
all matter does now scintillate.**

7. Mother Mary, awaken people to the reality that there needs to be an upsurge in the use and the recognition of the feminine wisdom. Right now this is mostly coming from women.

> I raise my voice and take my stand,
> a stop to war I do command,
> no more shall warring scar the earth,
> a golden age is given birth.

**O Mother Mary, generate,
the song that does accelerate,
the earth into a higher state,
all matter does now scintillate.**

8. Mother Mary, awaken people to the reality that many women who have taken up leadership positions have been seduced into thinking that, in order to get along in a male-dominated world, they have to become like men, at least when they are dealing with business or politics.

> As Mother Earth is free at last,
> disasters belong to the past,
> your Mother Light is so intense,
> that matter is now far less dense.

> **O Mother Mary, generate,**
> **the song that does accelerate,**
> **the earth into a higher state,**
> **all matter does now scintillate.**

9. Mother Mary, awaken people to the reality that it is not women alone who can bring this change. Men also need to do so, those who are more intuitive.

> In Mother Light the earth is pure,
> the upward spiral will endure,
> prosperity is now the norm,
> God's vision manifest as form.

> **O Mother Mary, generate,**
> **the song that does accelerate,**
> **the earth into a higher state,**
> **all matter does now scintillate.**

Part 7

1. Mother Mary, I visualize the awakening of people to the true aspects of the Alpha and Omega form of wisdom and how to balance them through the Christ mind.

> O Blessed Mary's Song of Life,
> consuming every form of strife.
> As I attune to sound so fair,
> each cell is healthy, I declare.

**O Mother Mary, generate,
the song that does accelerate,
my mind into a peaceful state,
God's perfect love I radiate.**

2. Mother Mary, I call forth the uniting of the feminine and the masculine wisdom to form that Christ discernment, that Christ vision, that does not swing towards either of the dualistic extremes but stays on the middle way.

As life's own song I ever hear,
it does consume all sense of fear.
In tune with Mother's symphony,
from all diseases I AM free.

**O Mother Mary, generate,
the song that does accelerate,
my mind into a peaceful state,
God's perfect love I radiate.**

3. Mother Mary, awaken people to the reality that Christ wisdom acknowledges that, as long as we are in embodiment, there will be an oscillating movement. This is the characteristic of an unascended sphere, and it will be there until the sphere ascends.

In Mother's love I do transcend,
and all my struggles hereby end.
For when with Mother's eye I see,
no imperfection touches me.

> **O Mother Mary, generate,**
> **the song that does accelerate,**
> **my mind into a peaceful state,**
> **God's perfect love I radiate.**

4. Mother Mary, awaken people to the reality that it is not a matter of stopping the oscillating movement. It is a matter of pulling it into an upward spiral.

> I see that healing must begin
> by finding Living Christ within.
> For as I see with single eye,
> each cell the light does amplify.

> **O Mother Mary, generate,**
> **the song that does accelerate,**
> **my mind into a peaceful state,**
> **God's perfect love I radiate.**

5. Mother Mary, awaken people to the reality that it is the oscillations that give us the kind of experiences we need to have in an unascended sphere, and we do not seek to stop that which is the key to growth. We make sure that is does not become the source of standstill or the downward spiral.

> In Mother's music I am free,
> from memories of a lesser me.
> My vision in a perfect state,
> that all my cells regenerate.

**O Mother Mary, generate,
the song that does accelerate,
my mind into a peaceful state,
God's perfect love I radiate.**

6. Mother Mary, I call for you and the angels of the Divine Mother to consume the opposition to the uniting of the masculine and feminine wisdom.

O Mother's Love, sweet melody,
from imperfections I AM free.
O Mother Mary, sound of sounds,
within my heart your love abounds.

**O Mother Mary, generate,
the song that does accelerate,
my mind into a peaceful state,
God's perfect love I radiate.**

7. Mother Mary, awaken people to the reality that there is no greater manifestation of anti-love than this perversion, this separation of the masculine and feminine wisdom.

Through Mother's beauty so sublime,
transcending bounds of space and time.
All cells beyond the mortal tomb,
as they are whole in Mother's womb.

**O Mother Mary, generate,
the song that does accelerate,
my mind into a peaceful state,
God's perfect love I radiate.**

8. Mother Mary, awaken people to the reality that there is nothing that the fallen beings and the dark forces oppose more than the uniting of the two.

> In resonance with life's own song,
> in life's harmonics I belong.
> The blueprint of my perfect state
> does every cell reconsecrate.
>
> **O Mother Mary, generate,**
> **the song that does accelerate,**
> **my mind into a peaceful state,**
> **God's perfect love I radiate.**

9. Mother Mary, awaken people to the reality that the fallen beings have no power to stop us unless they can deceive us into stopping ourselves. Awaken all people to our real power to rise above the past and manifest balance in our personal lives an our societies.

> The tuning fork in every cell
> is now attuned to Mother's bell.
> From curse of death I AM now free,
> I claim my immortality.
>
> **O Mother Mary, generate,**
> **the song that does accelerate,**
> **my mind into a peaceful state,**
> **God's perfect love I radiate.**

Sealing

In the name of the Divine Mother, I call to Mother Mary for the sealing of myself and all people in my circle of influence in the creative flow of the Divine Mother, the River of Life. I call for the multiplication of my calls by all representatives of the Divine Mother, so that we form the perfect figure-eight flow of "As Above, so below." Thus, I accept that this is fully manifest, because the mouth of the Lord, the Divine Mother that I AM, has spoken it. Amen.

18 | A MIGHTY ACTION OF SOUL HEALING

I AM the Ascended Master Mother Mary. I come filled with gratitude for your presence, for your coming together, for the work you have performed. Truly a very significant clearance of the European continent has taken place in all four octaves, and as you have made the calls, much energy has been transformed. Many dark beings, many fallen beings, have been removed, and this has been a very significant clearance. It is, of course, the Alpha action where you call into action the Ascended Host to remove the darkness and bring the light. As the Divine Mother, I, of course, also see the Omega aspect. I truly see how many people embodied on the European continent are suffering because in past lives they experienced some of the incredibly traumatic events that have taken place here.

You have made calls on the wars of Europe, but there have been so many other events that have traumatized people, created wounds in their souls, split their souls, so that they often have soul parts in many different countries. Many have been soldiers and have been killed on various battlefields and may have soul parts that are still trapped there. Even though much darkness has been removed, this does not mean that the people are healed. Thus I come to elicit your help in performing a healing action for the people of Europe.

Healing the souls of Europeans

This can, of course, be turned into an invocation that you can give as an invocation on your own. But for this particular purpose I ask you to remain silent, I ask you to close your eyes, and I ask you to visualize as you hear me speak. What we will do is go through all of the countries of Europe, and I will make certain calls for the healing of the people and for the return and integration of any soul parts. I ask you, as best you remember European geography, to all put your attention on that one country I am mentioning. I know that you are from many different countries, and I know you have a stronger affinity with your own country, but there is great value in all of you together at the same time putting your attention on one country.

> **I now call for the divine healing of the souls of all people who embody in Norway. I call for the return of all soul parts, and I call for these soul parts to be integrated so the people can be whole in their lower beings, and therefore be more free to integrate with their higher beings. I call for the healing of those souls who have the potential to embody the flame that Norway holds for the earth.**

I now call for the healing of all souls who embody in Sweden. I call for the return of their soul parts, for them to be integrated, and for them to be whole so they can find their way to manifest their divine plans and to bring the gift that they are here to bring, and that the country of Sweden can bring to the world.

I call for the healing of all souls who embody in the country of Finland. I call for the return of their soul parts, for them to be integrated so that the people can be whole, to flow with the Holy Spirit and bring forth that gift that is theirs to bring to this planet.

I call for the healing of all souls who embody in the country of Denmark. I call for the return of their soul parts, for them to be integrated so that they can be whole, to lock in to the Mother Flame and bring that unique gift that Denmark can bring to the nations.

I call for the healing of the souls of all people who embody in the country of Estonia. I call for the return of their soul parts, for them to be integrated so that the people can be free to bring that gift, that flame, that Estonia can bring to the people of the world.

I call for the healing of the souls of all people who embody in the country of Latvia. I call for the return of their soul parts, for them to be integrated so the people may be whole and be in attunement with their higher selves, and bring that gift to the world that is theirs to give.

I call for the healing of the souls of all people who embody in the country of Lithuania. I call for the return of their soul parts and for their integration so that the people will be whole and be able to know and bring their gift to the world.

I call for the healing of all people who embody in the country of Russia. I call for the return of their soul parts, for their integration that the people will be whole and be able to know and dare to express their gift to the world.
I call for the healing again of all souls who embody in the country of Russia. I call for the return of their soul parts, for their integration that the people will be whole.
I call for the healing of all people who embody in the country of Russia, for the return of their soul parts, and their integration that the people will be whole.

I call for the healing of the souls of all people who embody in the country of Belarus. I call for the return of their soul parts and for their integration so that the people will be free, will be whole, to bring their gift to the world.

I call for the healing of all people who embody in the country of Poland. I call for the return of their soul parts, for their integration so that the people will be whole and have the Heart Flame to bring their gift to the world.
I call for the healing of all people who embody in the country of Poland, for the return of their soul parts, for their integration so that the people will be whole and be free.

I call for the healing of the souls of all people who embody in the country of Germany. I call for the return of their soul parts and for their integration so that the people will be whole and be free to bring their gift to the world.
I call for the healing of the souls of all people who embody in the country of Germany. I call for their integration that the people will be whole.
I call for the healing of the souls of all people who embody in the country of Germany. I call for the return of their soul parts and the integration so that the people will be whole.

I call for the healing of the souls of all people who embody in Czechia and Slovakia, the former Czechoslovakia. I call for the return of their soul parts and for their integration so that the people will be whole.

I call for the healing of the souls of all people who embody in the country of Hungary. I call for the return of their soul parts and their integration so that the people will be whole and free to bring their gift to the world.

I call for the healing of all people who embody in the country of Austria. I call for the return of their soul parts and for their integration so that the people will be whole.

I call for the healing of all people who embody in the country of Switzerland. I call for the return of their soul parts and their integration so that the people will be whole and be able to bring their gift to the world.

I call for the healing of the souls of all people who embody in the country of France. I call for the return of their soul parts and their reintegration so that the people will be truly free to bring their gift. I call for the healing of the souls of all people who embody in the country of France. I call for the return of their soul parts and for their integration so the people will be whole.

I call for the healing of the souls of all people who embody in the country of Belgium. I call for the return of their soul parts and their integration so the people will be whole and free to bring their gift.

I call for the healing of the souls of all people who embody in the country of the Netherlands and Holland. I call for the reintegration of their soul parts, for the return of those soul parts so the people will be whole and will be free to bring their gift.

I call for the healing of all people who embody in the country of England. I call for the return of their soul parts and their reintegration so that the people will be whole and will be free.
I call for the healing of all people who embody in the country of England. I call for the return of their soul parts and their reintegration so the people will be able to bring their gift to the world.

I call for the healing of the souls of all people who embody in the country of Ireland. I call for the return of their soul parts and their reintegration so that the people will be whole.

I call for the healing of the souls of all people who embody in the country of Scotland. I call for the

return of their soul parts and their reintegration so
the people will be whole.

I call for the healing of the souls of all people
who embody in the country of Spain. I call for the
return of their soul parts and their reintegration so
that the people will be whole.
I call for the healing of all people who embody in
the country of Spain. I call for the return of their
soul parts and their integration so the people will
be free to bring their gift.

I call for the healing of all people who embody
in the country of Portugal. I call for the return of
their soul parts and their reintegration so that the
people will be whole.

I call for the healing of the souls of all people who
embody in the Basque regions of Spain. I call for
the return of their soul parts and their integration
so that the people will be whole and free to bring
their gift.

I call for the healing of the souls of all people who
embody in the nation of Italy. I call for the return
of their soul parts and for their integration so the
people will be whole and be able to bring their
gift.
I call for the healing of all people who embody in

Italy and for the return of their soul parts so that the people will be whole and free.

I call for the healing of all souls who embody in the Balkan nations of the former Yugoslavia. I call for the return of their soul parts, for their integration so the people will be whole.
I call for the healing of all people who embody in the former Yugoslavia and for the return of their soul parts, their integration so the people will be free to bring their gift.

I call for the healing of the souls of all people who embody in the former Albania. I call for the return of their soul parts and their integration so that the people will be whole.

I call for the healing of the souls of all people who embody in the country of Greece. I call for the return of their soul parts and their integration so the people will be whole.

I call for the healing of the souls of all people who embody in the country of Bulgaria. I call for the return of their soul parts and their integration so the people will be whole.

I call for the healing of the souls of all people who embody in the country of Romania. I call for the return of their soul parts and their reintegration so that the people will be whole.

I call for the healing of all people who embody in the country of Turkey. I call for the return of their soul parts and their integration so that the people will be free to bring their gift to the world.

I call for the healing of the souls of all people who embody in the countries around the Black Sea. I call for the return of their soul parts and their reintegration so that the people will be whole.

I call for the healing of the people, of the souls of all people, who embody in Ukraine. I call for the return of their soul parts and their reintegration so the people will be whole.
I call for the healing of the souls of all people who embody in Ukraine. I call for the return of their soul parts and their integration so that the people will be free to bring their gift to the world.

I call for the healing of all mothers on the European continent who have seen their sons and husbands and fathers be killed in war. I call for the return of their soul parts, for their integration so that the people will be whole and will be free to bring their gift of motherhood to the European continent.

I call for the souls, for the healing of the souls of all fathers on the European continent who have seen their sons go off to war and be killed. I call for the return of their soul parts and their integration so that they will be able to bring their gift of the Alpha Flame of Fatherhood to this continent.

I call for the healing of the souls of all sons on the European continent who have been taken from their families and killed on the battlefields of Europe. I call for the return of their soul parts, their integration so that the people will be whole and be able to hold that Flame of the Divine Son for this continent.

I call for the healing of all daughters on the European continent who have seen their brothers and fathers and sons be killed in war, who have seen their homes destroyed, their cities laid waste. I call for the return of their soul parts and their integration so that they will be free to hold that Flame of the Divine Feminine for this continent.

I call for the healing of all children on the European continent, those who have in past lives been killed by war or other atrocities in their childhood, without receiving the opportunity to grow into adulthood, and who thus carry scars in their souls. I call for the return of their soul parts and their integration so that they will be free to be the Divine Child in embodiment and to have that innocence of the childlike mind returned to them.

I call for the healing of all of the gnomes in the physical elemental kingdom over the European continent. I call for them to be healed, to be freed of their burdens that they may be able to fulfill their task of service to human beings.

I call for the healing of all of the undines of the water element over Europe, that they may be healed and be whole and be free to give their service to human beings.

I call for the healing of the sylphs of the air over the European continent. I call for them to be whole, that they may be able to give service to humankind.

I call for the healing of the fiery salamanders of the identity realm over the European continent. I call for them to be whole that they may be able to fulfill their highest service to mankind.

A cleansing action for Europe

I AM the Divine Mother, manifesting my presence in the physical, releasing almost infinite quantities of healing water over the European continent. This water is charged with the highest possible vibration of the emotional octave, healing the emotional bodies of all people on earth. This water falls like a gentle rain, and when it reaches the emotional bodies of the people in embodiment in Europe, it gently washes away all of the misqualified energies.

These energies are washed out of the emotional body onto the ground, where they keep running towards the lowest point. They gather in the rivers of Europe. They flow through those rivers. They are carried towards the sea, and there the angels of all of the Chohans, all of the Archangels, all of the Elohim of the seven rays are waiting to consume and transform those energies.

I AM the Divine Mother, and I release the healing air currents over the European continent. This gentle wind of the Holy Spirit blows through the mental bodies of the people in embodiment in Europe. It gently dislodges and blows away all of the imperfect thoughts and ideas inserted into people's mental bodies.

It gathers them like dust, carries them up higher, carries them beyond the clouds. And there, the angels of the Chohans, the Archangels and the Elohim are waiting to consume and transform these energies, so that the people may be free to receive the ideas from the ascended masters in their mental bodies.

I AM the Divine Mother in physical manifestation, and I release the fire of the identity realm over the European continent. This fire enters the identity bodies of all people in embodiment. It forms a mighty, hot wind that blows away the false sense of identity, blows it out of the identity bodies, carries it upwards.

There, as it comes closer and closer to the physical sun, it is met by the light of the angels of the Chohans, the Archangels and the Elohim. Thus, it is consumed before it even reaches the physical sun.

I am visualizing the European continent being covered by a gentle snowfall of white crystals. They fall gently like the snow, gently falling on the first days of autumn. They fall through the identity octave, through the mental realm, through the emotional realm and then they manifest physically. They fall as white, perfect, symmetrical crystals that carry with them the white light of the Divine Mother. They fall onto the ground, they cover the ground, and then they are absorbed into the ground where they go below the surface. They go through deeper and deeper layers of the earth, and as they go, they consume the records of all the blood that has soaked into the ground on this continent throughout the ages beyond known history.

They carry all of these records with them as they come closer to the center of the earth. There they are consumed finally and fully by the angels of the Chohans, the Archangels and the Elohim. Then, the crystals begin to rise back up towards the surface where they remain in the upper layers of the soil over Europe. Every country is covered in them, and they will remain there as the receivers and transmitters of the purifying white light of the Divine Mother.

I now ask you to fully accept this clearing action as a manifest reality:

I first ask you to accept it as a manifest reality in the identity realm and visualize the entire European continent with the identity realm above it.

I now ask you to accept this clearance as a manifest reality in the mental realm over the European continent.

I now ask you to accept the clearance in the emotional body of the European continent.

And I ask you to accept the clearance at the physical level over the European continent.

I ask you to center in your heart and to sense that inner knowing that this clearance is real, that it is manifest, and that Europe will never be the same. Do you accept this? I must be hard of hearing, my beloved. Do you accept this? All: Yes!

Thank you! I realize I am taking you quickly out of a very meditative action to an outgoing action. I truly am grateful for your presence. I am grateful for your willingness to be the open doors for this figure-eight flow from above to below—from us Above to you below, from the Alpha to the Omega, and then back to the Alpha, so that the figure-eight flow is closed from you, and we can multiply it and send even more.

The origin of hatred of the Mother

Life is a wonderful gift. I know that so many millions of people on the European continent would not be able to accept this statement. They have such burdens, such scars in their souls, in their four lower bodies, that if they were to hear this statement spoken, they would rebel against it. They might denounce the messenger or the being speaking the message. They might say

I am unreal, that this is all fantasy. It is truly because their wounds are so intense that they cannot acknowledge the existence of the Divine Mother. It is because it is one thing to receive a wound in the soul through a traumatic event, but it is another to have the overlay – the emotional, mental and even in the identity realm have the overlay – that if the Divine Mother was real, she would have prevented this from happening. Truly, there are so many people who feel that they have been so hurt by the matter realm, by the Mother realm, that they will not even accept the concept that there is a Divine Mother. For they feel that she should have protected them from these wounds, these traumas.

This has led to the condition that I have called hatred of the Mother. Truly, this originated with the fallen beings, as I have explained, who rebelled against the Mother realm. But it has been so contagious that it has spread to the people, even those of the original inhabitants of the earth, and even those who have come here on a rescue mission. Many feel that these wounds, their wounds, are so deep, so painful, so intense, that they cannot possibly accept that there should be a benevolent being representing the Divine Mother. Why would the Mother not step in and protect them and their children from these calamities?

I fully understand why people cannot understand this. I know that you have received some answers and teachings that will help you understand this and understand how the law of free will works. I ask you then to open yourself up to the wisdom of the Divine Mother that can help you, in your own mind, resolve this dilemma, this paradox, this unanswered question. I ask you also to visualize and make the calls that the people of Europe who have been so wounded will also be able to receive some portion of the wisdom of the Divine Mother, which will allow them to see that they have a misconception of what the Mother is and what the role of the Mother is: The role of the Mother is to protect, to heal, to guide, but never to force.

The trauma that people have experienced has come through force, but that force has not come from the Divine Mother. It is not a feature of the Mother, and therefore it cannot be stopped by the Mother, for the free will of both the fallen beings and the original inhabitants of the earth must be allowed to outplay itself. The Mother can only reflect back what people are sending out, when they are not open to the wisdom of the Mother that they can receive from within, or even from those who have been able to tune in throughout the ages to some aspect of the wisdom and share it with the people.

The Divine Mother loves all people

Truly, truly, the Divine Mother loves everyone. I would much prefer that people would understand this, so they would not reject the love, so they could experience my love for them and know that, even though my love cannot prevent the outplaying of free will, my love can indeed heal each and every wound you have received through the outplaying of free will – both that of yourselves and the other inhabitants on this planet. There is no hurt, no wound, no scar, that the love of the Divine Mother cannot heal.

It is not a matter of looking to the past and regretting what happened. It is a matter of accepting that what happened has happened as an outplaying of free will, as an outplaying, a manifestation, of a certain state of consciousness. What happened has happened, and it is over with, at least in that manifestation of it. When you do not seek to recreate the past and to undo what cannot be undone, in your acceptance that this happened, you can look at the fact that it can continue to affect you only when you hold on to it.

Then you can come to the point of realizing, as I have said before, that the only path to freedom from the past is to forgive. To forgive all, to forgive unconditionally, because in forgiving you are releasing. When you are releasing the matrices in your mind that you are holding on to, then you open yourself up for the love of the Divine Mother.

There are so many people who have been tricked by the fallen beings into believing that when they have been healed, then they can forgive and let go. But as you all know, the consciousness must come before the physical manifestation. You must be willing to forgive and let go, and then you are healed.

There are some images of the Divine Mother that show her with a heart pierced with a dagger. That is because the Divine Mother's heart has been pierced by the pain of her children. Now, you may visualize one of these images of the figure of the Divine Mother with a physical heart visible and a dagger sticking through it, and then you may visualize that I, the Ascended Master Mother Mary, am reaching my hand down, grabbing the handle of this dagger, and pulling it out of the heart of the Divine Mother, the Divine Feminine.

Thereby, I pull it out of the heart of all people in embodiment who have been hurt by these traumas. I take this dagger, and I throw it into the fire of the Divine Mother where it is instantly consumed. Thus, I do not wish you to hold these images in your mind anymore, but accept that the Divine Mother over the European continent is healed. Her heart is whole. Visualize that the hearts of all people are whole, that they are no more pierced, that they are no more divided. There is the wholeness of heart that opens up the rose of the heart chakra to receive the unconditional love of the Divine Mother.

[Messenger exhales.] I breathe out the healing energy of the Divine Mother. I am grateful for your presence and your willingness to serve as the physical anchors for the release of this healing action. Mother Mary I AM.

19 | HEALING PEOPLE'S PAST TRAUMAS

NOTE: You can adapt this invocation for other nations and continents by substituting names. You can mention the name of some countries several times to fit the number of verses. You can give the entire invocation for one nation only.

In the name I AM THAT I AM, Jesus Christ, I call to all representatives of the Divine Mother, especially Maraytaii, Nada, Kuan Yin, Mother Mary, Portia, Liberty, Venus and Omega for the healing of people's past soul traumas. Heal people of all conditions that prevent them from moving into an upward spiral, including…

[Make personal calls.]

Part 1

1. Maraytaii, heal the four lower bodies of all people who are suffering because in past lives they experienced some of the traumatic events that have taken place on the European continent and other continents.

> O Cosmic Mother, sound the gong,
> that calls me home where I belong.
> I know you love me tenderly,
> and in that knowing I am free.
>
> **Maraytaii, I resonate**
> **with song that opens cosmic gate.**
> **Your melody makes me vibrate**
> **my sense of self I recreate.**

2. Maraytaii, heal the four lower bodies of all people who have been soldiers and have been killed on various battlefields and have soul parts that are still trapped there.

> O Cosmic Mother, hold me tight,
> I resonate with your own light.
> Your music purifies my heart,
> your love to all I do impart.
>
> **Maraytaii, I resonate**
> **with song that opens cosmic gate.**
> **Your melody makes me vibrate**
> **my sense of self I recreate.**

3. Maraytaii, I call for the divine healing of the souls of all people who embody in Norway. I call for the return of all soul parts, and I call for these soul parts to be integrated so the people can be whole in their lower beings, and therefore be more free to integrate with their higher beings. I call for the healing of those souls who have the potential to embody the flame that Norway holds for the earth.

> O Cosmic Mother, we are one,
> your heart is like a blazing sun.
> My being can but amplify,
> the sacred sound you magnify.
>
> **Maraytaii, I resonate**
> **with song that opens cosmic gate.**
> **Your melody makes me vibrate**
> **my sense of self I recreate.**

4. Maraytaii, I call for the healing of all souls who embody in Sweden. I call for the return of their soul parts, for them to be integrated, and for them to be whole so they can find their way to manifest their divine plans and to bring the gift that they are here to bring, and that the country of Sweden can bring to the world.

> O Cosmic Mother, I now hear,
> the subtle sound of Sacred Sphere.
> As I attune to Cosmic Hum,
> the lesser self I overcome.

> **Maraytaii, I resonate**
> **with song that opens cosmic gate.**
> **Your melody makes me vibrate**
> **my sense of self I recreate.**

5. Maraytaii, I call for the healing of all souls who embody in the country of Finland. I call for the return of their soul parts, for them to be integrated so that the people can be whole, to flow with the Holy Spirit and bring forth that gift that is theirs to bring to this planet.

> O Cosmic Mother, take me home,
> I am in sync with Sacred OM,
> The sound of sounds will raise me up,
> so only light is in my cup.

> **Maraytaii, I resonate**
> **with song that opens cosmic gate.**
> **Your melody makes me vibrate**
> **my sense of self I recreate.**

6. Maraytaii, I call for the healing of all souls who embody in the country of Denmark. I call for the return of their soul parts, for them to be integrated so that they can be whole, to lock in to the Mother Flame and bring the unique gift that Denmark can bring to the nations.

> O Cosmic Mother, I will be,
> a part of cosmic symphony.
> All that I AM, an instrument,
> for sound that is from heaven sent.

> **Maraytaii, I resonate
> with song that opens cosmic gate.
> Your melody makes me vibrate
> my sense of self I recreate.**

7. Maraytaii, I call for the healing of the souls of all people who embody in the country of Estonia. I call for the return of their soul parts, for them to be integrated so that the people can be free to bring the gift, that flame, that Estonia can bring to the people of the world.

> O Cosmic Mother, I now call,
> to enter sacred music hall.
> I will be part of life's ascent,
> towards the starry firmament.

> **Maraytaii, I resonate
> with song that opens cosmic gate.
> Your melody makes me vibrate
> my sense of self I recreate.**

8. Maraytaii, I call for the healing of the souls of all people who embody in the country of Latvia. I call for the return of their soul parts, for them to be integrated so the people may be whole and be in attunement with their higher selves, and bring that gift to the world that is theirs to give.

> O Cosmic Mother, tune my strings,
> my total being with you sings.
> Your song I now reverberate,
> as cosmic love I celebrate.

> Maraytaii, I resonate
> with song that opens cosmic gate.
> Your melody makes me vibrate
> my sense of self I recreate.

9. Maraytaii, I call for the healing of the souls of all people who embody in the country of Lithuania. I call for the return of their soul parts and for their integration so that the people will be whole and be able to know and bring their gift to the world.

> O Cosmic Mother, I love you,
> your love song keeps me ever true.
> You fill me with your sacred tone,
> and thus I never feel alone.

> Maraytaii, I resonate
> with song that opens cosmic gate.
> Your melody makes me vibrate
> my sense of self I recreate.

Part 2

1. Beloved Nada, I call for the healing of all people who embody in the country of Russia. I call for the return of their soul parts, for their integration that the people will be whole and be able to know and dare to express their gift to the world.

19 | Healing people's past traumas

O Nada, blessed cosmic grace,
filling up my inner space.
Your song is like a sacred balm,
my mind a sea of perfect calm.

**With Nada's secret melody,
my mind remains forever free.
Conducting Nada's symphony,
eternal peace I do decree.**

2. Beloved Nada, I call for the healing of all souls who embody in the country of Russia. I call for the return of their soul parts, for their integration that the people will be whole.

O Nada, in your Buddhic mind,
my inner peace I truly find.
As I your song reverberate,
your love I do assimilate.

**With Nada's secret melody,
my mind remains forever free.
Conducting Nada's symphony,
eternal peace I do decree.**

3. Beloved Nada, I call for the healing of all people who embody in the country of Russia, for the return of their soul parts, and their integration that the people will be whole.

O Nada, beauty so sublime,
I follow you beyond all time.
In soundless sound we do immerse,
to recreate the universe.

**With Nada's secret melody,
my mind remains forever free.
Conducting Nada's symphony,
eternal peace I do decree.**

4. Beloved Nada, I call for the healing of the souls of all people who embody in the country of Belarus. I call for the return of their soul parts and for their integration so that the people will be free, will be whole, to bring their gift to the world.

> O Nada, future we predict
> where nothing Christhood can restrict.
> With Buddhic mind we do perceive,
> a better future we conceive.

**With Nada's secret melody,
my mind remains forever free.
Conducting Nada's symphony,
eternal peace I do decree.**

5. Beloved Nada, I call for the healing of all people who embody in the country of Poland. I call for the return of their soul parts, for their integration so that the people will be whole and have the Heart Flame to bring their gift to the world.

> O Nada, future we rewrite,
> where might is never, ever right.
> Instead, the mind of Christ is king,
> we see the Christ in every thing.

> **With Nada's secret melody,
> my mind remains forever free.
> Conducting Nada's symphony,
> eternal peace I do decree.**

6. Beloved Nada, I call for the healing of all people who embody in the country of Poland, for the return of their soul parts, for their integration so that the people will be whole and be free.

> O Nada, peace is now the norm,
> my Spirit is beyond all form.
> To form I will no more adapt,
> I use potential yet untapped.

> **With Nada's secret melody,
> my mind remains forever free.
> Conducting Nada's symphony,
> eternal peace I do decree.**

7. Beloved Nada, I call for the healing of the souls of all people who embody in the country of Germany. I call for the return of their soul parts and for their integration so that the people will be whole and be free to bring their gift to the world.

> O Nada, such resplendent joy,
> my life I truly can enjoy.
> I am allowed to have some fun,
> my solar plexus like a sun.

> **With Nada's secret melody,
> my mind remains forever free.
> Conducting Nada's symphony,
> eternal peace I do decree.**

8. Beloved Nada, I call for the healing of the souls of all people who embody in the country of Germany. I call for their integration that the people will be whole.

> O Nada, service is the key,
> to living in reality.
> For I see now that life is one,
> my highest service has begun.
>
> **With Nada's secret melody,**
> **my mind remains forever free.**
> **Conducting Nada's symphony,**
> **eternal peace I do decree.**

9. Beloved Nada, I call for the healing of the souls of all people who embody in the country of Germany. I call for the return of their soul parts and the integration so that the people will be whole.

> O Nada, we do now decree,
> that life on earth shall be carefree.
> With Jesus we complete the quest,
> God's kingdom is now manifest.
>
> **With Nada's secret melody,**
> **my mind remains forever free.**
> **Conducting Nada's symphony,**
> **eternal peace I do decree.**

Part 3

1. Kuan Yin, I call for the healing of the souls of all people who embody in the Czech Republic. I call for the return of their soul parts and for their integration so that the people will be whole.

> O Kuan Yin, what sacred name,
> fill me now with Mercy's Flame.
> In giving mercy I am free,
> forgiving all is magic key.
>
> **In Kuan Yin's sweet melody,**
> **I am set free my Self to be.**
> **In Kuan Yin's vitality,**
> **I claim my immortality.**

2. Kuan Yin, I call for the healing of the souls of all people who embody in Slovakia. I call for the return of their soul parts and for their integration so that the people will be whole.

> O Kuan Yin, I now let go,
> of all attachments here below.
> All pent-up feelings I release,
> free from emotional disease.
>
> **In Kuan Yin's sweet melody,**
> **I am set free my Self to be.**
> **In Kuan Yin's vitality,**
> **I claim my immortality.**

3. Kuan Yin, I call for the healing of the souls of all people who embody in the country of Hungary. I call for the return of their soul parts and their integration so that the people will be whole and free to bring their gift to the world.

> O Kuan Yin, why must I feel,
> that life falls short of my ideal?
> All expectations I give up,
> my mind is now an empty cup.

> **In Kuan Yin's sweet melody,**
> **I am set free my Self to be.**
> **In Kuan Yin's vitality,**
> **I claim my immortality.**

4. Kuan Yin, I call for the healing of all people who embody in the country of Austria. I call for the return of their soul parts and for their integration so that the people will be whole.

> O Kuan Yin, transcend the past,
> as all resentment gone at last.
> From future nothing I expect,
> eternal now I won't reject.

> **In Kuan Yin's sweet melody,**
> **I am set free my Self to be.**
> **In Kuan Yin's vitality,**
> **I claim my immortality.**

5. Kuan Yin, I call for the healing of all people who embody in the country of Switzerland. I call for the return of their soul parts and their integration so that the people will be whole and be able to bring their gift to the world.

O Kuan Yin, uplifting me,
beyond Samsara's raging sea.
All safe inside your Prajna boat,
the farther shore no more remote.

**In Kuan Yin's sweet melody,
I am set free my Self to be.
In Kuan Yin's vitality,
I claim my immortality.**

6. Kuan Yin, I call for the healing of the souls of all people who embody in the country of France. I call for the return of their soul parts and their reintegration so that the people will be truly free to bring their gift.

O Kuan Yin, your alchemy,
with miracles you set me free.
As I forgive, I am forgiven,
by guilt I am no longer driven.

**In Kuan Yin's sweet melody,
I am set free my Self to be.
In Kuan Yin's vitality,
I claim my immortality.**

7. Kuan Yin, I call for the healing of the souls of all people who embody in the country of France. I call for the return of their soul parts and for their integration so the people will be whole.

> O Kuan Yin, all worries gone,
> with nothing done, no thing undone.
> Through separate self I will not do,
> and thus I rest, all one with you.
>
> **In Kuan Yin's sweet melody,**
> **I am set free my Self to be.**
> **In Kuan Yin's vitality,**
> **I claim my immortality.**

8. Kuan Yin, I call for the healing of the souls of all people who embody in the country of Belgium. I call for the return of their soul parts and their integration so the people will be whole and free to bring their gift.

> O Kuan Yin, your sanity,
> now sets me free from vanity.
> For truly, what is that to me;
> I just let go and follow thee.
>
> **In Kuan Yin's sweet melody,**
> **I am set free my Self to be.**
> **In Kuan Yin's vitality,**
> **I claim my immortality.**

9. Kuan Yin, I call for the healing of the souls of all people who embody in the country of the Netherlands and Holland. I call for the reintegration of their soul parts, for the return of those soul parts so the people will be whole and will be free to bring their gift.

O Kuan Yin, so sweet the sound,
that emanates from holy ground.
As I let go of ego's chore,
I find myself on farther shore.

**In Kuan Yin's sweet melody,
I am set free my Self to be.
In Kuan Yin's vitality,
I claim my immortality.**

Part 4

1. Mother Mary, I call for the healing of all people who embody in the country of England. I call for the return of their soul parts and their reintegration so that the people will be whole and will be free.

O Blessed Mary's Song of Life,
consuming every form of strife.
As I attune to sound so fair,
each cell is healthy, I declare.

**O Mother Mary, generate,
the song that does accelerate,
my mind into a peaceful state,
God's perfect love I radiate.**

2. Mother Mary, I call for the healing of all people who embody in the country of England. I call for the return of their soul parts and their reintegration so the people will be able to bring their gift to the world.

As life's own song I ever hear,
it does consume all sense of fear.
In tune with Mother's symphony,
from all diseases I AM free.

**O Mother Mary, generate,
the song that does accelerate,
my mind into a peaceful state,
God's perfect love I radiate.**

3. Mother Mary, I call for the healing of the souls of all people who embody in the country of Ireland. I call for the return of their soul parts and their reintegration so that the people will be whole.

In Mother's love I do transcend,
and all my struggles hereby end.
For when with Mother's eye I see,
no imperfection touches me.

**O Mother Mary, generate,
the song that does accelerate,
my mind into a peaceful state,
God's perfect love I radiate.**

4. Mother Mary, I call for the healing of the souls of all people who embody in the country of Scotland. I call for the return of their soul parts and their reintegration so the people will be whole.

I see that healing must begin
by finding Living Christ within.
For as I see with single eye,
each cell the light does amplify.

O Mother Mary, generate,
the song that does accelerate,
my mind into a peaceful state,
God's perfect love I radiate.

5. Mother Mary, I call for the healing of the souls of all people who embody in the country of Spain. I call for the return of their soul parts and their reintegration so that the people will be whole.

In Mother's music I am free,
from memories of a lesser me.
My vision in a perfect state,
that all my cells regenerate.

O Mother Mary, generate,
the song that does accelerate,
my mind into a peaceful state,
God's perfect love I radiate.

6. Mother Mary, I call for the healing of all people who embody in the country of Spain. I call for the return of their soul parts and their integration so the people will be free to bring their gift.

O Mother's Love, sweet melody,
from imperfections I AM free.
O Mother Mary, sound of sounds,
within my heart your love abounds.

**O Mother Mary, generate,
the song that does accelerate,
my mind into a peaceful state,
God's perfect love I radiate.**

7. Mother Mary, I call for the healing of all people who embody in the country of Portugal. I call for the return of their soul parts and their reintegration so that the people will be whole.

Through Mother's beauty so sublime,
transcending bounds of space and time.
All cells beyond the mortal tomb,
as they are whole in Mother's womb.

**O Mother Mary, generate,
the song that does accelerate,
my mind into a peaceful state,
God's perfect love I radiate.**

8. Mother Mary, I call for the healing of all people who embody in Italy and for the return of their soul parts so that the people will be whole and free.

In resonance with life's own song,
in life's harmonics I belong.
The blueprint of my perfect state
does every cell reconsecrate.

> **O Mother Mary, generate,**
> **the song that does accelerate,**
> **my mind into a peaceful state,**
> **God's perfect love I radiate.**

9. Mother Mary, I call for the healing of the souls of all people who embody in the nation of Italy. I call for the return of their soul parts and for their integration so the people will be whole and be able to bring their gift.

> The tuning fork in every cell
> is now attuned to Mother's bell.
> From curse of death I AM now free,
> I claim my immortality.

> **O Mother Mary, generate,**
> **the song that does accelerate,**
> **my mind into a peaceful state,**
> **God's perfect love I radiate.**

Part 5

1. Beloved Portia, I call for the healing of the souls of all people who embody in the Basque regions of Spain. I call for the return of their soul parts and their integration so that the people will be whole and free to bring their gift.

> O Portia, in your own retreat,
> with Mother's Love you do me greet.
> As all my tests I now complete,
> old patterns I no more repeat.

> O Portia, opportunity,
> I am beyond duality.
> I focus now internally,
> with you I grow eternally.

2. Beloved Portia, I call for the healing of all souls who embody in Bosnia and Herzegovina. I call for the return of their soul parts, for their integration so the people will be whole.

> O Portia, Justice is your name,
> upholding Cosmic Honor Flame,
> No longer will I play the game,
> of seeking to remain the same.

> **O Portia, opportunity,**
> **I am beyond duality.**
> **I focus now internally,**
> **with you I grow eternally.**

3. Beloved Portia, I call for the healing of all souls who embody in Croatia. I call for the return of their soul parts, for their integration so the people will be whole.

> O Portia, in the cosmic flow,
> one with you, I ever grow.
> I am the chalice here below,
> of cosmic justice you bestow.

> **O Portia, opportunity,**
> **I am beyond duality.**
> **I focus now internally,**
> **with you I grow eternally.**

4. Beloved Portia, I call for the healing of all souls who embody in Macedonia. I call for the return of their soul parts, for their integration so the people will be whole.

> O Portia, cosmic balance bring,
> eternal hope, my heart does sing.
> Protected by your Mother's wing,
> I feel at one with everything.
>
> **O Portia, opportunity,**
> **I am beyond duality.**
> **I focus now internally,**
> **with you I grow eternally.**

5. Beloved Portia, I call for the healing of all souls who embody in Montenegro. I call for the return of their soul parts, for their integration so the people will be whole.

> O Portia, bring the Mother Light,
> to set all free from darkest night.
> Your Love Flame shines forever bright,
> with Saint Germain now hold me tight.
>
> **O Portia, opportunity,**
> **I am beyond duality.**
> **I focus now internally,**
> **with you I grow eternally.**

6. Beloved Portia, I call for the healing of all souls who embody in Serbia. I call for the return of their soul parts, for their integration so the people will be whole.

O Portia, in your mastery,
I feel transforming chemistry.
In your light of reality,
I find the golden alchemy.

**O Portia, opportunity,
I am beyond duality.
I focus now internally,
with you I grow eternally.**

7. Beloved Portia, I call for the healing of all souls who embody in Slovenia. I call for the return of their soul parts, for their integration so the people will be whole.

O Portia, in the cosmic stream,
I am awake from human dream.
Removing now the ego's beam,
I earn my place on cosmic team.

**O Portia, opportunity,
I am beyond duality.
I focus now internally,
with you I grow eternally.**

8. Beloved Portia, I call for the healing of the souls of all people who embody in Albania. I call for the return of their soul parts and their integration so that the people will be whole.

O Portia, you come from afar,
you are a cosmic avatar.
So infinite your repertoire,
you are for earth a guiding star.

> O Portia, opportunity,
> I am beyond duality.
> I focus now internally,
> with you I grow eternally.

9. Beloved Portia, I call for the healing of the souls of all people who embody in the country of Greece. I call for the return of their soul parts and their integration so the people will be whole.

> O Portia, I am confident,
> I am a cosmic instrument.
> I came to earth from heaven sent,
> to help bring forward her ascent.

> O Portia, opportunity,
> I am beyond duality.
> I focus now internally,
> with you I grow eternally.

Part 6

1. Mother Liberty, I call for the healing of the souls of all people who embody in the country of Bulgaria. I call for the return of their soul parts and their integration so the people will be whole.

> O Liberty now set me free
> from devil's curse of poverty.
> I blame not Mother for my lack,
> O Blessed Mother, take me back.

**O Cosmic Mother Liberty,
conduct Abundance Symphony.
My highest service I now see,
abundance is now real for me.**

2. Mother Liberty, I call for the healing of the souls of all people who embody in the country of Romania. I call for the return of their soul parts and their reintegration so that the people will be whole.

> O Liberty, from distant shore,
> I come with longing to be More.
> I see abundance is a flow,
> abundance consciousness I grow.

**O Cosmic Mother Liberty,
conduct Abundance Symphony.
My highest service I now see,
abundance is now real for me.**

3. Mother Liberty, I call for the healing of all people who embody in the country of Turkey. I call for the return of their soul parts and their integration so that the people will be free to bring their gift to the world.

> O Liberty, expose the lie,
> that limitations can me tie.
> The Ma-ter light is not my foe,
> true opulence it does bestow.

> O Cosmic Mother Liberty,
> conduct Abundance Symphony.
> My highest service I now see,
> abundance is now real for me.

4. Mother Liberty, I call for the healing of the souls of all people who embody in Armenia. I call for the return of their soul parts and their reintegration so that the people will be whole.

> O Liberty, expose the plot,
> projected by the fallen lot.
> O Cosmic Mother, I now see,
> that Mother's not my enemy.

> O Cosmic Mother Liberty,
> conduct Abundance Symphony.
> My highest service I now see,
> abundance is now real for me.

5. Mother Liberty, I call for the healing of the souls of all people who embody in Georgia. I call for the return of their soul parts and their reintegration so that the people will be whole.

> O Liberty, with opened eyes,
> I now reject the devil's lies.
> I now embrace the Mother realm,
> for I see Father at the helm.

> O Cosmic Mother Liberty,
> conduct Abundance Symphony.
> My highest service I now see,
> abundance is now real for me.

6. Mother Liberty, I call for the healing of the souls of all people who embody in Moldova. I call for the return of their soul parts and their reintegration so that the people will be whole.

> O Liberty, a chalice pure,
> my lower bodies are for sure.
> Release through me your symphony,
> your gift of Cosmic Liberty.
>
> **O Cosmic Mother Liberty,**
> **conduct Abundance Symphony.**
> **My highest service I now see,**
> **abundance is now real for me.**

7. Mother Liberty, I call for the healing of the people, of the souls of all people, who embody in Ukraine. I call for the return of their soul parts and their reintegration so the people will be whole.

> O Liberty, the open door,
> I am for Symphony of More.
> In chakras mine light you release,
> the flow of love shall never cease.
>
> **O Cosmic Mother Liberty,**
> **conduct Abundance Symphony.**
> **My highest service I now see,**
> **abundance is now real for me.**

8. Mother Liberty, I call for the healing of the souls of all people who embody in Ukraine. I call for the return of their soul parts and their integration so that the people will be free to bring their gift to the world.

O Liberty, release the flow,
of opulence that you bestow.
For I am willing to receive,
the Golden Fleece that you now weave.

**O Cosmic Mother Liberty,
conduct Abundance Symphony.
My highest service I now see,
abundance is now real for me.**

9. Mother Liberty, I call for the healing of the souls of all people who embody in Ukraine. I call for the return of their soul parts and their integration so that the people will be free to bring their gift to the world.

O Liberty, release the cure,
to free the tired and the poor.
The huddled masses are set free,
by loving Song of Liberty.

**O Cosmic Mother Liberty,
conduct Abundance Symphony.
My highest service I now see,
abundance is now real for me.**

Part 7

1. Beloved Venus, I call for the healing of all mothers on the European continent who have seen their sons and husbands and fathers be killed in war. I call for the return of their soul parts, for their integration so that the people will be whole and will be free to bring their gift of motherhood to the European continent.

> O Venus, show me how to serve,
> your cosmic beauty I observe.
> What love from Venus you now bring,
> our planets do in tandem sing.
>
> **O Venus, service so divine,**
> **you are for earth a cosmic sign.**
> **Your selfless service is now mine,**
> **a life in service I define.**

2. Beloved Venus, I call for the healing of the souls of all fathers on the European continent who have seen their sons go off to war and be killed. I call for the return of their soul parts and their integration so that they will be able to bring their gift of the Alpha Flame of Fatherhood to this continent.

> O Venus, your love is the key,
> the hardened hearts on earth are free.
> Embracing future bright and bold,
> our planet's story is retold.

19 | Healing people's past traumas

**O Venus, service so divine,
you are for earth a cosmic sign.
Your selfless service is now mine,
a life in service I define.**

3. Beloved Venus, I call for the healing of the souls of all sons on the European continent who have been taken from their families and killed on the battlefields of Europe. I call for the return of their soul parts, their integration so that the people will be whole and be able to hold that Flame of the Divine Son for this continent.

O Venus, loving Mother mine,
my heart your love does now refine.
I am the open door for love,
descending like a Holy Dove.

**O Venus, service so divine,
you are for earth a cosmic sign.
Your selfless service is now mine,
a life in service I define.**

4. Beloved Venus, I call for the healing of all daughters on the European continent who have seen their brothers and fathers and sons be killed in war, who have seen their homes destroyed, their cities laid waste. I call for the return of their soul parts and their integration so that they will be free to hold that Flame of the Divine Feminine for this continent.

O Venus, play the secret note,
that is for hatred antidote.
All poisoned hearts you gently heal,
as love's true story you reveal.

> **O Venus, service so divine,**
> **you are for earth a cosmic sign.**
> **Your selfless service is now mine,**
> **a life in service I define.**

5. Beloved Venus, I call for the healing of all children on the European continent, those who have in past lives been killed by war or other atrocities in their childhood, without receiving the opportunity to grow into adulthood, and who thus carry scars in their souls. I call for the return of their soul parts and their integration so that they will be free to be the Divine Child in embodiment and to have that innocence of the childlike mind returned to them.

> O Venus, love fills every need,
> for truly, love is God's first seed.
> O let it blossom, let it grow,
> sweep earth into your loving flow.

> **O Venus, service so divine,**
> **you are for earth a cosmic sign.**
> **Your selfless service is now mine,**
> **a life in service I define.**

6. Beloved Venus, I call for the healing of all of the gnomes in the physical elemental kingdom over the European continent. I call for them to be healed, to be freed of their burdens that they may be able to fulfill their task of service to human beings.

> O Venus, music of the spheres,
> heard by those who God reveres.
> Our voices now as one we raise,
> singing in adoring praise.

**O Venus, service so divine,
you are for earth a cosmic sign.
Your selfless service is now mine,
a life in service I define.**

7. Beloved Venus, I call for the healing of all of the undines of the water element over Europe, that they may be healed and be whole and be free to give their service to human beings.

O Venus, we are joining ranks,
Sanat Kumara we give thanks.
Our planet has received new life,
to lift her out of war and strife.

**O Venus, service so divine,
you are for earth a cosmic sign.
Your selfless service is now mine,
a life in service I define.**

8. Beloved Venus, I call for the healing of the sylphs of the air over the European continent. I call for them to be whole, that they may be able to give service to humankind.

O Venus, your sweet melody,
consumes veil of duality.
Absorbed in tones of Cosmic Love,
all conflict we now rise above.

**O Venus, service so divine,
you are for earth a cosmic sign.
Your selfless service is now mine,
a life in service I define.**

9. Beloved Venus, I call for the healing of the fiery salamanders of the identity realm over the European continent. I call for them to be whole, that they may be able to fulfill their highest service to mankind.

> O Venus, shining Morning Star,
> a cosmic herald, that you are.
> The earth set free by sacred sound,
> our planet is now heaven-bound.
>
> **O Venus, service so divine,**
> **you are for earth a cosmic sign.**
> **Your selfless service is now mine,**
> **a life in service I define.**

Part 8

1. Beloved Omega, I call forth the manifestation of your Presence in the physical, releasing infinite quantities of healing water over the European continent. This water is charged with the highest possible vibration of the emotional octave, healing the emotional bodies of all people on earth. This water falls like a gentle rain, and when it reaches the emotional bodies of the people in embodiment in Europe, it gently washes away all of the misqualified energies.

> Omega, I now meditate,
> upon your throne in cosmic gate.
> I'm born out of the figure-eight,
> that Alpha and you co-create.

**O Song of Life, you vitalize,
all hearts you truly synchronize.
O Sacred Sound, you alchemize,
turn earth into a paradise.**

2. Beloved Omega, these energies are washed out of the emotional body onto the ground, where they keep running towards the lowest point. They gather in the rivers of Europe. They flow through those rivers. They are carried towards the sea, and there the angels of all of the Chohans, all of the Archangels, all of the Elohim of the seven rays are waiting to consume and transform those energies.

Omega, in your sacred space,
my cosmic parents I embrace.
I see that it is such a grace,
that I take part in cosmic race.

**O Song of Life, you vitalize,
all hearts you truly synchronize.
O Sacred Sound, you alchemize,
turn earth into a paradise.**

3. Beloved Omega, I call for you to release the healing air currents over the European continent. This gentle wind of the Holy Spirit blows through the mental bodies of the people in embodiment in Europe. It gently dislodges and blows away all of the imperfect thoughts and ideas inserted into people's mental bodies.

Omega in the Central Sun,
you show me life is cosmic fun.
And thus a victory is won,
my homeward journey has begun.

**O Song of Life, you vitalize,
all hearts you truly synchronize.
O Sacred Sound, you alchemize,
turn earth into a paradise.**

4. Beloved Omega, your healing wind gathers them like dust, carries them up higher, carries them beyond the clouds. And there, the angels of the Chohans, the Archangels and the Elohim are waiting to consume and transform these energies, so that the people may be free to receive the ideas from the ascended masters in their mental bodies.

Omega, femininity
is doorway to infinity.
With you I have affinity,
to know my own divinity.

**O Song of Life, you vitalize,
all hearts you truly synchronize.
O Sacred Sound, you alchemize,
turn earth into a paradise.**

5. Beloved Omega, I call forth the Divine Mother in physical manifestation to release the fire of the identity realm over the European continent. This fire enters the identity bodies of all people in embodiment. It forms a mighty, hot wind that blows away the false sense of identity, blows it out of the identity bodies, carries it upwards. As it comes closer and closer to the physical sun, it is met by the light of the angels of the Chohans, the Archangels and the Elohim. Thus, it is consumed before it even reaches the physical sun.

> Omega, in your cosmic flow,
> my plan divine I clearly know.
> My heart is now a lamp aglow,
> as love on all I do bestow.
>
> **O Song of Life, you vitalize,**
> **all hearts you truly synchronize.**
> **O Sacred Sound, you alchemize,**
> **turn earth into a paradise.**

6. Beloved Omega, I am visualizing the European continent being covered by a gentle snowfall of white crystals. They fall gently like the snow falling on the first days of autumn. They fall through the identity octave, through the mental realm, through the emotional realm and then they manifest physically.

> Omega, cosmic Mother Flame,
> this is the light from which I came.
> As I take part in cosmic game,
> Christ victory I do proclaim.

**O Song of Life, you vitalize,
all hearts you truly synchronize.
O Sacred Sound, you alchemize,
turn earth into a paradise.**

7. Beloved Omega, I visualize the white crystals falling as white, perfect, symmetrical crystals that carry with them the white light of the Divine Mother. They fall onto the ground, they cover the ground, and then they are absorbed into the ground where they go below the surface. They go through deeper and deeper layers of the earth, and as they go, they consume the records of all the blood that has soaked into the ground on this continent throughout the ages beyond known history.

Omega, I now comprehend,
why I did to earth descend.
And thus I fully do intend,
to help this planet to ascend.

**O Song of Life, you vitalize,
all hearts you truly synchronize.
O Sacred Sound, you alchemize,
turn earth into a paradise.**

8. Beloved Omega, I visualize the crystals carry all of these records with them as they come closer to the center of the earth. There they are consumed finally and fully by the angels of the Chohans, the Archangels and the Elohim.

Omega, I do now aspire,
to join the ranks of cosmic choir.
My heart burns with a Christic fire,
that is this planet's sanctifier.

**O Song of Life, you vitalize,
all hearts you truly synchronize.
O Sacred Sound, you alchemize,
turn earth into a paradise.**

9. Beloved Omega, I visualize the crystals begin to rise back up towards the surface where they remain in the upper layers of the soil over Europe. Every country is covered in them, and they will remain there as the receivers and transmitters of the purifying white light of the Divine Mother.

Omega, my heart is ablaze,
my life is in an upward phase.
Come teach me now the secret phrase,
so that I can this planet raise.

**O Song of Life, you vitalize,
all hearts you truly synchronize.
O Sacred Sound, you alchemize,
turn earth into a paradise.**

Part 9

1. Mother Mary, I now fully accept this clearing action as a manifest reality.

O blessed Mary, Mother mine,
there is no greater love than thine,
as we are one in heart and mind,
my place in hierarchy I find.

**O Mother Mary, generate,
the song that does accelerate,
the earth into a higher state,
all matter does now scintillate.**

2. Mother Mary, I accept it as a manifest reality in the identity realm and I visualize the entire European continent with the identity realm above it.

I came to earth from heaven sent,
as I am in embodiment,
I use Divine authority,
commanding you to set earth free.

**O Mother Mary, generate,
the song that does accelerate,
the earth into a higher state,
all matter does now scintillate.**

3. Mother Mary, I accept this clearance as a manifest reality in the mental realm over the European continent.

I call now in God's sacred name,
for you to use your Mother Flame,
to burn all fear-based energy,
restoring sacred harmony.

**O Mother Mary, generate,
the song that does accelerate,
the earth into a higher state,
all matter does now scintillate.**

4. Mother Mary, I accept the clearance in the emotional body of the European continent.

> Your sacred name I hereby praise,
> collective consciousness you raise,
> no more of fear and doubt and shame,
> consume it with your Mother Flame.
>
> **O Mother Mary, generate,**
> **the song that does accelerate,**
> **the earth into a higher state,**
> **all matter does now scintillate.**

5. Mother Mary, I accept the clearance at the physical level over the European continent.

> All darkness from the earth you purge,
> your light moves as a mighty surge,
> no force of darkness can now stop,
> the spiral that goes only up.
>
> **O Mother Mary, generate,**
> **the song that does accelerate,**
> **the earth into a higher state,**
> **all matter does now scintillate.**

6. Mother Mary, I center in my heart and I sense with my inner knowing that this clearance is real, that it is manifest, and that Europe will never be the same. I accept this.

All elemental life you bless,
removing from them man-made stress,
the nature spirits are now free,
outpicturing Divine decree.

**O Mother Mary, generate,
the song that does accelerate,
the earth into a higher state,
all matter does now scintillate.**

7. Mother Mary, I am willing to be the open door for the figure-eight flow from above to below.

I raise my voice and take my stand,
a stop to war I do command,
no more shall warring scar the earth,
a golden age is given birth.

**O Mother Mary, generate,
the song that does accelerate,
the earth into a higher state,
all matter does now scintillate.**

8. Mother Mary, I am willing to be the open door for the figure-eight flow from you Above to me below, from the Alpha to the Omega.

As Mother Earth is free at last,
disasters belong to the past,
your Mother Light is so intense,
that matter is now far less dense.

**O Mother Mary, generate,
the song that does accelerate,
the earth into a higher state,
all matter does now scintillate.**

9. Mother Mary, I am willing to be the open door for the figure-eight flow back to the Alpha, so that the figure-eight flow is closed from me, and you can multiply it and send even more.

In Mother Light the earth is pure,
the upward spiral will endure,
prosperity is now the norm,
God's vision manifest as form.

**O Mother Mary, generate,
the song that does accelerate,
the earth into a higher state,
all matter does now scintillate.**

Sealing

In the name of the Divine Mother, I call to Maraytaii, Nada, Kuan Yin and Mother Mary for the sealing of myself and all people in my circle of influence in the creative flow of the Divine Mother, the River of Life. I call for the multiplication of my calls by all representatives of the Divine Mother, so that we form the perfect figure-eight flow of "As Above, so below." Thus, I accept that this is fully manifest, because the mouth of the Lord, the Divine Mother that I AM, has spoken it. Amen.

20 | HEALING PEOPLE FROM HATRED OF THE MOTHER

In the name I AM THAT I AM, Jesus Christ, I call to all representatives of the Divine Mother, especially Mother Mary to heal people from all hatred of the Mother realm. Help people see the lies and wounds that prevent them from accepting the love of the Divine Mother and feeling love for the material realm, including…

[Make personal calls.]

Part 1

1. Mother Mary, life is a wonderful gift.

   O Blessed Mary's Song of Life,
   consuming every form of strife.
   As I attune to sound so fair,
   each cell is healthy, I declare.

> **O Mother Mary, generate,**
> **the song that does accelerate,**
> **my mind into a peaceful state,**
> **God's perfect love I radiate.**

2. Mother Mary, I call for the healing of the many millions of people who cannot accept this statement.

> As life's own song I ever hear,
> it does consume all sense of fear.
> In tune with Mother's symphony,
> from all diseases I AM free.

> **O Mother Mary, generate,**
> **the song that does accelerate,**
> **my mind into a peaceful state,**
> **God's perfect love I radiate.**

3. Mother Mary, I call for the healing of the many millions of people who have such burdens, such scars in their souls, in their four lower bodies, that if they were to hear this statement spoken, they would rebel against it. They would say you are unreal, that this is all fantasy.

> In Mother's love I do transcend,
> and all my struggles hereby end.
> For when with Mother's eye I see,
> no imperfection touches me.

> **O Mother Mary, generate,**
> **the song that does accelerate,**
> **my mind into a peaceful state,**
> **God's perfect love I radiate.**

4. Mother Mary, I call for the healing of the many millions of people whose wounds are so intense that they cannot acknowledge the existence of the Divine Mother.

> I see that healing must begin
> by finding Living Christ within.
> For as I see with single eye,
> each cell the light does amplify.
>
> **O Mother Mary, generate,**
> **the song that does accelerate,**
> **my mind into a peaceful state,**
> **God's perfect love I radiate.**

5. Mother Mary, I call for the healing of the many millions of people who have received a wound in the soul through a traumatic event, but who also have the overlay – the emotional, mental and identity realm overlay – that if the Divine Mother was real, she would have prevented this from happening.

> In Mother's music I am free,
> from memories of a lesser me.
> My vision in a perfect state,
> that all my cells regenerate.
>
> **O Mother Mary, generate,**
> **the song that does accelerate,**
> **my mind into a peaceful state,**
> **God's perfect love I radiate.**

6. Mother Mary, I call for the healing of the many millions of people who feel that they have been so hurt by the matter realm, by the Mother realm, that they will not even accept the concept that there is a Divine Mother. For they feel that she should have protected them from these wounds, these traumas.

> O Mother's Love, sweet melody,
> from imperfections I AM free.
> O Mother Mary, sound of sounds,
> within my heart your love abounds.
>
> **O Mother Mary, generate,**
> **the song that does accelerate,**
> **my mind into a peaceful state,**
> **God's perfect love I radiate.**

7. Mother Mary, I call for the healing of the many millions of people who are affected by the condition called hatred of the Mother.

> Through Mother's beauty so sublime,
> transcending bounds of space and time.
> All cells beyond the mortal tomb,
> as they are whole in Mother's womb.
>
> **O Mother Mary, generate,**
> **the song that does accelerate,**
> **my mind into a peaceful state,**
> **God's perfect love I radiate.**

8. Mother Mary, I call for you to help people see that hatred of the Mother originated with the fallen beings who rebelled against the Mother realm. But it has been so contagious that it has spread to the people, even those of the original inhabitants of the earth, and even those who have come here on a rescue mission.

> In resonance with life's own song,
> in life's harmonics I belong.
> The blueprint of my perfect state
> does every cell reconsecrate.
>
> **O Mother Mary, generate,**
> **the song that does accelerate,**
> **my mind into a peaceful state,**
> **God's perfect love I radiate.**

9. Mother Mary, I call for the healing of the many millions of people who feel that their wounds are so deep, so painful, so intense, that they cannot possibly accept that there should be a benevolent being representing the Divine Mother. Why would the Mother not step in and protect them and their children from these calamities?

> The tuning fork in every cell
> is now attuned to Mother's bell.
> From curse of death I AM now free,
> I claim my immortality.
>
> **O Mother Mary, generate,**
> **the song that does accelerate,**
> **my mind into a peaceful state,**
> **God's perfect love I radiate.**

Part 2

1. Mother Mary, help people receive the answers and teachings that will help them understand this and understand how the law of free will works.

> O Blessed Mary's Song of Life,
> consuming every form of strife.
> As I attune to sound so fair,
> each cell is healthy, I declare.
>
> **O Mother Mary, generate,**
> **the song that does accelerate,**
> **my mind into a peaceful state,**
> **God's perfect love I radiate.**

2. Mother Mary, help people open themselves to the wisdom of the Divine Mother that can help them, in their own minds, resolve this dilemma, this paradox, this unanswered question.

> As life's own song I ever hear,
> it does consume all sense of fear.
> In tune with Mother's symphony,
> from all diseases I AM free.
>
> **O Mother Mary, generate,**
> **the song that does accelerate,**
> **my mind into a peaceful state,**
> **God's perfect love I radiate.**

3. Mother Mary, help people who have been so wounded to be able to receive some portion of the wisdom of the Divine Mother.

> In Mother's love I do transcend,
> and all my struggles hereby end.
> For when with Mother's eye I see,
> no imperfection touches me.
>
> **O Mother Mary, generate,**
> **the song that does accelerate,**
> **my mind into a peaceful state,**
> **God's perfect love I radiate.**

4. Mother Mary, help people see that they have a misconception of what the Mother is and what the role of the Mother is.

> I see that healing must begin
> by finding Living Christ within.
> For as I see with single eye,
> each cell the light does amplify.
>
> **O Mother Mary, generate,**
> **the song that does accelerate,**
> **my mind into a peaceful state,**
> **God's perfect love I radiate.**

5. Mother Mary, help people see that the role of the Mother is to protect, to heal, to guide, but never to force.

In Mother's music I am free,
from memories of a lesser me.
My vision in a perfect state,
that all my cells regenerate.

**O Mother Mary, generate,
the song that does accelerate,
my mind into a peaceful state,
God's perfect love I radiate.**

6. Mother Mary, help people see that the trauma they have experienced has come through force, but that force has not come from the Divine Mother.

O Mother's Love, sweet melody,
from imperfections I AM free.
O Mother Mary, sound of sounds,
within my heart your love abounds.

**O Mother Mary, generate,
the song that does accelerate,
my mind into a peaceful state,
God's perfect love I radiate.**

7. Mother Mary, help people see that force is not a feature of the Mother, and therefore it cannot be stopped by the Mother, for the free will of both the fallen beings and the original inhabitants of the earth must be allowed to outplay itself.

Through Mother's beauty so sublime,
transcending bounds of space and time.
All cells beyond the mortal tomb,
as they are whole in Mother's womb.

20 | Healing people from hatred of the Mother

**O Mother Mary, generate,
the song that does accelerate,
my mind into a peaceful state,
God's perfect love I radiate.**

8. Mother Mary, help people see that the Mother can only reflect back what people are sending out.

In resonance with life's own song,
in life's harmonics I belong.
The blueprint of my perfect state
does every cell reconsecrate.

**O Mother Mary, generate,
the song that does accelerate,
my mind into a peaceful state,
God's perfect love I radiate.**

9. Mother Mary, help people see that when they are not open to the wisdom of the Mother that they can receive from within, or even from those who have been able to tune in throughout the ages, they can only learn through the School of Hard Knocks.

The tuning fork in every cell
is now attuned to Mother's bell.
From curse of death I AM now free,
I claim my immortality.

**O Mother Mary, generate,
the song that does accelerate,
my mind into a peaceful state,
God's perfect love I radiate.**

Part 3

1. Mother Mary, help people accept that the Divine Mother loves everyone.

> O Blessed Mary's Song of Life,
> consuming every form of strife.
> As I attune to sound so fair,
> each cell is healthy, I declare.
>
> **O Mother Mary, generate,**
> **the song that does accelerate,**
> **my mind into a peaceful state,**
> **God's perfect love I radiate.**

2. Mother Mary, help people understand this, so they will not reject your love.

> As life's own song I ever hear,
> it does consume all sense of fear.
> In tune with Mother's symphony,
> from all diseases I AM free.
>
> **O Mother Mary, generate,**
> **the song that does accelerate,**
> **my mind into a peaceful state,**
> **God's perfect love I radiate.**

3. Mother Mary, help people experience your love for them and accept that your love cannot prevent the outplaying of free will.

20 | Healing people from hatred of the Mother

In Mother's love I do transcend,
and all my struggles hereby end.
For when with Mother's eye I see,
no imperfection touches me.

**O Mother Mary, generate,
the song that does accelerate,
my mind into a peaceful state,
God's perfect love I radiate.**

4. Mother Mary, help people experience that your love can indeed heal each and every wound we have received through the outplaying of free will – both that of ourselves and the other inhabitants on this planet.

I see that healing must begin
by finding Living Christ within.
For as I see with single eye,
each cell the light does amplify.

**O Mother Mary, generate,
the song that does accelerate,
my mind into a peaceful state,
God's perfect love I radiate.**

5. Mother Mary, help people experience that there is no hurt, no wound, no scar, that the love of the Divine Mother cannot heal.

In Mother's music I am free,
from memories of a lesser me.
My vision in a perfect state,
that all my cells regenerate.

**O Mother Mary, generate,
the song that does accelerate,
my mind into a peaceful state,
God's perfect love I radiate.**

6. Mother Mary, help people realize that it is not a matter of looking to the past and regretting what happened.

O Mother's Love, sweet melody,
from imperfections I AM free.
O Mother Mary, sound of sounds,
within my heart your love abounds.

**O Mother Mary, generate,
the song that does accelerate,
my mind into a peaceful state,
God's perfect love I radiate.**

7. Mother Mary, help people realize that it is a matter of accepting that what happened has happened as an outplaying of free will, as an outplaying, a manifestation, of a certain state of consciousness.

Through Mother's beauty so sublime,
transcending bounds of space and time.
All cells beyond the mortal tomb,
as they are whole in Mother's womb.

**O Mother Mary, generate,
the song that does accelerate,
my mind into a peaceful state,
God's perfect love I radiate.**

8. Mother Mary, help people accept that what happened has happened, and it is over with, at least in that manifestation of it.

> In resonance with life's own song,
> in life's harmonics I belong.
> The blueprint of my perfect state
> does every cell reconsecrate.
>
> **O Mother Mary, generate,**
> **the song that does accelerate,**
> **my mind into a peaceful state,**
> **God's perfect love I radiate.**

9. Mother Mary, help people accept that when we do not seek to recreate the past and to undo what cannot be undone, in our acceptance that this happened, we can look at the fact that it can continue to affect us only when we hold on to it.

> The tuning fork in every cell
> is now attuned to Mother's bell.
> From curse of death I AM now free,
> I claim my immortality.
>
> **O Mother Mary, generate,**
> **the song that does accelerate,**
> **my mind into a peaceful state,**
> **God's perfect love I radiate.**

Part 4

1. Mother Mary, help people realize that the only path to freedom from the past is to forgive, to forgive all, to forgive unconditionally, because in forgiving we are releasing.

> O Blessed Mary's Song of Life,
> consuming every form of strife.
> As I attune to sound so fair,
> each cell is healthy, I declare.
>
> **O Mother Mary, generate,**
> **the song that does accelerate,**
> **my mind into a peaceful state,**
> **God's perfect love I radiate.**

2. Mother Mary, help people accept that when we are releasing the matrices in our mind that we are holding on to, then we open ourselves up for the love of the Divine Mother.

> As life's own song I ever hear,
> it does consume all sense of fear.
> In tune with Mother's symphony,
> from all diseases I AM free.
>
> **O Mother Mary, generate,**
> **the song that does accelerate,**
> **my mind into a peaceful state,**
> **God's perfect love I radiate.**

3. Mother Mary, help people rise above the illusion of the fallen beings that when we have been healed, then we can forgive and let go. Help people accept that the consciousness must come before the physical manifestation. We must be willing to forgive and let go, and then we are healed.

> In Mother's love I do transcend,
> and all my struggles hereby end.
> For when with Mother's eye I see,
> no imperfection touches me.
>
> **O Mother Mary, generate,**
> **the song that does accelerate,**
> **my mind into a peaceful state,**
> **God's perfect love I radiate.**

4. Mother Mary, I now visualize an image of the Divine Mother with a physical heart visible and a dagger sticking through it, and I visualize that you are reaching your hand down, grabbing the handle of this dagger, and pulling it out of the heart of the Divine Mother, the Divine Feminine.

> I see that healing must begin
> by finding Living Christ within.
> For as I see with single eye,
> each cell the light does amplify.
>
> **O Mother Mary, generate,**
> **the song that does accelerate,**
> **my mind into a peaceful state,**
> **God's perfect love I radiate.**

5. Mother Mary, I visualize and accept that you are pulling the dagger out of the heart of all people in embodiment who have been hurt by these traumas.

> In Mother's music I am free,
> from memories of a lesser me.
> My vision in a perfect state,
> that all my cells regenerate.
>
> **O Mother Mary, generate,**
> **the song that does accelerate,**
> **my mind into a peaceful state,**
> **God's perfect love I radiate.**

6. Mother Mary, I visualize and accept that you take this dagger, and you throw it into the fire of the Divine Mother where it is instantly consumed.

> O Mother's Love, sweet melody,
> from imperfections I AM free.
> O Mother Mary, sound of sounds,
> within my heart your love abounds.
>
> **O Mother Mary, generate,**
> **the song that does accelerate,**
> **my mind into a peaceful state,**
> **God's perfect love I radiate.**

7. Mother Mary, I accept that the Divine Mother over the [European] continent is healed. Her heart is whole.

Through Mother's beauty so sublime,
transcending bounds of space and time.
All cells beyond the mortal tomb,
as they are whole in Mother's womb.

**O Mother Mary, generate,
the song that does accelerate,
my mind into a peaceful state,
God's perfect love I radiate.**

8. Mother Mary, I visualize that the hearts of all people are whole, that they are no more pierced, that they are no more divided. There is the wholeness of heart that opens up the rose of the heart chakra to receive the unconditional love of the Divine Mother.

In resonance with life's own song,
in life's harmonics I belong.
The blueprint of my perfect state
does every cell reconsecrate.

**O Mother Mary, generate,
the song that does accelerate,
my mind into a peaceful state,
God's perfect love I radiate.**

9. Mother Mary, I breathe out the healing energy of the Divine Mother. I am willing to serve as the physical anchor for the release of this healing action.

The tuning fork in every cell
is now attuned to Mother's bell.
From curse of death I AM now free,
I claim my immortality.

**O Mother Mary, generate,
the song that does accelerate,
my mind into a peaceful state,
God's perfect love I radiate.**

Sealing

In the name of the Divine Mother, I call to Mother Mary for the sealing of myself and all people in my circle of influence in the creative flow of the Divine Mother, the River of Life. I call for the multiplication of my calls by all representatives of the Divine Mother, so that we form the perfect figure-eight flow of "As Above, so below." Thus, I accept that this is fully manifest, because the mouth of the Lord, the Divine Mother that I AM, has spoken it. Amen.

21 | A BUDDHIC PERSPECTIVE ON OVERCOMING THE PAST

The Buddha I AM. The Ascended Master Gautama Buddha I AM. I come for multiple purposes this day. I come, first of all, to give an action to the European continent to multiply what you have brought to the altar during this conference. Because you have exceeded the potential for the conference, I am able to step in and bring forth the judgment of the Buddha of certain fallen beings that we had not planned could be removed at this time. Because of your willingness to step up and transcend the consciousness embodied by these fallen beings, it has been possible for me, as the Lord of the World, to step in and say that these beings shall now be removed from the four levels of matter over the European continent.

This requires, as we have said, that there are those who have reached a certain level of consciousness comparable to that which the fallen beings had attained before they fell. There are some of you who have attained this, and there are others on the European continent, some not affiliated with this movement, who have attained a sufficient level that this can be done. Yet it still requires the intercession of the Lord of the World to make this a manifest reality. This is not a mechanical consequence of what people have done. It is a gift that I have decided to give, based on the purity of the intention and the hearts of yourselves and many other people in embodiment in Europe.

The paradox of buddhic awareness

You will often think of the Buddha as sitting, as you see the messenger sitting, in a cross-legged position with closed eyes and a slight smile, seeming detached from the world. This is an image I have given in order to help people at a certain phase of the spiritual path extricate themselves from the intense struggle created by the fallen beings. The fallen beings and the dark forces have, of course, attempted to pull people into this struggle and to keep them there indefinitely. It was necessary to bring forth ideas and thoughtforms that could help people attain that non-attachment to the demons of Mara, so they would not be tempted into a reactionary pattern.

Nevertheless I want you to know that as the Ascended Master Gautama Buddha, I hold a spiritual office for the earth, the office of the Lord of the World. As a result of this office, I am perfectly aware of everything that is happening on earth. I know the suffering of all people in embodiment. I feel the compassion and the love for them, for I know also that they are extensions of the One Mind, that the Buddha nature is in them. I am, of course, still in the ascended state of consciousness and therefore not attached to people's experiences, but I do experience what people experience. This is part of my office. You might look at it as a burden, and it *would* be a burden from the unascended state of consciousness, but it is not a burden from the ascended state of consciousness. This I would discourse on, because it is almost impossible when you are in embodiment to resolve this seeming paradox. How can the Buddha experience what people on earth experience and not be burdened by it? You yourselves can cultivate this ability, not quite to the same degree as when you are ascended, but you can cultivate it. It is a matter, as we have touched upon earlier, of realizing that everything that happens in the matter realm is like a movie projected onto a screen. It is a matter of realizing what science, to some degree, has attempted to achieve: that it is possible to look at what happens on earth in an objective or detached manner where you do not judge. You simply see what is, without applying a value judgment of should this or should this not happen.

Now again, I know that this instantly engenders a reaction from the collective consciousness, because it will say: "Are you then saying that everything that is happening is okay? That there are not things happening on earth that should not be happening? Can you really say that the Holocaust is just an event like any other event? Are you saying that it doesn't matter whether it happened or did not happen?"

Do you see? This reaction comes from the consciousness that is attached and therefore pulls you into the reactionary pattern where the fallen beings want to keep you indefinitely. An event on earth is just an event. There is, as we have touched upon before, a fundamental difference between the event and your perception of it.

There are people who believe that, before they themselves can be free of the earth, certain changes need to happen on earth. Certain manifestations cannot be here, or they cannot be at peace, or they cannot be free. You will not ascend from earth until you free yourself from this pull. You who are in embodiment today should not count on waiting until the earth is in some perfect state before you ascend. For the foreseeable future there will be many imperfections on earth so unless you want to postpone your ascension for a very long time, you need to realize that you will have to ascend even though the earth is not in a perfect state.

The difference between event and perception

How do you ascend when there is imperfection in the physical octave? You do so by recognizing the difference between the event and your perception of it, and then taking command over your perception. From my office of the Lord of the World, I see an event from the outside and the inside at the same time. I am experiencing what the people involved with this event are experiencing, how they are reacting to it. I am also seeing the event from the outside, from the objective, detached perspective. I see what most people do not see, namely that no matter how the event takes form, and no matter what meaning people project onto it, no matter how they react emotionally, mentally, and at the identity level, it is all part of the forward movement of life.

This does not mean that an event such as the Holocaust had to happen. It does not mean that the ascended masters wanted it to happen. It does not mean that I am saying this was a beneficial event. It was obviously an event that created deep wounds in the souls of many people, and those wounds are keeping them trapped in the reactionary pattern.

It is still part of the forward progression of life, in the sense that those who will not learn directly from the ascended masters must learn by seeing the Mother realm outpicture as physical events their state of consciousness. Even though the actual events can be absolutely horrible to experience, it is the only way that people learn when they are not open to learning from Above. When you are not open to learning from the Father element that we of the ascended masters represent to earth, you must learn from the Mother element. Therefore, the most horrible event on earth is an outpicturing in matter of a very horrible, unbalanced state of consciousness.

By having it outpictured in matter, it becomes far more difficult for people to ignore or deny it, as they had been ignoring or denying that state of consciousness for a very long time before the physical event had been carried through the three higher levels and crossed into the material realm. I see that whatever happens is, in a sense, necessary. Since the people were not able to reach a higher form of learning, it was necessary for their liberation that they saw the physical outpicturing of the consciousness behind it.

I also, as the Lord of the World, have no attachment and pass no judgment on which path an individual or even a group of people, even humankind as a whole, should or should not follow towards their liberation from matter. How can I pass such judgment when I respect free will, and when I have taken the vow that I will hold space for the lifestreams on earth, and thereby make it possible for them to outpicture any state of consciousness as a physical reality?

How the masters respect free will

Do you understand that the earth is not a high planet? There are many higher planets where the wars and the torture that you see on earth could not be physically manifest. Matter itself on those planets has been raised to such a level that it could not even take on these forms that you see on earth. The elementals would refuse to manifest such forms. On earth it is possible for such forms to manifest. Why is this possible? Because we of the ascended masters give many opportunities to the beings who have become trapped in duality.

After I made my ascension from this earth, I could have moved on. I could have said: "Enough with this earth. I do not want to be associated with this planet anymore." Or I could have said: "Enough with a certain manifestation of darkness on earth. I will not allow this anymore." But what would that have meant? It would have meant that a large number of lifestreams would have had to be removed. This would have made it more difficult for them to grow because the earth is at a certain level where it provides an opportunity to grow for a large number of lifestreams who are in a sort of in-between state. I decided after my ascension to accept the Office of the Lord of the World and set a certain level that would allow the largest number of lifestreams to receive an opportunity to grow in the schoolroom of earth.

This could have been done in many other ways, but for a number of complex reasons, as a result of a complex calculation on my part, I set a certain level. Therefore, I have held the balance, so to speak, that has made it possible for some of these very dark events and manifestations to take place. You may think this is not spiritual, not enlightened, not what the Buddha should be doing, but then you are looking at the Buddha not with the mind of the Buddha, but with the mind of the anti-Buddha. I am a teacher. If you will not listen to me directly, I could choose to reject you as a student, or I could do what I have decided to do—hold the balance, hold the space, that will allow you to outpicture your state of consciousness to a terrifying degree. This was my decision to make.

Raising the consciousness of Europe

It is my decision to adjust, based on the growth of the people in embodiment. As I said in the beginning, I have decided to make an adjustment whereby the level of the lowest possible consciousness in the European continent has been raised higher by several degrees. We have talked about the 144 levels of consciousness, and we have said that as humankind progresses, this level will be raised higher. For the European continent the level has been raised so that it is no longer possible for lifestreams below a certain level of consciousness to embody here. This is not yet a planetary phenomenon. It may become so in the years to come. We shall see what can be accomplished in the United States this summer. It is, my beloved, a significant victory for the European continent. It is a significant shift.

You cannot overestimate the importance of raising the level of consciousness. It is, however, necessary for you who are the spiritual people to continue doing the work. Even though a certain group of fallen beings can be removed, they have left traces of themselves in the physical, the emotional, the mental and the identity realms. These traces are in people's consciousness.

You understand that what has happened today is that I have raised the level so that beings in the state of consciousness that precipitated the Nazi death camps can no longer embody on earth. Auschwitz is not possible today. Yet the many people who were hurt directly by the concentration camps, and the many people who have been hurt indirectly by knowing about these events, are still holding on to and feeding a certain matrix in the three higher bodies. As you can see, there is a museum in the physical of Auschwitz and other concentration camps, and there is a parallel in the three higher bodies.

Although it would not be possible to manifest the death camps today, this does not mean that the earth is free from the records of them. There is certainly a need to make the calls for the records to be consumed, for the energies to be transformed. There is also a need for forgiveness because, as we have said, people will not be free until they forgive and let it go.

Compassion at the buddhic level

We have given you teachings about how you create spirits through your consciousness. You understand that today a certain group of fallen beings have been removed. Those fallen beings are not on earth anymore in any of the four octaves. But the spirits that people have created because of the events precipitated by these fallen beings are still there and are still alive, in the sense that they have the power to steal energy from people.

What I am asking you to consider as mature spiritual students is to strive to cultivate the consciousness I have described. Now, many of you are in embodiment on earth because you have to some degree fulfilled that Bodhisattva ideal where you hear the cries of the world, and you feel compassion, and you do not want to leave the earth behind until other beings are free. What I am talking about here is not necessarily your ascension. Earth is a dark planet. Many of the spiritual people on earth were not among the original inhabitants of earth, those who took it into a downward spiral. You have volunteered to come here after having embodied on other planets. This did not mean that you ascended from those other planets. It meant that you reached a certain level of maturity, and then you decided that you wanted to step up your service by embodying on a darker planet.

Now, you may go in on a dark planet and create a karmic spiral for yourself by fighting, for example, the fallen beings or other groups of people. This could prevent you from moving on from that planet. But many of the spiritual people have not done so, at least not for many lifetimes. There can be a point where, even though you are not ready for your ascension, you have a right to decide: "I want to move on from the earth. I have had enough of this darkness. I want to move to a lighter planet to complete the process of my ascension there." Truly, earth is a very difficult planet on which to earn your ascension. What I am saying is that you have decided to stay with this planet, most of you, even though you could have moved on, and you have done this out of compassion. I am asking you to step up your compassion to the buddhic level where you attain this neutral, non-attached way of looking at events.

It is not that you are not concerned about people. It is not that you do not feel compassion. You feel the compassion for people without feeling the pain of the people. This is almost the only way, on a planet as dark as earth, to earn your ascension. As long as you feel the pain of the people, you will be pulled into some emotional reaction. When you see such dark events unfolding as you are seeing even today in the Middle East, and you allow yourself to be pulled into an emotional reaction, then as long as you have that emotional reaction, you cannot ascend. You are not free. Neither are you free to give the highest service where you are holding a balance, a spiritual balance, and you are pulling up on the collective consciousness. I am asking you to consider this slight shift in consciousness, where you can look at events on earth without being pulled into that strong emotional reaction.

You can feel a higher sense of compassion for the people. You can make the calls, but you are not even making the calls with an attachment to the result. You are not attached to bringing about physical changes, in the sense that you are not feeling this urge to produce a certain change or to prevent a certain event. You are, as I said, locked in to the reality of free will: that people must learn in whatever way they can learn, and that even seemingly dark events can be the only teacher people can respond to. While you are making the appropriate calls, you are non-attached to the outcome. Because you know that even the calls to the ascended masters must be answered with respect for the very complex equation of free will.

The Karmic Board and its calculations

You have heard about a group of ascended masters called the Great Karmic Board. The calculations they face are incredibly complex, my beloved. You would be amazed at the complexity. We have mentioned this before, but I want to touch upon it. Because it simply would not be possible for anyone in embodiment to grasp the complexity of how karmic ties between people and groups of people must be allowed to be outplayed in certain physical events, in order to give the people involved the maximum opportunity to shift their consciousness.

You understand what I am saying? When people do not listen to a spiritual teacher, their only teacher is physical events. The Karmic Board is constantly walking this tightrope of allowing physical events to happen that are necessary for people's learning, but doing everything that can be done to prevent those physical events from escalating into a self-reinforcing downward spiral. What you can gain from this is that there are certain events that need to be taken to a certain level for the sake of people's learning, but they may not have to be accelerated beyond that level. What you realize from your perspective of being in embodiment on earth is that when you make the calls for a certain situation, you need to respect that the ascended masters cannot necessarily stop certain events from happening because it is necessary for the learning.

You simply will not be able to grasp this with the outer mind, and therefore you need to be respectful of the fact that this is beyond your outer comprehension. You do not expect to understand this. Especially, do not expect to understand it with the rational mind because there is no rational reason for it. It is all a reason in consciousness, in people's perception. A certain event can shatter or challenge people's perception filter, but you cannot understand this rationally. You could not even understand it with the current level of science that is so linear because it is much more multidimensional, spherical.

You need to have that non-attachment where you do not become frustrated, or do not feel that your calls are not working, or: "What's the point because I have made the calls to stop this war, and it is still going on?"

The far-reaching effects of the Holocaust

What you need to recognize is that if we take an event like the Holocaust, the reason this could happen was that it was necessary for the learning process of most people on earth to see an extreme outpicturing of what prejudice against other people can lead to. This was not just a racial prejudice against the Jews. The Holocaust challenged the perception filters of many people that it is okay to have prejudices against other groups of people, and to generalize that all members of a certain group are bad because a few individuals are bad. The effect of the

Holocaust has been very far-reaching in terms of challenging people's perception filters so it was necessary that the Holocaust would go to a certain level.

What then happens is that when this is allowed to precipitate as a physical event, the fallen beings and the dark forces, especially in the astral plane, always attempt to manipulate people into taking it much further than was necessary for the learning process. The dark forces attempt to escalate the event. You know, for example, that there are situations in the physical octave where air can start swirling, water can start swirling, and there is upheaval, there is movement, there is a chaotic movement. But then a shift can occur, and all of a sudden a vortex is formed that becomes a tornado, or a maelstrom in the ocean, or an earthquake on land or many of these other processes. It is as if there is a turmoil that is visible up until a certain level, and then all of a sudden a shift happens, and now a self-reinforcing spiral has been created. It just pulls people into it, and they seem to be unable to stop it.

How dark forces escalate events

This is what the dark forces always attempt to create in any event, in any conflict situation. They always attempt to escalate it by inserting certain ideas into people's minds and by pulling on their emotions so that they act out of hatred or anger against other people. They become completely irrational and they all get pulled into this blindness. It is as if the physical madness, the physical events, have to reach a certain climax before people are then again able to extract themselves from it and suddenly see how mad it was. You see in the Second World War how first the German population was pulled into supporting Hitler, and then many other nations were pulled

21 | A Buddhic perspective on overcoming the past

into this absolute determination to defeat the enemy, which made them go into the same mindset as the enemy.

As has been said, the challenge of war is that, in order to defeat the enemy, you have to be as ruthless as the enemy. You just have to hope you do not become worse than your enemy, and that is indeed what can happen in many situations.

It is, of course, not constructive that people look upon the Nazis as creating hatred against the Jews, but the people themselves have a greater hatred of the Nazis so the spiral keeps escalating. What I am saying here is that you, as the spiritual people when making the calls, can often prevent that a teaching event escalates into a downward spiral. You will again not see this physically because you will not see what *does not* happen physically, and you will not know how bad the potential was for that situation to escalate.

Cultivating detachment from results

I am asking you again to step up to this more detached view. You realize you are in embodiment, you realize you have the opportunity to make the calls for certain events, but you are not attached to the physical outcome. Of course, you also need to realize that even when an event has happened, it is still a matter of people's choices whether they will actually use that event to challenge their perception filters. I, from my view as the Lord of the World, am always respectful of people's choices. I am not attached to them making certain choices, and you need to cultivate that non-attachment in yourselves where you can have that respect for free will so that you are not personally pulled into a reaction when people do not make the highest possible choice. I know there are many of you, as spiritual people, cannot even watch the news because it is too painful for you. This also shows that you have not yet attained that detachment. I am not hereby saying that you *should* watch the news or, especially, overindulge in it because you will be overwhelmed by the information stream. I am only pointing out to you that if you have an emotional reaction where you cannot watch the news, then you can help yourself by contemplating the ideas I have given you of stepping up to this detachment of the Buddha where you see what is going on without being pulled into a reactionary spiral. This will make it so much easier for you to be in embodiment on this very turbulent planet.

You see what I am saying here? There are many people on earth who deliberately, at least at subconscious levels, are not aware of what is going on on the planet. They do not want to put their attention on how people are suffering in other parts of the world. This is necessary for you at a certain level because it would disturb you too much.

You cannot make your ascension from a given planet until you have looked at every state of consciousness found on that planet and transcended it. What is the path of walking up through the 144 levels? It is that you must look at every level which corresponds to a certain state of consciousness and then, through a conscious choice, transcend it.

There is a phase where you are blind because you need to be blind. Then there is a phase where you begin to go beyond the blindness. You are willing to look at certain things, and in that phase you are inevitably disturbed by what you see and you are pulled into an emotional reaction.

What I am giving you here is that there is a higher phase where now you can look at what is happening and you are not pulled into a reaction. You can be aware, you can make the calls, but it does not disturb you. It does not take you away from that centeredness in the Buddhic mind.

Being centered as the Buddha, being at peace as the Buddha, does not mean that I am blind to what is happening in the world. It means that I see, but I see it from the inside and the outside at the same time. I see it from every perspective possible on the 144 levels, and I see it even beyond. It is easy to be non-attached if you are not aware, but the challenge is to be aware and be non-attached.

The trauma of being vulnerable

Now, I will touch upon the topic of what other masters have called your initial or cosmic birth trauma, when you first came into embodiment on this planet. Most of you, as I said, reached a certain level of maturity on other planets before you decided to embody on earth. You had not ascended from those planets so you still had some unresolved psychology before you came to this earth. This means that when you first came to this earth, you came here to bring your light. You came here with an awareness of how things are in the higher identity realm and in the spiritual realm. You came here with some awareness of how beings treat each other. When you came to this earth, you were shocked at seeing what human beings will do to each other, and you are, of course, still somewhat shocked today.

What you have achieved in this conference is that you have found a way to interact with each other that is close to what we do as ascended masters. We do not have the many ego games. We are not seeking to manipulate. You have experienced a touch of heaven here.

Now, you will be going out and going back into your daily lives, and you will be confronted with whatever consciousness is in your lives at this point. What I want you to consider here is that when you first came to this earth, you came with an intention to bring change. It was a good intention, it was a positive intention, but it was not quite as mature, quite as detached, as the Buddhic perspective I have given you. You had a clear intention of changing things, and then, when you encountered the density of this realm, you were shocked at what is going on. Then, you became even more determined to change things. How are you going to change things? By expressing your light on this planet.

Now, you had a discussion last night where several of you realized that you have always been afraid of revealing who you are, expressing who you are, expressing your light, because you felt it would be rejected. It would be too much for people. This is exactly what you almost all did in your first embodiment. You encountered the density, and you decided that you would express your light to the absolute maximum capacity you had, in order to change that condition.

What you did not quite realize is the equation of the physical octave. You see, when you have a certain amount of light, the fallen beings in the lower identity realm cannot overcome you. They cannot force you because your light can withstand their attacks in the identity body. If you have a certain amount of light, you can withstand anything the fallen beings can throw at you in the mental body. Likewise, you can withstand anything they can throw at you in the emotional body.

You had a certain sense when you came here that – because you were invulnerable in the identity body, in the mental body, and in the emotional body – you expected that you would also be invulnerable in the physical body. You expected that, because you had greater light than most of the people in embodiment, they would not be able to touch you, and therefore you were safe in expressing your light. You expected that your light could overcome any challenge in the physical octave, but this is not the case in the physical octave.

When you are in a physical body, your physical body can be attacked by human beings who are in a far lower state of consciousness than yourself. These human beings cannot directly hurt your emotional, mental and identity bodies, but they *can* hurt your physical body. As you know from this planet, there are innumerable methods for producing pain in the physical body.

How we started hiding our light

Here you come with the best of intentions, with a certain expectation that you will be invulnerable, and suddenly the dark forces in the three higher octaves take over the minds of certain people in embodiment and they use them to kill you, to imprison you, to torture you, and to cause all kinds of pain to your physical body.

Then, you go into feeling that your light is rejected, that nobody wants it on this planet. You go into feeling that perhaps God the Father should not have allowed your physical body to be tortured. Or you feel that God the Mother should not have allowed you to feel such intense pain. All of a sudden you are taken away from your original intention. You are either scared into hiding your light or you feel: "What is the point in sharing it when it has no effect?" This is part of the wound you have been carrying where you have not dared to express your light.

Here is how this ties in with my saying that you start out being blind, then you become seeing and you become disturbed, and then you can go to the third level where you are seeing but you are non-attached. You start coming here with the best of intentions, but you are blind to how the physical octave works. Then you become attacked, and now you go into this tumultuous period where you are disturbed by what is going on.

You are beginning to realize how dark a planet you are on, and you are beginning to realize how merciless the physical octave can be. You are beginning to see, but you are very disturbed, and it is so painful that you go into this reactionary spiral. The third level up is to come to the point where you are seeing how this planet works. You are seeing people's state of consciousness. You are seeing the wisdom of the Mother and knowing how the material world works. But you have the detachment that allows you to still express your light.

Only now you do not do it with the intention you had in the beginning of changing or forcing other people. You do it in a much more balanced way, as we discussed yesterday. The wisdom of the Mother allows you to look at: What does that particular person need in order to take the next step? Then you don't express more than that.

You are not blasting people with the fullness of your light, because you are not doing it because you need to see some change. You have that respect for the outplaying of free will. You have that total respect for the people around you: that they are at a certain level of consciousness, that they have a right to be at that consciousness, that it is not your job to force them. It is your role to inspire them, to show them an example that there is an alternative, but never to force.

Overcoming the desire to use force

Do you understand what I am actually saying here, my beloved? When you came to this planet, you came here to bring change, and you were using your light with force. This is what created an opposite reaction from the fallen beings so that they attacked you to try to prevent the light from destroying their grip on the people. It was *your* force in *your* immaturity that created this reaction.

When you begin to see this, you can look at this original trauma, you can look at the hurt, you can look at the anger against the Mother or the anger against the Father, and you can come to the point where you can let it go. You realize that even though you have experienced much pain to the physical body, even though you have wounds in your soul, your four lower bodies, nothing has touched what we have called the Conscious You. Because it is still pure awareness, the pure awareness of the Buddha that sees but is not attached.

You see the events that are happening on earth, but they cannot pull you into a reaction. Therefore you know, you suddenly realize, that what has happened and been done to your physical body has indeed affected your emotional body, your mental body, and your identity body. But it is not the dark forces that have directly influenced your three higher bodies. It is *your* reaction that has influenced the three higher bodies.

By transcending, by accelerating yourself beyond that reaction, you again come to the point where you are invulnerable to the dark forces in the three higher bodies. When you have the detachment in the physical octave where you are not seeking to force others, you will also be in a certain sense invulnerable at the physical level.

Then you can begin to truly fulfill your mission by sharing your light, rather than seeking to force it upon others. This is the inner peace that has been attained in the past by very few people, but that should not stop you from attaining it in the present, in the present age, for you are, many of you, mature lifestreams. What I am talking about here is not some far-flung level that is high above your present attainment. I am not saying it could take decades for you to achieve this non-attachment.

For many of you it is just a slight turn of the dial of consciousness, a slight switch. For some of you it will require several shifts, but it is certainly something where, if you can hear and read this message, you are capable of making the switch. Those who were not capable would not have been willing to read or hear to this point. I am not asking you to do something that is impossible. I am asking you to accept that this is possible.

Expressing our light without force

You have had some experience during this conference of how you can be in this free- flowing, loving state of mind where you are not seeking to force each other in any way. You are sharing, and thereby you are creating that upward spiral. But you can do this individually in your own mind, where you are in that upward spiral. You are just sharing yourself, but you have no intention of forcing other people or forcing a certain reaction from the physical octave. It has been said that when you are in a truly loving frame of mind, the entire universe will support you. When you are seeking to force – you understand – the matter realm, the Mother element, must reflect back to you what you are sending out. You experience that as an opposing force, and then you think that the Mother is opposing you.

When you are no longer seeking to force, then what will the matter realm reflect back to you? Only that which supports the expression of your light, of your being, of your individuality, and your further growth on the spiritual path. The spiritual path will, at a certain level, be ups and downs, but there can come a point where you go beyond the ups and downs, and it is not standstill but a steady progression.

You see that, as Mother Mary has explained, there are always the swings, the oscillations, because you are in the physical octave, but they are not taking you from one stop to another stop, to another crisis, to another terrible event. They are just swinging, but there is an upward movement so that you are taken up in an ascending spiral. You realize that the fallen beings have put a fear in you that they can destroy you, they can stop your path, they can take you on a false path, but you can go beyond that fear when you realize that you are constantly moving in an upward spiral. You know that no force in the four octaves of earth can stop that.

You are aware that you are an extension of the ascended masters, and that the light of the masters is more powerful, of a higher vibration, than anything on earth. This is your frame of reference. This is your lodestone. When you attune to it, you can look beyond any condition, and it can take you in this constant upward spiral that reaches towards a greater and greater sense of peace, a greater and greater sense of joy, of enthusiasm, of fulfillment. You can come to the point where you look at life, you look at this earth, as complex as it is, you look at everything that is going on, and you still feel what a wonderful opportunity to be alive, what a privilege to be in embodiment on this planet. This is not easy for many people to attain. There are many people who can hardly dare to envision that they could attain it, but it is possible.

The frame of mind from which we ascend

You can come to a point where you look at this planet, and whether you stay in embodiment or ascend—I will not say it does not matter to you, but you could go either way. Do you understand, my beloved, that this is the only frame of mind from which you can ascend? When you are no longer trying to run away from the conditions on earth, when you are no longer seeking to change the conditions on earth, *then* you are free to ascend.

When can you ascend? When you no longer feel that you have to, when you are non-attached, when you are free. You are completely free to make the choice to stay in embodiment, and you are equally free to make the choice to ascend.

Then you make that choice. You walk through that gate. and before you take that final step through the gate, you look back on earth, as I did under the Bo tree, and you must look at all the demons of Mara. You must look at each and every one of the demons that have affected you in the past. You must look with that complete detachment where you see but you have no reaction, no value judgment, no desire to force. You see and then you decide: "I am walking through that gate to the ascended realm."

Even before you ascend, you can come to that point where you have the choice. Even though you are not physically ascending, you are not going out of the body, you can say: "I am walking into that mindset of the non-attachment of the Buddha."

What I am pointing out to you is that many of you are coming close to the point where you are free to make that decision. I am making you aware of it because I am, of course, hoping that all of you will, within not too long a time span, be able to make that decision and therefore attain that state of inner peace I experienced in the later years that I was in embodiment.

Truly, it is a joy to be in embodiment when you have that state of inner peace. That is when you can have that Buddhic smile where whatever happens in the outer, whatever happens in the physical, you still have that Buddhic non-attachment. You see but you do not react.

The Buddha I AM. It has been my joy, my privilege, to be with you. I have been with you for this entire conference whether you have felt my Presence or not. It is my joy to have spoken to you today, to have shared my Presence in a more physical way, and I hope you will be able to carry my Presence with you and know that, wherever you are, I am there with you.

For I hold space. There is no place on earth that you could go where the Buddha was not present. I hope you will have some awareness that I too am with you always. My peace I give to you. Gautama I AM.

22 | HELPING PEOPLE ATTAIN NON-ATTACHMENT

In the name I AM THAT I AM, Jesus Christ, I call to all representatives of the Divine Father, especially Gautama Buddha, and all representatives of the Divine Mother, especially Kuan Yin to help people develop Buddhic non-attachment. Help people see their reactionary patterns that pull them into negative spirals, including...

[Make personal calls.]

Part 1

1. Gautama Buddha, I call forth the judgment of the Buddha on the fallen beings that can be removed from the four levels of matter at this time.

Gautama, show my mental state
that does give rise to love and hate,
your exposé I do endure,
so my perception will be pure.

**Gautama, Flame of Cosmic Peace,
unruly thoughts do hereby cease,
we radiate from you and me
the peace to still Samsara's Sea.**

2. Gautama Buddha, help people extricate themselves from the intense struggle created by the fallen beings.

Gautama, in your Flame of Peace,
the struggling self I now release,
the Buddha Nature I now see,
it is the core of you and me.

**Gautama, Flame of Cosmic Peace,
unruly thoughts do hereby cease,
we radiate from you and me
the peace to still Samsara's Sea.**

3. Gautama Buddha, help people attain non-attachment to the demons of Mara so they cannot be tempted into a reactionary pattern.

Gautama, I am one with thee,
Mara's demons do now flee,
your Presence like a soothing balm,
my mind and senses ever calm.

> Gautama, Flame of Cosmic Peace,
> unruly thoughts do hereby cease,
> we radiate from you and me
> the peace to still Samsara's Sea.

4. Gautama Buddha, help people resolve the paradox so we can be in embodiment and recognize people's suffering while not being burdened by it.

> Gautama, I now take the vow,
> to live in the eternal now,
> with you I do transcend all time,
> to live in present so sublime.

> Gautama, Flame of Cosmic Peace,
> unruly thoughts do hereby cease,
> we radiate from you and me
> the peace to still Samsara's Sea.

5. Gautama Buddha, help people realize that everything that happens in the matter realm is like a movie projected onto a screen.

> Gautama, I have no desire,
> to nothing earthly I aspire,
> in non-attachment I now rest,
> passing Mara's subtle test.

> Gautama, Flame of Cosmic Peace,
> unruly thoughts do hereby cease,
> we radiate from you and me
> the peace to still Samsara's Sea.

6. Gautama Buddha, help people realize that it is possible to look at what happens on earth in an objective and detached manner where we do not judge. We simply see what is, without applying a value judgment of should this or should this not happen.

> Gautama, I melt into you,
> my mind is one, no longer two,
> immersed in your resplendent glow,
> Nirvana is all that I know.
>
> **Gautama, Flame of Cosmic Peace,**
> **unruly thoughts do hereby cease,**
> **we radiate from you and me**
> **the peace to still Samsara's Sea.**

7. Gautama Buddha, help people overcome the reaction from the collective consciousness that says that if an event is just an event, then everything must be acceptable.

> Gautama, in your timeless space,
> I am immersed in Cosmic Grace,
> I know the God beyond all form,
> to world I will no more conform.
>
> **Gautama, Flame of Cosmic Peace,**
> **unruly thoughts do hereby cease,**
> **we radiate from you and me**
> **the peace to still Samsara's Sea.**

8. Gautama Buddha, help people accept that an event on earth really is just an event. There is a fundamental difference between the event and our perception of it.

> Gautama, I am now awake,
> I clearly see what is at stake,
> and thus I claim my sacred right
> to be on earth the Buddhic Light.
>
> **Gautama, Flame of Cosmic Peace,**
> **unruly thoughts do hereby cease,**
> **we radiate from you and me**
> **the peace to still Samsara's Sea.**

9. Gautama Buddha, help people overcome the illusion that before they themselves can be free of the earth, certain changes need to happen on earth. Certain manifestations cannot be here, or they cannot be at peace, or they cannot be free.

> Gautama, with your thunderbolt,
> we give the earth a mighty jolt,
> I know that some will understand,
> and join the Buddha's timeless band.
>
> **Gautama, Flame of Cosmic Peace,**
> **unruly thoughts do hereby cease,**
> **we radiate from you and me**
> **the peace to still Samsara's Sea.**

Part 2

1. Gautama Buddha, help people see that we will not ascend from earth until we free ourselves from this pull. We cannot wait until the earth is in some perfect state before we ascend. We have to ascend even though the earth is not in a perfect state.

> O Kuan Yin, what sacred name,
> fill me now with Mercy's Flame.
> In giving mercy I am free,
> forgiving all is magic key.
>
> **In Kuan Yin's sweet melody,**
> **I am set free my Self to be.**
> **In Kuan Yin's vitality,**
> **I claim my immortality.**

2. Gautama Buddha, help people recognize the difference between an event and our perception of it. Help us take command over our perception.

> O Kuan Yin, I now let go,
> of all attachments here below.
> All pent-up feelings I release,
> free from emotional disease.
>
> **In Kuan Yin's sweet melody,**
> **I am set free my Self to be.**
> **In Kuan Yin's vitality,**
> **I claim my immortality.**

3. Gautama Buddha, help people see that no matter how an event takes form, and no matter what meaning we project onto it, no matter how we react emotionally, mentally, and at the identity level, it is all part of the forward movement of life.

> O Kuan Yin, why must I feel,
> that life falls short of my ideal?
> All expectations I give up,
> my mind is now an empty cup.
>
> **In Kuan Yin's sweet melody,**
> **I am set free my Self to be.**
> **In Kuan Yin's vitality,**
> **I claim my immortality.**

4. Gautama Buddha, help people see that this does not mean that an event had to happen, that the ascended masters wanted it to happen or that it was a beneficial event.

> O Kuan Yin, transcend the past,
> as all resentment gone at last.
> From future nothing I expect,
> eternal now I won't reject.
>
> **In Kuan Yin's sweet melody,**
> **I am set free my Self to be.**
> **In Kuan Yin's vitality,**
> **I claim my immortality.**

5. Gautama Buddha, help people see that even when an event creates deep wounds in the souls of many people, it is still part of the forward progression of life. Those who will not learn directly from the ascended masters, must learn by seeing the Mother realm outpicture as physical events their state of consciousness.

> O Kuan Yin, uplifting me,
> beyond Samsara's raging sea.
> All safe inside your Prajna boat,
> the farther shore no more remote.
>
> **In Kuan Yin's sweet melody,**
> **I am set free my Self to be.**
> **In Kuan Yin's vitality,**
> **I claim my immortality.**

6. Gautama Buddha, help people see that even though an event can be horrible to experience, it is the only way that people learn when they are not open to learning from Above.

> O Kuan Yin, your alchemy,
> with miracles you set me free.
> As I forgive, I am forgiven,
> by guilt I am no longer driven.
>
> **In Kuan Yin's sweet melody,**
> **I am set free my Self to be.**
> **In Kuan Yin's vitality,**
> **I claim my immortality.**

7. Gautama Buddha, help people see that when we are not open to learning from the Father element, that the ascended masters represent to earth, we must learn from the Mother element. The most horrible event on earth is an outpicturing in matter of a very unbalanced state of consciousness.

> O Kuan Yin, all worries gone,
> with nothing done, no thing undone.
> Through separate self I will not do,
> and thus I rest, all one with you.
>
> **In Kuan Yin's sweet melody,**
> **I am set free my Self to be.**
> **In Kuan Yin's vitality,**
> **I claim my immortality.**

8. Gautama Buddha, help people see that by having it outpictured in matter, it becomes more difficult for people to ignore or deny it, as they had been ignoring or denying that state of consciousness for a very long time before the physical event took place.

> O Kuan Yin, your sanity,
> now sets me free from vanity.
> For truly, what is that to me;
> I just let go and follow thee.
>
> **In Kuan Yin's sweet melody,**
> **I am set free my Self to be.**
> **In Kuan Yin's vitality,**
> **I claim my immortality.**

9. Gautama Buddha, help people see that whatever happens is necessary. When people are not able to reach a higher form of learning, it is necessary for their liberation that they see the physical outpicturing of the consciousness behind it.

> O Kuan Yin, so sweet the sound,
> that emanates from holy ground.
> As I let go of ego's chore,
> I find myself on farther shore.
>
> **In Kuan Yin's sweet melody,**
> **I am set free my Self to be.**
> **In Kuan Yin's vitality,**
> **I claim my immortality.**

Part 3

1. Gautama Buddha, help people overcome the trap of thinking they have to have attachments and pass judgments on which path an individual or even a group of people, even humankind as a whole, should or should not follow towards their liberation from matter.

> Gautama, show my mental state
> that does give rise to love and hate,
> your exposé I do endure,
> so my perception will be pure.

> Gautama, Flame of Cosmic Peace,
> unruly thoughts do hereby cease,
> we radiate from you and me
> the peace to still Samsara's Sea.

2. Gautama Buddha, help people see that we cannot pass judgment when we respect free will, which makes it possible for people to outpicture any state of consciousness as a physical reality.

> Gautama, in your Flame of Peace,
> the struggling self I now release,
> the Buddha Nature I now see,
> it is the core of you and me.

> Gautama, Flame of Cosmic Peace,
> unruly thoughts do hereby cease,
> we radiate from you and me
> the peace to still Samsara's Sea.

3. Gautama Buddha, help people see that the earth is not a high planet. There are many higher planets where the wars and the torture that we see on earth could not be physically manifest.

> Gautama, I am one with thee,
> Mara's demons do now flee,
> your Presence like a soothing balm,
> my mind and senses ever calm.

> Gautama, Flame of Cosmic Peace,
> unruly thoughts do hereby cease,
> we radiate from you and me
> the peace to still Samsara's Sea.

4. Gautama Buddha, help people see that imperfections are possible on earth because the ascended masters give many opportunities to the beings who have become trapped in duality.

> Gautama, I now take the vow,
> to live in the eternal now,
> with you I do transcend all time,
> to live in present so sublime.

> **Gautama, Flame of Cosmic Peace,**
> **unruly thoughts do hereby cease,**
> **we radiate from you and me**
> **the peace to still Samsara's Sea.**

5. Gautama Buddha, help people see that the earth is at a level where it provides an opportunity to grow for a large number of lifestreams who are in an in-between state. The masters have set a level that allows the largest number of lifestreams to receive an opportunity to grow in the schoolroom of earth.

> Gautama, I have no desire,
> to nothing earthly I aspire,
> in non-attachment I now rest,
> passing Mara's subtle test.

> **Gautama, Flame of Cosmic Peace,**
> **unruly thoughts do hereby cease,**
> **we radiate from you and me**
> **the peace to still Samsara's Sea.**

6. Gautama Buddha, help people see that you have held the balance and made it possible for some very dark events and manifestations to take place in order to help humankind grow the only way people can grow.

> Gautama, I melt into you,
> my mind is one, no longer two,
> immersed in your resplendent glow,
> Nirvana is all that I know.

> **Gautama, Flame of Cosmic Peace,**
> **unruly thoughts do hereby cease,**
> **we radiate from you and me**
> **the peace to still Samsara's Sea.**

7. Gautama Buddha, help people see that instead of rejecting many students, you have chosen to hold the balance, hold the space, that will allow people to outpicture their state of consciousness to a certain degree.

> Gautama, in your timeless space,
> I am immersed in Cosmic Grace,
> I know the God beyond all form,
> to world I will no more conform.

> **Gautama, Flame of Cosmic Peace,**
> **unruly thoughts do hereby cease,**
> **we radiate from you and me**
> **the peace to still Samsara's Sea.**

8. Gautama Buddha, I call upon you to make an adjustment whereby the level of the lowest possible consciousness on earth will be raised as much as possible.

Gautama, I am now awake,
I clearly see what is at stake,
and thus I claim my sacred right
to be on earth the Buddhic Light.

**Gautama, Flame of Cosmic Peace,
unruly thoughts do hereby cease,
we radiate from you and me
the peace to still Samsara's Sea.**

9. Gautama Buddha, I call for the clearing out of all records and traces of the fallen beings who can be removed. I call for the clearing of the traces in the physical, the emotional, the mental and the identity realms, the traces that are in people's consciousness.

Gautama, with your thunderbolt,
we give the earth a mighty jolt,
I know that some will understand,
and join the Buddha's timeless band.

**Gautama, Flame of Cosmic Peace,
unruly thoughts do hereby cease,
we radiate from you and me
the peace to still Samsara's Sea.**

Part 4

1. Gautama Buddha, help the many people who were hurt directly by the concentration camps, and the many people who have been hurt indirectly by knowing about these events, to stop holding on to and feeding the matrix in the three higher bodies.

> O Kuan Yin, what sacred name,
> fill me now with Mercy's Flame.
> In giving mercy I am free,
> forgiving all is magic key.
>
> **In Kuan Yin's sweet melody,**
> **I am set free my Self to be.**
> **In Kuan Yin's vitality,**
> **I claim my immortality.**

2. Gautama Buddha, I call for the records of Auschwitz and other concentration camps to be cleared from the emotional, mental and identity realms and for the energies to be transformed.

> O Kuan Yin, I now let go,
> of all attachments here below.
> All pent-up feelings I release,
> free from emotional disease.
>
> **In Kuan Yin's sweet melody,**
> **I am set free my Self to be.**
> **In Kuan Yin's vitality,**
> **I claim my immortality.**

3. Gautama Buddha, help people see that they need to forgive even the concentration camps because they will not be free until they forgive and let it go.

> O Kuan Yin, why must I feel,
> that life falls short of my ideal?
> All expectations I give up,
> my mind is now an empty cup.
>
> **In Kuan Yin's sweet melody,**
> **I am set free my Self to be.**
> **In Kuan Yin's vitality,**
> **I claim my immortality.**

4. Gautama Buddha, I call for the binding or consuming of the spirits that people have created as a result of being exposed to the events precipitated by the fallen beings who have now been removed.

> O Kuan Yin, transcend the past,
> as all resentment gone at last.
> From future nothing I expect,
> eternal now I won't reject.
>
> **In Kuan Yin's sweet melody,**
> **I am set free my Self to be.**
> **In Kuan Yin's vitality,**
> **I claim my immortality.**

5. Gautama Buddha, help all mature spiritual students cultivate the consciousness of non-attachment. Help them see if they have taken the Bodhisattva vow and do not want to leave the earth behind until other beings are free.

> O Kuan Yin, uplifting me,
> beyond Samsara's raging sea.
> All safe inside your Prajna boat,
> the farther shore no more remote.
>
> **In Kuan Yin's sweet melody,**
> **I am set free my Self to be.**
> **In Kuan Yin's vitality,**
> **I claim my immortality.**

6. Gautama Buddha, help the spiritual people see if they have attained the right to decide that they want to move on from this dark planet. Help them see if they have decided to stay with this planet out of compassion.

> O Kuan Yin, your alchemy,
> with miracles you set me free.
> As I forgive, I am forgiven,
> by guilt I am no longer driven.
>
> **In Kuan Yin's sweet melody,**
> **I am set free my Self to be.**
> **In Kuan Yin's vitality,**
> **I claim my immortality.**

7. Gautama Buddha, help the spiritual people step up their compassion to the buddhic level where they attain the neutral, non-attached way of looking at events. Help them feel the compassion for people without feeling the pain of the people.

O Kuan Yin, all worries gone,
with nothing done, no thing undone.
Through separate self I will not do,
and thus I rest, all one with you.

In Kuan Yin's sweet melody,
I am set free my Self to be.
In Kuan Yin's vitality,
I claim my immortality.

8. Gautama Buddha, help the spiritual people see that on a dark planet like earth, this is the only way to earn our ascension. As long as we feel the pain of the people, we will be pulled into some emotional reaction and then we cannot ascend.

O Kuan Yin, your sanity,
now sets me free from vanity.
For truly, what is that to me;
I just let go and follow thee.

In Kuan Yin's sweet melody,
I am set free my Self to be.
In Kuan Yin's vitality,
I claim my immortality.

9. Gautama Buddha, help the spiritual people be free to give the highest service where we are holding a spiritual balance and we are pulling up the collective consciousness. Help us make a slight shift in consciousness, where we can look at events on earth without being pulled into a strong emotional reaction.

O Kuan Yin, so sweet the sound,
that emanates from holy ground.
As I let go of ego's chore,
I find myself on farther shore.

In Kuan Yin's sweet melody,
I am set free my Self to be.
In Kuan Yin's vitality,
I claim my immortality.

Part 5

1. Gautama Buddha, help the spiritual people feel a higher sense of compassion for the people where we can make the calls, but we have no attachment to the result, we are not attached to bringing about physical changes.

Gautama, show my mental state
that does give rise to love and hate,
your exposé I do endure,
so my perception will be pure.

Gautama, Flame of Cosmic Peace,
unruly thoughts do hereby cease,
we radiate from you and me
the peace to still Samsara's Sea.

2. Gautama Buddha, help the spiritual people lock in to the reality of free will: that people must learn in whatever way they *can* learn, and that even seemingly dark events can be the only teacher people can respond to.

> Gautama, in your Flame of Peace,
> the struggling self I now release,
> the Buddha Nature I now see,
> it is the core of you and me.
>
> **Gautama, Flame of Cosmic Peace,
> unruly thoughts do hereby cease,
> we radiate from you and me
> the peace to still Samsara's Sea.**

3. Gautama Buddha, help the spiritual people make the appropriate calls while being non-attached to the outcome because they know that even the calls to the ascended masters must be answered with respect for the very complex equation of free will.

> Gautama, I am one with thee,
> Mara's demons do now flee,
> your Presence like a soothing balm,
> my mind and senses ever calm.
>
> **Gautama, Flame of Cosmic Peace,
> unruly thoughts do hereby cease,
> we radiate from you and me
> the peace to still Samsara's Sea.**

4. Gautama Buddha, help the spiritual people understand that the Great Karmic Board deals with calculations that are incredibly complex. We who are in embodiment cannot grasp the complexity of how karmic ties between people and groups of people must be allowed to be outplayed in certain physical events, in order to give the people involved the maximum opportunity to shift their consciousness.

Gautama, I now take the vow,
to live in the eternal now,
with you I do transcend all time,
to live in present so sublime.

**Gautama, Flame of Cosmic Peace,
unruly thoughts do hereby cease,
we radiate from you and me
the peace to still Samsara's Sea.**

5. Gautama Buddha, help the spiritual people accept that when people do not listen to a spiritual teacher, their only teacher is physical events. The Karmic Board is constantly walking a tightrope of allowing physical events to happen that are necessary for people's learning, but doing everything that can be done to prevent those physical events from escalating into a self-reinforcing downward spiral.

Gautama, I have no desire,
to nothing earthly I aspire,
in non-attachment I now rest,
passing Mara's subtle test.

**Gautama, Flame of Cosmic Peace,
unruly thoughts do hereby cease,
we radiate from you and me
the peace to still Samsara's Sea.**

6. Gautama Buddha, help the spiritual people accept that there are certain events that need to be taken to a certain level for the sake of people's learning, but they may not have to be accelerated beyond that level. When we make the calls for a certain situation, we need to respect that the ascended masters cannot necessarily stop certain events from happening because it is necessary for the learning process.

Gautama, I melt into you,
my mind is one, no longer two,
immersed in your resplendent glow,
Nirvana is all that I know.

**Gautama, Flame of Cosmic Peace,
unruly thoughts do hereby cease,
we radiate from you and me
the peace to still Samsara's Sea.**

7. Gautama Buddha, help the spiritual people grasp this with the outer mind, and therefore be respectful of the fact that we do not need to understand this with the rational mind because there is no rational reason for it. It is all a reason in consciousness, in people's perception.

Gautama, in your timeless space,
I am immersed in Cosmic Grace,
I know the God beyond all form,
to world I will no more conform.

**Gautama, Flame of Cosmic Peace,
unruly thoughts do hereby cease,
we radiate from you and me
the peace to still Samsara's Sea.**

8. Gautama Buddha, help the spiritual people know that a certain event can shatter or challenge people's perception filter, but we cannot understand this rationally.

> Gautama, I am now awake,
> I clearly see what is at stake,
> and thus I claim my sacred right
> to be on earth the Buddhic Light.
>
> **Gautama, Flame of Cosmic Peace,**
> **unruly thoughts do hereby cease,**
> **we radiate from you and me**
> **the peace to still Samsara's Sea.**

9. Gautama Buddha, help the spiritual people attain the non-attachment where we do not become frustrated, do not feel that our calls are not working or think that there is no point because we have made the calls and the event is still going on.

> Gautama, with your thunderbolt,
> we give the earth a mighty jolt,
> I know that some will understand,
> and join the Buddha's timeless band.
>
> **Gautama, Flame of Cosmic Peace,**
> **unruly thoughts do hereby cease,**
> **we radiate from you and me**
> **the peace to still Samsara's Sea.**

Sealing

In the name of the Divine Mother, I call to Kuan Yin and Mother Mary for the sealing of myself and all people in my circle of influence in the creative flow of the Divine Mother, the River of Life. I call for the multiplication of my calls by all representatives of the Divine Mother, so that we form the perfect figure-eight flow of "As Above, so below." Thus, I accept that this is fully manifest, because the mouth of the Lord, the Divine Mother that I AM, has spoken it. Amen.

23 | HELPING PEOPLE ATTAIN NON-REACTIVENESS

In the name I AM THAT I AM, Jesus Christ, I call to all representatives of the Divine Father, especially Gautama Buddha, and all representatives of the Divine Mother, especially Kuan Yin to help people develop Buddhic non-reactiveness. Help people see their reactionary patterns that prevent them from letting go of the past, including...

[Make personal calls.]

Part 1

1. Gautama Buddha, help people see that the Holocaust could happen because it was necessary for the learning process of most people on earth to see an extreme outpicturing of what prejudice against other people can lead to.

Gautama, show my mental state
that does give rise to love and hate,
your exposé I do endure,
so my perception will be pure.

**Gautama, Flame of Cosmic Peace,
unruly thoughts do hereby cease,
we radiate from you and me
the peace to still Samsara's Sea.**

2. Gautama Buddha, help people see that the Holocaust challenged the perception filters of many people who thought that it is acceptable to have prejudices against other groups of people, and to generalize that all members of a certain group are bad because a few individuals are bad.

Gautama, in your Flame of Peace,
the struggling self I now release,
the Buddha Nature I now see,
it is the core of you and me.

**Gautama, Flame of Cosmic Peace,
unruly thoughts do hereby cease,
we radiate from you and me
the peace to still Samsara's Sea.**

3. Gautama Buddha, help people see that the effect of the Holocaust has been very far-reaching in terms of challenging people's perception filters so it was necessary that the Holocaust would go to a certain level.

23 | Helping people attain non-reactiveness

> Gautama, I am one with thee,
> Mara's demons do now flee,
> your Presence like a soothing balm,
> my mind and senses ever calm.
>
> **Gautama, Flame of Cosmic Peace,**
> **unruly thoughts do hereby cease,**
> **we radiate from you and me**
> **the peace to still Samsara's Sea.**

4. Gautama Buddha, help people see that when something is allowed to precipitate as a physical event, the fallen beings and the dark forces always attempt to manipulate people into taking it much further than was necessary for the learning process. The dark forces attempt to escalate the event.

> Gautama, I now take the vow,
> to live in the eternal now,
> with you I do transcend all time,
> to live in present so sublime.
>
> **Gautama, Flame of Cosmic Peace,**
> **unruly thoughts do hereby cease,**
> **we radiate from you and me**
> **the peace to still Samsara's Sea.**

5. Gautama Buddha, help people see the mechanism whereby the fallen beings seek to precipitate a self-reinforcing spiral that pulls people into it, and they seem to be unable to stop it. The dark forces attempt to create this spiral in any event, in any conflict situation.

Gautama, I have no desire,
to nothing earthly I aspire,
in non-attachment I now rest,
passing Mara's subtle test.

**Gautama, Flame of Cosmic Peace,
unruly thoughts do hereby cease,
we radiate from you and me
the peace to still Samsara's Sea.**

6. Gautama Buddha, help people see how the fallen beings attempt to escalate a situation by inserting certain ideas into people's minds and by pulling on their emotions so that they act out of hatred or anger against other people.

Gautama, I melt into you,
my mind is one, no longer two,
immersed in your resplendent glow,
Nirvana is all that I know.

**Gautama, Flame of Cosmic Peace,
unruly thoughts do hereby cease,
we radiate from you and me
the peace to still Samsara's Sea.**

7. Gautama Buddha, help people see how people become completely irrational and they all get pulled into this blindness. Thereby, the physical events have to reach a certain climax before people are again able to extract themselves from it and suddenly see how mad it was.

23 | Helping people attain non-reactiveness

Gautama, in your timeless space,
I am immersed in Cosmic Grace,
I know the God beyond all form,
to world I will no more conform.

**Gautama, Flame of Cosmic Peace,
unruly thoughts do hereby cease,
we radiate from you and me
the peace to still Samsara's Sea.**

8. Gautama Buddha, help people see how, in the Second World War, first the German population was pulled into supporting Hitler. Then many other nations were pulled into the absolute determination to defeat the enemy, which made them go into the same mindset as the enemy.

Gautama, I am now awake,
I clearly see what is at stake,
and thus I claim my sacred right
to be on earth the Buddhic Light.

**Gautama, Flame of Cosmic Peace,
unruly thoughts do hereby cease,
we radiate from you and me
the peace to still Samsara's Sea.**

9. Gautama Buddha, help people see that it is not constructive that we look upon the Nazis as creating hatred against the Jews, but we ourselves have a greater hatred of the Nazis so the spiral keeps escalating.

Gautama, with your thunderbolt,
we give the earth a mighty jolt,
I know that some will understand,
and join the Buddha's timeless band.

Gautama, Flame of Cosmic Peace,
unruly thoughts do hereby cease,
we radiate from you and me
the peace to still Samsara's Sea.

Part 2

1. Gautama Buddha, help the spiritual people see that by making the calls, we can often prevent that a teaching event escalates into a downward spiral. We will not see this physically because we will not see what does not happen, and we will not know how bad the potential was for that situation to escalate.

O Kuan Yin, what sacred name,
fill me now with Mercy's Flame.
In giving mercy I am free,
forgiving all is magic key.

In Kuan Yin's sweet melody,
I am set free my Self to be.
In Kuan Yin's vitality,
I claim my immortality.

2. Gautama Buddha, help the spiritual people realize that we need to make the calls for certain events, but we are not attached to the physical outcome. Help us see that even when an event has happened, it is still a matter of people's choices whether they will use that event to challenge their perception filters.

> O Kuan Yin, I now let go,
> of all attachments here below.
> All pent-up feelings I release,
> free from emotional disease.
>
> **In Kuan Yin's sweet melody,**
> **I am set free my Self to be.**
> **In Kuan Yin's vitality,**
> **I claim my immortality.**

3. Gautama Buddha, help the spiritual people see that you, as the Lord of the World, are always respectful of people's choices. Help us cultivate non-attachment where we can have the respect for free will so that we are not personally pulled into a reaction when people do not make the highest possible choice.

> O Kuan Yin, why must I feel,
> that life falls short of my ideal?
> All expectations I give up,
> my mind is now an empty cup.
>
> **In Kuan Yin's sweet melody,**
> **I am set free my Self to be.**
> **In Kuan Yin's vitality,**
> **I claim my immortality.**

4. Gautama Buddha, help the spiritual people be able to watch the news with the detachment of the Buddha where we see what is going on without being pulled into a reactionary spiral.

O Kuan Yin, transcend the past,
as all resentment gone at last.
From future nothing I expect,
eternal now I won't reject.

**In Kuan Yin's sweet melody,
I am set free my Self to be.
In Kuan Yin's vitality,
I claim my immortality.**

5. Gautama Buddha, help the spiritual people overcome the desire for not wanting to know what is happening, not wanting to put our attention on how people are suffering in other parts of the world.

O Kuan Yin, uplifting me,
beyond Samsara's raging sea.
All safe inside your Prajna boat,
the farther shore no more remote.

**In Kuan Yin's sweet melody,
I am set free my Self to be.
In Kuan Yin's vitality,
I claim my immortality.**

6. Gautama Buddha, help the spiritual people see that we cannot make our ascension from a given planet until we have looked at every state of consciousness found on that planet and transcended it. We must look at every state of consciousness and then, through a conscious choice, transcend it.

O Kuan Yin, your alchemy,
with miracles you set me free.
As I forgive, I am forgiven,
by guilt I am no longer driven.

**In Kuan Yin's sweet melody,
I am set free my Self to be.
In Kuan Yin's vitality,
I claim my immortality.**

7. Gautama Buddha, help the spiritual people step up to the higher phase, where we can look at what is happening and we are not pulled into a reaction. We can be aware, we can make the calls, but it does not disturb us. It does not take us away from centeredness in the Buddhic mind.

O Kuan Yin, all worries gone,
with nothing done, no thing undone.
Through separate self I will not do,
and thus I rest, all one with you.

**In Kuan Yin's sweet melody,
I am set free my Self to be.
In Kuan Yin's vitality,
I claim my immortality.**

8. Gautama Buddha, help the spiritual people see that when we first came into embodiment on this planet, we had reached a certain level of maturity on other planets before we decided to embody on earth.

> O Kuan Yin, your sanity,
> now sets me free from vanity.
> For truly, what is that to me;
> I just let go and follow thee.
>
> **In Kuan Yin's sweet melody,**
> **I am set free my Self to be.**
> **In Kuan Yin's vitality,**
> **I claim my immortality.**

9. Gautama Buddha, help the spiritual people see that we had not ascended from those planets so we still had some unresolved psychology before we came to this earth.

> O Kuan Yin, so sweet the sound,
> that emanates from holy ground.
> As I let go of ego's chore,
> I find myself on farther shore.
>
> **In Kuan Yin's sweet melody,**
> **I am set free my Self to be.**
> **In Kuan Yin's vitality,**
> **I claim my immortality.**

Part 3

1. Gautama Buddha, help the spiritual people see that when we first came to this earth, we came here to bring our light. We came here with an awareness of how things are in the higher identity realm and in the spiritual realm. We came here with some awareness of how beings treat each other.

> Gautama, show my mental state
> that does give rise to love and hate,
> your exposé I do endure,
> so my perception will be pure.
>
> **Gautama, Flame of Cosmic Peace,**
> **unruly thoughts do hereby cease,**
> **we radiate from you and me**
> **the peace to still Samsara's Sea.**

2. Gautama Buddha, help the spiritual people see that when we came to this earth, we were shocked at seeing what human beings will do to each other, and we are still shocked today.

> Gautama, in your Flame of Peace,
> the struggling self I now release,
> the Buddha Nature I now see,
> it is the core of you and me.
>
> **Gautama, Flame of Cosmic Peace,**
> **unruly thoughts do hereby cease,**
> **we radiate from you and me**
> **the peace to still Samsara's Sea.**

3. Gautama Buddha, help the spiritual people see that when we first came to this earth, we came with an intention to bring change. It was a good intention, it was a positive intention, but it was not as mature and detached as the Buddhic perspective.

> Gautama, I am one with thee,
> Mara's demons do now flee,
> your Presence like a soothing balm,
> my mind and senses ever calm.
>
> **Gautama, Flame of Cosmic Peace,**
> **unruly thoughts do hereby cease,**
> **we radiate from you and me**
> **the peace to still Samsara's Sea.**

4. Gautama Buddha, help the spiritual people see that we had a clear intention of changing things. When we encountered the density of this realm, we were shocked and became even more determined to change things.

> Gautama, I now take the vow,
> to live in the eternal now,
> with you I do transcend all time,
> to live in present so sublime.
>
> **Gautama, Flame of Cosmic Peace,**
> **unruly thoughts do hereby cease,**
> **we radiate from you and me**
> **the peace to still Samsara's Sea.**

5. Gautama Buddha, help the spiritual people see that we can change things only by expressing our light on this planet.

> Gautama, I have no desire,
> to nothing earthly I aspire,
> in non-attachment I now rest,
> passing Mara's subtle test.
>
> **Gautama, Flame of Cosmic Peace,**
> **unruly thoughts do hereby cease,**
> **we radiate from you and me**
> **the peace to still Samsara's Sea.**

6. Gautama Buddha, help the spiritual people see that we are often afraid of revealing who we are, expressing who we are, expressing our light, because we feel it would be rejected. It would be too much for people.

> Gautama, I melt into you,
> my mind is one, no longer two,
> immersed in your resplendent glow,
> Nirvana is all that I know.
>
> **Gautama, Flame of Cosmic Peace,**
> **unruly thoughts do hereby cease,**
> **we radiate from you and me**
> **the peace to still Samsara's Sea.**

7. Gautama Buddha, help the spiritual people see that in our first embodiment we encountered the density, and we decided that we would express our light to the absolute maximum capacity we had in order to change a certain condition.

Gautama, in your timeless space,
I am immersed in Cosmic Grace,
I know the God beyond all form,
to world I will no more conform.

**Gautama, Flame of Cosmic Peace,
unruly thoughts do hereby cease,
we radiate from you and me
the peace to still Samsara's Sea.**

8. Gautama Buddha, help the spiritual people see that we did not understand the equation of the physical octave. When we have a certain amount of light, we can avoid the attacks of the fallen beings in the identity, mental and emotional realms.

Gautama, I am now awake,
I clearly see what is at stake,
and thus I claim my sacred right
to be on earth the Buddhic Light.

**Gautama, Flame of Cosmic Peace,
unruly thoughts do hereby cease,
we radiate from you and me
the peace to still Samsara's Sea.**

9. Gautama Buddha, help the spiritual people see that because we were invulnerable in the identity, mental and emotional body, we expected to also be invulnerable in the physical body.

Gautama, with your thunderbolt,
we give the earth a mighty jolt,
I know that some will understand,
and join the Buddha's timeless band.

**Gautama, Flame of Cosmic Peace,
unruly thoughts do hereby cease,
we radiate from you and me
the peace to still Samsara's Sea.**

Part 4

1. Gautama Buddha, help the spiritual people see that we expected that, because we had greater light than most of the people in embodiment, they would not be able to touch us, and therefore we were safe in expressing our light.

O Kuan Yin, what sacred name,
fill me now with Mercy's Flame.
In giving mercy I am free,
forgiving all is magic key.

**In Kuan Yin's sweet melody,
I am set free my Self to be.
In Kuan Yin's vitality,
I claim my immortality.**

2. Gautama Buddha, help the spiritual people see that we expected that our light could overcome any challenge in the physical octave, but this is not the case in the physical octave.

O Kuan Yin, I now let go,
of all attachments here below.
All pent-up feelings I release,
free from emotional disease.

**In Kuan Yin's sweet melody,
I am set free my Self to be.
In Kuan Yin's vitality,
I claim my immortality.**

3. Gautama Buddha, help the spiritual people see that when we are in a physical body, our physical body can be attacked by human beings who are in a far lower state of consciousness than ourselves.

O Kuan Yin, why must I feel,
that life falls short of my ideal?
All expectations I give up,
my mind is now an empty cup.

**In Kuan Yin's sweet melody,
I am set free my Self to be.
In Kuan Yin's vitality,
I claim my immortality.**

4. Gautama Buddha, help the spiritual people see that these human beings cannot directly hurt our emotional, mental and identity bodies, but they *can* hurt our physical bodies. There are innumerable methods for producing pain in the physical body.

O Kuan Yin, transcend the past,
as all resentment gone at last.
From future nothing I expect,
eternal now I won't reject.

**In Kuan Yin's sweet melody,
I am set free my Self to be.
In Kuan Yin's vitality,
I claim my immortality.**

5. Gautama Buddha, help the spiritual people see that we came with the best of intentions, with a certain expectation that we will be invulnerable. The dark forces in the three higher octaves took over the minds of certain people in embodiment and they used them to kill us, to imprison us, to torture us, and to cause all kinds of pain to our physical bodies.

> O Kuan Yin, uplifting me,
> beyond Samsara's raging sea.
> All safe inside your Prajna boat,
> the farther shore no more remote.

**In Kuan Yin's sweet melody,
I am set free my Self to be.
In Kuan Yin's vitality,
I claim my immortality.**

6. Gautama Buddha, help the spiritual people see that we reacted to this by feeling that our light was rejected, that nobody wanted it on this planet. We felt that God the Father should not have allowed our physical bodies to be tortured. Or we felt that God the Mother should not have allowed us to feel such intense pain.

> O Kuan Yin, your alchemy,
> with miracles you set me free.
> As I forgive, I am forgiven,
> by guilt I am no longer driven.

> **In Kuan Yin's sweet melody,**
> **I am set free my Self to be.**
> **In Kuan Yin's vitality,**
> **I claim my immortality.**

7. Gautama Buddha, help the spiritual people see that this caused us to be taken away from our original intention. We were either scared into hiding our light or we felt that there is no point in sharing it when it has no effect.

> O Kuan Yin, all worries gone,
> with nothing done, no thing undone.
> Through separate self I will not do,
> and thus I rest, all one with you.

> **In Kuan Yin's sweet melody,**
> **I am set free my Self to be.**
> **In Kuan Yin's vitality,**
> **I claim my immortality.**

8. Gautama Buddha, help the spiritual people see that this is part of the wound we have been carrying where we have not dared to express our light.

> O Kuan Yin, your sanity,
> now sets me free from vanity.
> For truly, what is that to me;
> I just let go and follow thee.

> **In Kuan Yin's sweet melody,**
> **I am set free my Self to be.**
> **In Kuan Yin's vitality,**
> **I claim my immortality.**

9. Gautama Buddha, help the spiritual people see that we came here with the best of intentions, but we were blind to how the physical octave works. Then we became attacked, and we went into a tumultuous period where we were disturbed by what was going on.

> O Kuan Yin, so sweet the sound,
> that emanates from holy ground.
> As I let go of ego's chore,
> I find myself on farther shore.
>
> **In Kuan Yin's sweet melody,**
> **I am set free my Self to be.**
> **In Kuan Yin's vitality,**
> **I claim my immortality.**

Part 5

1. Gautama Buddha, help the spiritual people see that as we began to realize how dark this planet is and how merciless the physical octave can be, we became very disturbed, and it was so painful that we went into a reactionary spiral.

> Gautama, show my mental state
> that does give rise to love and hate,
> your exposé I do endure,
> so my perception will be pure.

> **Gautama, Flame of Cosmic Peace,**
> **unruly thoughts do hereby cease,**
> **we radiate from you and me**
> **the peace to still Samsara's Sea.**

2. Gautama Buddha, help the spiritual people step up to a higher level where we are seeing how this planet works. We are seeing people's state of consciousness. We are seeing the wisdom of the Mother and knowing how the material world works. But we have the detachment that allows us to still express our light.

> Gautama, in your Flame of Peace,
> the struggling self I now release,
> the Buddha Nature I now see,
> it is the core of you and me.

> **Gautama, Flame of Cosmic Peace,**
> **unruly thoughts do hereby cease,**
> **we radiate from you and me**
> **the peace to still Samsara's Sea.**

3. Gautama Buddha, help the spiritual people transcend the intention we had in the beginning of changing or forcing other people. Help us express our light in a much more balanced way.

> Gautama, I am one with thee,
> Mara's demons do now flee,
> your Presence like a soothing balm,
> my mind and senses ever calm.

> **Gautama, Flame of Cosmic Peace,**
> **unruly thoughts do hereby cease,**
> **we radiate from you and me**
> **the peace to still Samsara's Sea.**

4. Gautama Buddha, help the spiritual people attain the wisdom of the Mother and look at what a particular person needs in order to take the next step. Then we don't express more than that.

> Gautama, I now take the vow,
> to live in the eternal now,
> with you I do transcend all time,
> to live in present so sublime.

> **Gautama, Flame of Cosmic Peace,**
> **unruly thoughts do hereby cease,**
> **we radiate from you and me**
> **the peace to still Samsara's Sea.**

5. Gautama Buddha, help the spiritual people avoid blasting people with the fullness of our light. We are not doing it because we need to see some change.

> Gautama, I have no desire,
> to nothing earthly I aspire,
> in non-attachment I now rest,
> passing Mara's subtle test.

> **Gautama, Flame of Cosmic Peace,**
> **unruly thoughts do hereby cease,**
> **we radiate from you and me**
> **the peace to still Samsara's Sea.**

6. Gautama Buddha, help the spiritual people have respect for the outplaying of free will. Help us respect the people around us and see that they are at a certain level of consciousness, that they have a right to be in that consciousness, that it is not our job to force them. It is our role to inspire them, to show them an example that there is an alternative, but never to force.

> Gautama, I melt into you,
> my mind is one, no longer two,
> immersed in your resplendent glow,
> Nirvana is all that I know.
>
> **Gautama, Flame of Cosmic Peace,**
> **unruly thoughts do hereby cease,**
> **we radiate from you and me**
> **the peace to still Samsara's Sea.**

7. Gautama Buddha, help the spiritual people see that when we came to this planet, we came here to bring change, and we were using our light with force. This is what created an opposite reaction from the fallen beings so that they attacked us to try to prevent the light from destroying their grip on the people. It was our force in our immaturity that created this reaction.

> Gautama, in your timeless space,
> I am immersed in Cosmic Grace,
> I know the God beyond all form,
> to world I will no more conform.

23 | Helping people attain non-reactiveness

**Gautama, Flame of Cosmic Peace,
unruly thoughts do hereby cease,
we radiate from you and me
the peace to still Samsara's Sea.**

8. Gautama Buddha, help the spiritual people look at the original trauma, look at the hurt, look at the anger against the Mother or the anger against the Father. Help us come to the point where we can let it go.

Gautama, I am now awake,
I clearly see what is at stake,
and thus I claim my sacred right
to be on earth the Buddhic Light.

**Gautama, Flame of Cosmic Peace,
unruly thoughts do hereby cease,
we radiate from you and me
the peace to still Samsara's Sea.**

9. Gautama Buddha, help the spiritual people realize that even though we have experienced much pain to the physical body, even though we have wounds in our souls, nothing has touched the Conscious You. It is still pure awareness, the pure awareness of the Buddha that sees but is not attached.

Gautama, with your thunderbolt,
we give the earth a mighty jolt,
I know that some will understand,
and join the Buddha's timeless band.

> Gautama, Flame of Cosmic Peace,
> unruly thoughts do hereby cease,
> we radiate from you and me
> the peace to still Samsara's Sea.

Part 6

1. Gautama Buddha, help the spiritual people see that what has been done to our physical body has affected our emotional, mental and identity bodies. But it is not the dark forces that have directly influenced our three higher bodies. It is our reaction that has influenced the three higher bodies.

> O Kuan Yin, what sacred name,
> fill me now with Mercy's Flame.
> In giving mercy I am free,
> forgiving all is magic key.
>
> **In Kuan Yin's sweet melody,**
> **I am set free my Self to be.**
> **In Kuan Yin's vitality,**
> **I claim my immortality.**

2. Gautama Buddha, help the spiritual people accelerate ourselves beyond that reaction and come to the point where we are invulnerable to the dark forces in the three higher bodies.

> O Kuan Yin, I now let go,
> of all attachments here below.
> All pent-up feelings I release,
> free from emotional disease.

> **In Kuan Yin's sweet melody,**
> **I am set free my Self to be.**
> **In Kuan Yin's vitality,**
> **I claim my immortality.**

3. Gautama Buddha, help the spiritual people have the detachment in the physical octave where we are not seeking to force others, and thereby we attain a sense of being invulnerable at the physical level.

> O Kuan Yin, why must I feel,
> that life falls short of my ideal?
> All expectations I give up,
> my mind is now an empty cup.

> **In Kuan Yin's sweet melody,**
> **I am set free my Self to be.**
> **In Kuan Yin's vitality,**
> **I claim my immortality.**

4. Gautama Buddha, help the spiritual people begin to fulfill our mission by sharing our light, rather than seeking to force it upon others. Help us have the inner peace that is not above our present attainment. Help us make a slight turn of the dial of consciousness, a slight switch.

> O Kuan Yin, transcend the past,
> as all resentment gone at last.
> From future nothing I expect,
> eternal now I won't reject.

> **In Kuan Yin's sweet melody,**
> **I am set free my Self to be.**
> **In Kuan Yin's vitality,**
> **I claim my immortality.**

5. Gautama Buddha, help the spiritual people attain the free-flowing, loving state of mind where we are not seeking to force each other. We are sharing, and thereby we are creating an upward spiral.

> O Kuan Yin, uplifting me,
> beyond Samsara's raging sea.
> All safe inside your Prajna boat,
> the farther shore no more remote.

> **In Kuan Yin's sweet melody,**
> **I am set free my Self to be.**
> **In Kuan Yin's vitality,**
> **I claim my immortality.**

6. Gautama Buddha, help the spiritual people create an upward spiral in our own minds. We are sharing ourselves, but we have no intention of forcing other people or forcing a certain reaction from the physical octave.

> O Kuan Yin, your alchemy,
> with miracles you set me free.
> As I forgive, I am forgiven,
> by guilt I am no longer driven.

**In Kuan Yin's sweet melody,
I am set free my Self to be.
In Kuan Yin's vitality,
I claim my immortality.**

7. Gautama Buddha, help the spiritual people see that when we are in a truly loving frame of mind, the entire universe will support us. When we are seeking to force the matter realm, the Mother element must reflect back to us what we are sending out. We experience that as an opposing force, and then we think that the Mother is opposing us.

O Kuan Yin, all worries gone,
with nothing done, no thing undone.
Through separate self I will not do,
and thus I rest, all one with you.

**In Kuan Yin's sweet melody,
I am set free my Self to be.
In Kuan Yin's vitality,
I claim my immortality.**

8. Gautama Buddha, help the spiritual people see that when we are no longer seeking to force, the matter realm will reflect back to us only that which supports the expression of our light, our being, our individuality and our further growth on the spiritual path.

O Kuan Yin, your sanity,
now sets me free from vanity.
For truly, what is that to me;
I just let go and follow thee.

> **In Kuan Yin's sweet melody,**
> **I am set free my Self to be.**
> **In Kuan Yin's vitality,**
> **I claim my immortality.**

9. Gautama Buddha, help the spiritual people see that the spiritual path will, at a certain level, be ups and downs. Help us come the point where we go beyond the ups and downs, and it is not standstill but a steady progression.

> O Kuan Yin, so sweet the sound,
> that emanates from holy ground.
> As I let go of ego's chore,
> I find myself on farther shore.

> **In Kuan Yin's sweet melody,**
> **I am set free my Self to be.**
> **In Kuan Yin's vitality,**
> **I claim my immortality.**

Part 7

1. Gautama Buddha, help the spiritual people see that there are always swings, oscillations, in the physical octave, but they are not taking us from one stop to another stop, to another crisis, to another terrible event. They are just swinging, but there is an upward movement so that we are taken up in an ascending spiral.

> Gautama, show my mental state
> that does give rise to love and hate,
> your exposé I do endure,
> so my perception will be pure.
>
> **Gautama, Flame of Cosmic Peace,**
> **unruly thoughts do hereby cease,**
> **we radiate from you and me**
> **the peace to still Samsara's Sea.**

2. Gautama Buddha, help the spiritual people realize that the fallen beings have put a fear in us that they can destroy us, they can stop our path, they can take us on a false path. We can go beyond that fear when we realize that we are constantly moving in an upward spiral.

> Gautama, in your Flame of Peace,
> the struggling self I now release,
> the Buddha Nature I now see,
> it is the core of you and me.
>
> **Gautama, Flame of Cosmic Peace,**
> **unruly thoughts do hereby cease,**
> **we radiate from you and me**
> **the peace to still Samsara's Sea.**

3. Gautama Buddha, help the spiritual people know that no force in the four octaves of earth can stop that. We are extensions of the ascended masters, and the light of the masters is more powerful than anything on earth.

> Gautama, I am one with thee,
> Mara's demons do now flee,
> your Presence like a soothing balm,
> my mind and senses ever calm.
>
> **Gautama, Flame of Cosmic Peace,**
> **unruly thoughts do hereby cease,**
> **we radiate from you and me**
> **the peace to still Samsara's Sea.**

4. Gautama Buddha, help the spiritual people see that the light is our frame of reference, our lodestone. When we attune to it, we can look beyond any condition. It can take us in this constant upward spiral that reaches towards a greater and greater sense of peace, joy, enthusiasm and fulfillment.

> Gautama, I now take the vow,
> to live in the eternal now,
> with you I do transcend all time,
> to live in present so sublime.
>
> **Gautama, Flame of Cosmic Peace,**
> **unruly thoughts do hereby cease,**
> **we radiate from you and me**
> **the peace to still Samsara's Sea.**

5. Gautama Buddha, help the spiritual people come to the point where we look at life, we look at this earth, we look at everything that is going on, and we still feel that it is a wonderful opportunity to be alive, a privilege to be in embodiment on this planet.

> Gautama, I have no desire,
> to nothing earthly I aspire,
> in non-attachment I now rest,
> passing Mara's subtle test.
>
> **Gautama, Flame of Cosmic Peace,**
> **unruly thoughts do hereby cease,**
> **we radiate from you and me**
> **the peace to still Samsara's Sea.**

6. Gautama Buddha, help the spiritual people come to a point where we look at this planet, and we accept that we can stay in embodiment or ascend. The only frame of mind from which we can ascend is when we are no longer trying to run away from the conditions on earth and we are no longer seeking to change them.

> Gautama, I melt into you,
> my mind is one, no longer two,
> immersed in your resplendent glow,
> Nirvana is all that I know.
>
> **Gautama, Flame of Cosmic Peace,**
> **unruly thoughts do hereby cease,**
> **we radiate from you and me**
> **the peace to still Samsara's Sea.**

7. Gautama Buddha, help the spiritual people see that before we can ascend, we must look back on earth and we must look at all the demons of Mara. We must look at each and every one of the demons that have affected us in the past. We must look with complete detachment where we see but we have no reaction, no value judgment, no desire to force. We see and then we decide: "I am walking through that gate to the ascended realm."

> Gautama, in your timeless space,
> I am immersed in Cosmic Grace,
> I know the God beyond all form,
> to world I will no more conform.
>
> **Gautama, Flame of Cosmic Peace,**
> **unruly thoughts do hereby cease,**
> **we radiate from you and me**
> **the peace to still Samsara's Sea.**

8. Gautama Buddha, help the spiritual people see that even if we are not physically ascending, we are not going out of the body, we can still say: "I am walking into the mindset of the non-attachment of the Buddha."

> Gautama, I am now awake,
> I clearly see what is at stake,
> and thus I claim my sacred right
> to be on earth the Buddhic Light.
>
> **Gautama, Flame of Cosmic Peace,**
> **unruly thoughts do hereby cease,**
> **we radiate from you and me**
> **the peace to still Samsara's Sea.**

9. Gautama Buddha, help the spiritual people see if we are coming close to the point where we are free to make that decision. Help us make that decision and therefore attain the state of inner peace you experienced in the later years that you were in embodiment. Help us attain the Buddhic smile where whatever happens in the physical, we still have that Buddhic non-attachment. We see but we do not react.

> Gautama, with your thunderbolt,
> we give the earth a mighty jolt,
> I know that some will understand,
> and join the Buddha's timeless band.
>
> **Gautama, Flame of Cosmic Peace,**
> **unruly thoughts do hereby cease,**
> **we radiate from you and me**
> **the peace to still Samsara's Sea.**

Sealing

In the name of the Divine Mother, I call to Kuan Yin and Mother Mary for the sealing of myself and all people in my circle of influence in the creative flow of the Divine Mother, the River of Life. I call for the multiplication of my calls by all representatives of the Divine Mother, so that we form the perfect figure-eight flow of "As Above, so below." Thus, I accept that this is fully manifest, because the mouth of the Lord, the Divine Mother that I AM, has spoken it. Amen.

24 | PROTECTION FROM DARK FORCES

NOTE: If you feel burdened by low-frequency energy, thoughts or feelings after giving the other invocations in this book, use the following invocation to protect yourself and the people around you from such energies and the dark forces projecting them.

In the name of the I AM THAT I AM, Jesus Christ, I call upon Mother Mary, Archangel Michael, Astrea and Saint Germain to help us accelerate ourselves beyond the reach of the dark forces. Awaken people to the reality that we are spiritual beings and that we can co-create a new future by working with the ascended masters. I especially call for …

[Make your own calls here.]

Part 1

1. Archangel Michael, I accept your total protection for myself and all people in my circle of influence from any backlash from the fallen beings in the form of physical accidents, mishaps or acts of violence.

> Archangel Michael, light so blue,
> my heart has room for only you.
> My mind is one, no longer two,
> your love for me is ever true.

> **Archangel Michael, you are here,**
> **your light consumes all doubt and fear.**
> **Your Presence is forever near,**
> **you are to me so very dear.**

2. Archangel Michael, I accept your total protection for myself and all people in my circle of influence from any backlash from the fallen beings in the form of disease or problems with the physical body.

> Archangel Michael, I will be,
> all one with your reality.
> No fear can hold me as I see,
> this world no power has o'er me.

> **Archangel Michael, you are here,**
> **your light consumes all doubt and fear.**
> **Your Presence is forever near,**
> **you are to me so very dear.**

3. Archangel Michael, I accept your total protection for myself and all people in my circle of influence from any backlash from the fallen beings in the form of emotional projections causing erratic or insane behavior.

> Archangel Michael, hold me tight,
> shatter now the darkest night.
> Clear my chakras with your light,
> restore to me my inner sight.

> **Archangel Michael, you are here,**
> **your light consumes all doubt and fear.**
> **Your Presence is forever near,**
> **you are to me so very dear.**

4. Archangel Michael, I accept your total protection for myself and all people in my circle of influence from any backlash from the fallen beings in the form of emotional projections causing depression or a sense of discouragement.

> Archangel Michael, now I stand,
> with you the light I do command.
> My heart I ever will expand,
> till highest truth I understand.

> **Archangel Michael, you are here,**
> **your light consumes all doubt and fear.**
> **Your Presence is forever near,**
> **you are to me so very dear.**

5. Archangel Michael, I accept your total protection for myself and all people in my circle of influence from any backlash from the fallen beings in the form of mental projections causing confusion or mental instability.

> Archangel Michael, in my heart,
> from me you never will depart.
> Of hierarchy I am a part,
> I now accept a fresh new start.

> **Archangel Michael, you are here,**
> **your light consumes all doubt and fear.**
> **Your Presence is forever near,**
> **you are to me so very dear.**

6. Archangel Michael, I accept your total protection for myself and all people in my circle of influence from any backlash from the fallen beings in the form of mental projections causing fanaticism or closed-mindedness.

> Archangel Michael, sword of blue,
> all darkness you are cutting through.
> My Christhood I do now pursue,
> discernment shows me what is true.

> **Archangel Michael, you are here,**
> **your light consumes all doubt and fear.**
> **Your Presence is forever near,**
> **you are to me so very dear.**

7. Archangel Michael, I accept your total protection for myself and all people in my circle of influence from any backlash from the fallen beings in the form of identity projections causing attachments to certain belief systems.

> Archangel Michael, in your wings,
> I now let go of lesser things.
> God's homing call in my heart rings,
> my heart with yours forever sings.

> **Archangel Michael, you are here,**
> **your light consumes all doubt and fear.**
> **Your Presence is forever near,**
> **you are to me so very dear.**

8. Archangel Michael, I accept your total protection for myself and all people in my circle of influence from any backlash from the fallen beings in the form of identity projections causing an identity crisis or fanaticism.

> Archangel Michael, take me home,
> in higher spheres I want to roam.
> I am reborn from cosmic foam,
> my life is now a sacred poem.

> **Archangel Michael, you are here,**
> **your light consumes all doubt and fear.**
> **Your Presence is forever near,**
> **you are to me so very dear.**

9. Archangel Michael, I accept your total protection for myself and all people in my circle of influence from any backlash from the fallen beings in the form of any opposition to our spiritual growth.

> Archangel Michael, light you are,
> shining like the bluest star.
> You are a cosmic avatar,
> with you I will go very far.
>
> **Archangel Michael, you are here,**
> **your light consumes all doubt and fear.**
> **Your Presence is forever near,**
> **you are to me so very dear.**

Part 2

1. Beloved Astrea, I accept that you are cutting free myself and all people in my circle of influence from any fallen beings in embodiment or any people controlled by fallen beings in the three higher octaves.

> Astrea, loving Being white,
> your Presence is my pure delight,
> your sword and circle white and blue,
> the astral plane is cutting through.
>
> **Astrea, come accelerate,**
> **with purity I do vibrate,**
> **release the fire so blue and white,**
> **my aura filled with vibrant light.**

2. Beloved Astrea, I accept that you are cutting free myself and all people in my circle of influence from any fallen beings, demons or entities in the astral plane.

> Astrea, calm the raging storm,
> so purity will be the norm,
> my aura filled with blue and white,
> with shining armor, like a knight.
>
> **Astrea, come accelerate,**
> **with purity I do vibrate,**
> **release the fire so blue and white,**
> **my aura filled with vibrant light.**

3. Beloved Astrea, I accept that you are cutting free myself and all people in my circle of influence from any fallen beings or demons in the mental realm.

> Astrea, come and cut me free,
> from every binding entity,
> let astral forces all be bound,
> true freedom I have surely found.
>
> **Astrea, come accelerate,**
> **with purity I do vibrate,**
> **release the fire so blue and white,**
> **my aura filled with vibrant light.**

4. Beloved Astrea, I accept that you are cutting free myself and all people in my circle of influence from any fallen beings or demons in the identity octave.

Astrea, I sincerely urge,
from demons all, do me purge,
consume them all and take me higher,
I will endure your cleansing fire.

**Astrea, come accelerate,
with purity I do vibrate,
release the fire so blue and white,
my aura filled with vibrant light.**

5. Beloved Astrea, I accept that you are binding and consuming the demons and fallen beings in the astral plane who are attacking myself or any people in my circle of influence as an act of revenge for me making the calls for putting a stop to war.

Astrea, do all spirits bind,
so that I am no longer blind,
I see the spirit and its twin,
the victory of Christ I win.

**Astrea, come accelerate,
with purity I do vibrate,
release the fire so blue and white,
my aura filled with vibrant light.**

6. Beloved Astrea, I accept that you are binding and consuming the demons and fallen beings in the mental realm who are attacking myself or any people in my circle of influence as an act of revenge for me making the calls for putting a stop to war.

> Astrea, clear my every cell,
> from energies of death and hell,
> my body is now free to grow,
> each cell emits an inner glow.
>
> **Astrea, come accelerate,**
> **with purity I do vibrate,**
> **release the fire so blue and white,**
> **my aura filled with vibrant light.**

7. Beloved Astrea, I accept that you are binding and consuming the demons and fallen beings in the identity realm who are attacking myself or any people in my circle of influence as an act of revenge for me making the calls for putting a stop to war.

> Astrea, clear my feeling mind,
> in purity my peace I find,
> with higher feeling you release,
> I co-create in perfect peace.
>
> **Astrea, come accelerate,**
> **with purity I do vibrate,**
> **release the fire so blue and white,**
> **my aura filled with vibrant light.**

8. Beloved Astrea, I accept that you are binding and consuming the demons and fallen beings who are aggressively seeking to discourage me from doing the work that will lead to their removal from the earth.

Astrea, clear my mental realm,
my Christ self always at the helm,
I see now how to manifest,
the matrix that for all is best.

**Astrea, come accelerate,
with purity I do vibrate,
release the fire so blue and white,
my aura filled with vibrant light.**

9. Beloved Astrea, I accept that you are binding and consuming the demons and fallen beings who are seeking to prevent anyone from using the teachings and tools of the ascended masters that will lead to their removal from the earth.

Astrea, with great clarity,
I claim a new identity,
etheric blueprint I now see,
I co-create more consciously.

**Astrea, come accelerate,
with purity I do vibrate,
release the fire so blue and white,
my aura filled with vibrant light.**

Part 3

1. Mother Mary, I accept that you are helping myself and all people in my circle of influence see and transcend all physical habits that are making us vulnerable to the attacks of the demons and fallen beings in all for octaves.

O blessed Mary, Mother mine,
there is no greater love than thine,
as we are one in heart and mind,
my place in hierarchy I find.

O Mother Mary, generate,
the song that does accelerate,
the earth into a higher state,
all matter does now scintillate.

2. Mother Mary, I accept that you are helping myself and all people in my circle of influence see and transcend all emotional patterns that are making us vulnerable to the attacks of the demons and fallen beings in all for octaves.

I came to earth from heaven sent,
as I am in embodiment,
I use Divine authority,
commanding you to set earth free.

O Mother Mary, generate,
the song that does accelerate,
the earth into a higher state,
all matter does now scintillate.

3. Mother Mary, I accept that you are helping myself and all people in my circle of influence see and transcend all mental illusions that are making us vulnerable to the attacks of the demons and fallen beings in all for octaves.

I call now in God's sacred name,
for you to use your Mother Flame,
to burn all fear-based energy,
restoring sacred harmony.

**O Mother Mary, generate,
the song that does accelerate,
the earth into a higher state,
all matter does now scintillate.**

4. Mother Mary, I accept that you are helping myself and all people in my circle of influence see and transcend all false sense of identity that is making us vulnerable to the attacks of the demons and fallen beings in all for octaves.

Your sacred name I hereby praise,
collective consciousness you raise,
no more of fear and doubt and shame,
consume it with your Mother Flame.

**O Mother Mary, generate,
the song that does accelerate,
the earth into a higher state,
all matter does now scintillate.**

5. Mother Mary, I accept that you are helping myself and all people in my circle of influence see and transcend any tendency to think we are in opposition to the fallen beings or other people.

> All darkness from the earth you purge,
> your light moves as a mighty surge,
> no force of darkness can now stop,
> the spiral that goes only up.
>
> **O Mother Mary, generate,**
> **the song that does accelerate,**
> **the earth into a higher state,**
> **all matter does now scintillate.**

6. Mother Mary, I accept that you are helping myself and all people in my circle of influence see and transcend any tendency to think we have to live an extremist or unbalanced lifestyle in order to fulfill our Divine plans.

> All elemental life you bless,
> removing from them man-made stress,
> the nature spirits are now free,
> outpicturing Divine decree.
>
> **O Mother Mary, generate,**
> **the song that does accelerate,**
> **the earth into a higher state,**
> **all matter does now scintillate.**

7. Mother Mary, I accept that you are helping myself and all people in my circle of influence see and transcend any tendency to go into a mindset where we produce inharmonious energies that actually feed the forces of war.

I raise my voice and take my stand,
a stop to war I do command,
no more shall warring scar the earth,
a golden age is given birth.

O Mother Mary, generate,
the song that does accelerate,
the earth into a higher state,
all matter does now scintillate.

8. Mother Mary, I accept that you are helping myself and all people in my circle of influence see and transcend the intent of the fallen beings to force us to go towards greater and greater extremes in order to defeat an enemy.

As Mother Earth is free at last,
disasters belong to the past,
your Mother Light is so intense,
that matter is now far less dense.

O Mother Mary, generate,
the song that does accelerate,
the earth into a higher state,
all matter does now scintillate.

9. Mother Mary, I accept that you are helping myself and all people in my circle of influence see and transcend any imbalance in the three higher bodies that leads to imbalances at the physical level.

In Mother Light the earth is pure,
the upward spiral will endure,
prosperity is now the norm,
God's vision manifest as form.

**O Mother Mary, generate,
the song that does accelerate,
the earth into a higher state,
all matter does now scintillate.**

Part 4

1. Saint Germain, send oceans of violet flame into the lives of myself and all people in my circle of influence. Transmute any karmic vulnerability to physical accidents, mishaps or other events that block our Divine plans.

O Saint Germain, you do inspire,
my vision raised forever higher,
with you I form a figure-eight,
your Golden Age I co-create.

**O Saint Germain, what love you bring,
it truly makes all matter sing,
your violet flame does all restore,
with you we are becoming more.**

2. Saint Germain, send oceans of violet flame into the physical bodies of myself and all people in my circle of influence. Transmute any karmic vulnerability to physical diseases or bodily imbalances that block our Divine plans.

O Saint Germain, what Freedom Flame,
released when we recite your name,
acceleration is your gift,
our planet it will surely lift.

**O Saint Germain, what love you bring,
it truly makes all matter sing,
your violet flame does all restore,
with you we are becoming more.**

3. Saint Germain, send oceans of violet flame into the emotional bodies of myself and all people in my circle of influence. Transmute any karmic ties to any beings in the emotional octave and any tendency for depression or emotional instability.

O Saint Germain, in love we claim,
our right to bring your violet flame,
from you Above, to us below,
it is an all-transforming flow.

**O Saint Germain, what love you bring,
it truly makes all matter sing,
your violet flame does all restore,
with you we are becoming more.**

4. Saint Germain, send oceans of violet flame into the mental bodies of myself and all people in my circle of influence. Transmute any karmic ties to any beings in the mental octave and any tendency for confusion or lack of clarity.

O Saint Germain, I love you so,
my aura filled with violet glow,
my chakras filled with violet fire,
I am your cosmic amplifier.

**O Saint Germain, what love you bring,
it truly makes all matter sing,
your violet flame does all restore,
with you we are becoming more.**

5. Saint Germain, send oceans of violet flame into the identity bodies of myself and all people in my circle of influence. Transmute any karmic ties to any beings in the identity octave and any tendency for fanaticism or closed-mindedness.

O Saint Germain, I am now free,
your violet flame is therapy,
transform all hang-ups in my mind,
as inner peace I surely find.

**O Saint Germain, what love you bring,
it truly makes all matter sing,
your violet flame does all restore,
with you we are becoming more.**

6. Saint Germain, send oceans of violet flame into the lives of myself and all people in my circle of influence. Transmute any karmic vulnerability that prevents us from walking a balanced path and living a balanced life.

O Saint Germain, my body pure,
your violet flame for all is cure,
consume the cause of all disease,
and therefore I am all at ease.

**O Saint Germain, what love you bring,
it truly makes all matter sing,
your violet flame does all restore,
with you we are becoming more.**

7. Saint Germain, send oceans of violet flame into the lives of myself and all people in my circle of influence. Transmute any karmic vulnerability that prevents us from finding the personal inner balance that allows us to make the calls that give the ascended masters the authority to remove war from the earth.

O Saint Germain, I'm karma-free,
the past no longer burdens me,
a brand new opportunity,
I am in Christic unity.

**O Saint Germain, what love you bring,
it truly makes all matter sing,
your violet flame does all restore,
with you we are becoming more.**

8. Saint Germain, send oceans of violet flame into the lives of myself and all people in my circle of influence. Transmute any illusion in our own consciousness that makes us vulnerable to the energies and attacks from the dark forces.

O Saint Germain, we are now one,
I am for you a violet sun,
as we transform this planet earth,
your Golden Age is given birth.

**O Saint Germain, what love you bring,
it truly makes all matter sing,
your violet flame does all restore,
with you we are becoming more.**

9. Saint Germain, send oceans of violet flame into the lives of myself and all people in my circle of influence. Transmute any karmic vulnerability and energies so that the fallen beings can no longer hurt us because we have accelerated our consciousness beyond their reach.

O Saint Germain, the earth is free,
from burden of duality,
in oneness we bring what is best,
your Golden Age is manifest.

**O Saint Germain, what love you bring,
it truly makes all matter sing,
your violet flame does all restore,
with you we are becoming more.**

Sealing

In the name of the I AM THAT I AM, I accept that Archangel Michael, Astrea and Shiva form an impenetrable shield around myself and all constructive people, sealing us from all fear-based energies in all four octaves. I accept that the Light of God is consuming and transforming all fear-based energies that make up the forces behind war!

www.ingramcontent.com/pod-product-compliance
Lightning Source LLC
Chambersburg PA
CBHW021147230426
43667CB00006B/284